First published in July 2008

ISBN 978-0-9556564-2-2
ISBN 978-0-9556564-3-9 (de Luxe edition)

Published by
Porter Press International Ltd.

PO Box 2, Tenbury Wells,
WR15 8XX, UK.
Tel: +44 (0)1584 781588
Fax: +44 (0)1584 781630
sales@porterpress.co.uk
www.porterpress.co.uk

Designed by Grafx Resource
Printed and bound in China through World Print Limited

COPYRIGHT

Every effort has been made to trace and acknowledge copyright holders. The author wishes to thank the Editors and
publishers of the named publications for their kind permission to reproduce cuttings, memos or photographs. Without their
co-operation, this publication would not have been possible.

ILLUSTRATIVE CREDITS

The majority of the images have been supplied by the Porsche Historical Archive in Stuttgart, Germany. However, additional
photographic material has been supplied by John Colley (page 141 – all; page 153 – top left; page 163 – right); Cartoonstock
(page 124 – bottom left; page 142 – bottom left); RUF Automobile (page 133 – top right; page 153 – right); album cover 'Turbo'
by Judas Priest, reproduced by kind permission of Sony BMG Music Entertainment (UK) Ltd. (page 163 – left); "Turbo Lover"
Words and Music by Glenn Raymond Tipton, Robert Halford and Kenneth Downing © 1986, reproduced by permission of
EMI Songs Ltd/ EMI Music Publishing Ltd, London W8 5SW.

I would also like to thank Dr. Wolfgang Porsche for agreeing to provide an endorsement for this book. Currently the Chairman
of the Porsche Supervisory Board, Dr. Wolfgang Porsche has been intimately involved in the development of the 911 for many
years. I am most grateful that he could find the time to provide these kind words in his busy schedule.

Porsche 911 Scrapbook

Glen Smale

Design by Andrew Garman

Porter Press International

BREAKING COVER

The year 1948 was a tentative one for Porsche as a company in what was generally a very dynamic and unsettled period in world history, but Ferry Porsche, son of company founder Professor Ferdinand Porsche, was focussed and single-minded. With hindsight, however, the company never looked as though it could fail because Ferry assembled a team of talented and committed engineers with whom he built his dream – the dream that he and his father had had many years earlier, of building a sports car bearing the family name.

It must be remembered that immediately post-War, commercial opportunities were plentiful but material and financial resources were not. Frequently, therefore, start-up companies around this time had to rely on a rather large dose of enthusiasm and belief on the part of its employees that the product being manufactured was worthy of their efforts and that the company would, in return, provide a stable income for their families in the years to come. Coupled with this trusting relationship, and weighing quite heavily in Porsche's favour, was the strong German tradition of hard work and attention to detail.

With a solid foundation of talent, skills and determination to build on, Porsche set about making the diminutive 356 model which would put the company on the motoring map. In the early days, solid reliability and encouraging achievements on the race tracks of the world fuelled further development until it was felt that the 356 had reached its ultimate progression and a new model was needed to take the company forward. Porsche needed to modernise its product range, as so many of its competitors were doing at that time.

The Porsche 356 had begun life back in 1948 in an old converted sawmill in the town of Gmünd in the picturesque Austrian Alps, but production moved to Stuttgart in 1950 in order to benefit from the developing German economy and industrial infrastructure. The 1950s had been spent fruitfully, as the reputation of the little 356 had impressed sports car drivers and public alike. It had also sold well beyond the forecast number of units planned by Ferry Porsche, but then the company had always been conservative in this area.

The 356 enjoyed three model revisions in its life cycle - the 356 A-B-C - and reached its ultimate development potential with the last iteration, the 356 C Carrera 2.0-litre. This was indeed a powerful sports car for its day, but was by now clearly becoming outdated. Besides, Ferry Porsche was itching to take the company forward. There was a concern, though, by the late 1950s that the Porsche 356 was considered small and not particularly powerful in comparison to other sports cars at its lofty price level. If truth be told, the 356 represented a car designed in an earlier era, but finding a suitable replacement was not a step to be taken lightly due to its fanatically loyal following.

From the start, Porsche intended to be nothing other than a manufacturer of high quality, performance sports cars. With the attractive 356 approaching the end of its product life cycle by the late 1950s, work on a successor to this model began to gather momentum in the drawing and design offices of the Porsche factory in Stuttgart-Zuffenhausen. After a production run of 77,766 units, the last of the 356 models finally rolled off the production line as late as 1965, once production of its successor was well under way.

TIMELINE (1959-1966):

1959	1962	1963	1964	1965	1966
Design work begins on the 356 replacement.	Typ 644 T8 begins to show 901 final style.	Typ 901 announced at the Frankfurt Motor Show.	First deliveries of new Typ 901.	Porsche 912 introduced.	More power for 1967 model.
			Model name changed to 911 in October.	End of 356C production.	

Ferry Porsche pictured here with his father Ferdinand Porsche in 1934. He had worked in his father's design office ever since the establishment of 'Dr. Ing. h.c. F. Porsche GmbH' three years earlier

Porsche 911 Scrapbook

Glen Smale

Design by Andrew Garman

Porter Press International

ACKNOWLEDGEMENTS

Generally, authors draw on the knowledge of others in their research and writing on a particular subject. This project was no exception, and I am constantly amazed at, and grateful for, the willingness of others to give of their time and knowledge so freely.

A large proportion of the images in this book have been provided by the Porsche Archiv in Stuttgart. For his tireless work in this respect, I would like to single out Jens Torner who, at my request, has time after time gone back into the vast Porsche archives to seek out some additional piece of obscure Porsche history. Without his enthusiasm and dedication to the subject, this book would not have been possible.

In addition, I would like to thank Michael Cotton, retired head of PR at Porsche in Great Britain, who graciously suggested that I take on this project. Michael has also kindly assisted with photos, history and valuable contacts. Anne Hope of Motor Industry Publishing has proved an invaluable source of both information and inspiration, and I am most grateful to her for the many hours spent in her vast archive.

Stephen Mummery, editor of *Porsche Post*, the Porsche Club of Great Britain official magazine, has also provided many photos and much information relating to Porsche's early days in the UK. I would also like to thank Peter Cook, Porsche Club archivist, for his assistance with similar material. I am very grateful to Derek Smith of Haynes Publishing and Kevin Quinn of Veloce Publishing for their help with sourcing images and book details relating to the many books published by them on the subject of Porsche.

And then there is the team at Porter Press International, who have all contributed enormously in their own way to the production of this book. For his patience and constant encouragement, Philip Porter has been a tremendous help as has editor Mark Holman, a world away in New Zealand. As always, Andy Garman's creative skills have made my rather mundane ramblings into something special and Abigail Humphries has provided invaluable support behind the scenes. The one remaining member of the Porter team is Claire Bryan, whose move to the Continent, I was relieved to find out, had nothing to do with my missing deadlines nor my constant demands for assistance of various kinds. Claire has been a pillar of strength and I appreciate her input throughout this journey.

Last, and by no means least, I would like to thank my wife Elke for her steadfast support throughout this project. Writing is a lonely profession, and all too often when I could not see the light at the end of the tunnel, it was she who did, and I would like to express my appreciation of her unwavering belief in my abilities.

INTRODUCTION

From a very young age, I have always considered Porsche cars to be a cut above the rest as they were usually driven faster than most other sports cars which impressed me no end as a schoolboy. Later, however, when I was able to drive and experience the Porsche 911 for myself, the car's design integrity and quality of engineering impressed me more than anything else.

The 911 is an extraordinary vehicle in what is today a sea of mediocrity. Its success can be put down to several factors, one of which is the 911's solid but simple construction as a sports car. Another reason no doubt is the 911's enviable motor sport record, which spans the whole spectrum of the sport from club events to international endurance racing. The 911, like the 356, has created a reputation of being a 'giant killer', and this has undoubtedly benefited the image of the roadgoing models.

Following its birth in 1963, the 911 has grown, matured, been threatened with the chop and suffered the roller-coaster effects of the economy and the markets, and yet risen once again as a market leader. Through a solid product development plan, good management and a strong commitment from the Porsche family and staff, the 911 has adapted to meet market demands, and today is widely regarded as an icon in the sports car market.

The story of the evergreen 911 is quite simply one of the most intriguing in the history of the motor industry, a fact which has fuelled solid sales for almost 50 years. Although the 911's silhouette has remained largely unchanged since its inception, sports car enthusiasts, and in particular those many devoted Porschephiles, continue to remain loyal to the 911 as though it were the only car on the planet. The magic of the 911 will live on as long as the development engineers in Stuttgart can find new boundaries for the 911 to conquer – long may it continue.

I hope that, through uncovering some of the lesser known 911 facts, including previously unseen photographs and fresh insights, this book will enable you to see this marvellous sports car in an altogether different, and even more interesting, light.

Glen Smale
Carmarthenshire, Wales
April 2008

INTRODUCTION BY DR WOLFGANG PORSCHE,
Chairman of the Porsche Supervisory Board

The Porsche 911 has undoubtedly been the mainstay of the Porsche model range since 1963, and during this time it has won over many enthusiasts around the world.

The secret to the survival of the 911 can be put down to its simple yet highly original design, excellent build quality and continuous development over the years. Since the introduction of this sports car, the 911 range has continued to adapt to the changing global market conditions, and combined with its outstanding motor sport record, this has helped the 911 to remain a market leader.

It makes us proud that the 911 has proved so popular and we hope that the 'Eleven' will continue to bring excitement to our customers for many more years.

BREAKING COVER

The year 1948 was a tentative one for Porsche as a company in what was generally a very dynamic and unsettled period in world history, but Ferry Porsche, son of company founder Professor Ferdinand Porsche, was focussed and single-minded. With hindsight, however, the company never looked as though it could fail because Ferry assembled a team of talented and committed engineers with whom he built his dream – the dream that he and his father had had many years earlier, of building a sports car bearing the family name.

It must be remembered that immediately post-War, commercial opportunities were plentiful but material and financial resources were not. Frequently, therefore, start-up companies around this time had to rely on a rather large dose of enthusiasm and belief on the part of its employees that the product being manufactured was worthy of their efforts and that the company would, in return, provide a stable income for their families in the years to come. Coupled with this trusting relationship, and weighing quite heavily in Porsche's favour, was the strong German tradition of hard work and attention to detail.

With a solid foundation of talent, skills and determination to build on, Porsche set about making the diminutive 356 model which would put the company on the motoring map. In the early days, solid reliability and encouraging achievements on the race tracks of the world fuelled further development until it was felt that the 356 had reached its ultimate progression and a new model was needed to take the company forward. Porsche needed to modernise its product range, as so many of its competitors were doing at that time.

The Porsche 356 had begun life back in 1948 in an old converted sawmill in the town of Gmünd in the picturesque Austrian Alps, but production moved to Stuttgart in 1950 in order to benefit from the developing German economy and industrial infrastructure. The 1950s had been spent fruitfully, as the reputation of the little 356 had impressed sports car drivers and public alike. It had also sold well beyond the forecast number of units planned by Ferry Porsche, but then the company had always been conservative in this area.

The 356 enjoyed three model revisions in its life cycle - the 356 A-B-C - and reached its ultimate development potential with the last iteration, the 356 C Carrera 2.0-litre. This was indeed a powerful sports car for its day, but was by now clearly becoming outdated. Besides, Ferry Porsche was itching to take the company forward. There was a concern, though, by the late 1950s that the Porsche 356 was considered small and not particularly powerful in comparison to other sports cars at its lofty price level. If truth be told, the 356 represented a car designed in an earlier era, but finding a suitable replacement was not a step to be taken lightly due to its fanatically loyal following.

From the start, Porsche intended to be nothing other than a manufacturer of high quality, performance sports cars. With the attractive 356 approaching the end of its product life cycle by the late 1950s, work on a successor to this model began to gather momentum in the drawing and design offices of the Porsche factory in Stuttgart-Zuffenhausen. After a production run of 77,766 units, the last of the 356 models finally rolled off the production line as late as 1965, once production of its successor was well under way.

TIMELINE (1959-1966):

1959	1962	1963	1964	1965	1966
Design work begins on the 356 replacement.	Typ 644 T8 begins to show 901 final style.	Typ 901 announced at the Frankfurt Motor Show.	First deliveries of new Typ 901.	Porsche 912 introduced.	More power for 1967 model.
			Model name changed to 911 in October.	End of 356C production.	

Ferry Porsche pictured here with his father Ferdinand Porsche in 1934. He had worked in his father's design office ever since the establishment of 'Dr. Ing. h.c. F. Porsche GmbH' three years earlier

The Porsche Shield

The story goes that when Porsche needed to print its first owners' handbook in 1951, the printer had claret coloured paper in stock which was similar to the colour that existed on certain company literature at that time. With coloured paper being in short supply after the War, it was decided to use this shade and so the claret colour found its way onto more of Porsche's internal stationery, as well as the car's steering wheel emblem and hubcaps as from 1952.

Inspiration for a company crest and car badge is said to have been initiated by Max Hoffman, the company's American importer, who said that the American public liked to have badges on their cars. To this end, Ferry Porsche wanted to create some 'heraldry' and so decided to devise a coat of arms. The prancing horse in the centre of the shield is the horse from the City of Stuttgart's own coat of arms, because many centuries ago large stables existed in part of what is now Stuttgart. The red (originally claret) and black stripes are also the stripes of Württemberg, the administrative region for Stuttgart, further cementing the company's Swabian roots. These elements are interspersed with a stag's antlers.

The company name is then emblazoned across the top of the shield leaving one with no doubt as to which car you are looking at. The design work for this emblem was carried out by Porsche's own creative studio, Style Porsche, under the guidance of freelance graphic artist, Erich Strenger.

Ferdinand Porsche is seen holding a stopwatch at the Nürburgring in 1950. Behind him to the right is Ferry Porsche. Sadly, Dr.-Ing. h.c. Ferdinand Porsche died on January 30, 1951 and this was probably one of the last motor racing events he attended

Attending the first Frankfurt Motor Show, or Internationale Automobil-Ausstellung (IAA) in Frankfurt/Main, which was held from April 19-29, 1951, is Ferry Porsche (left) in discussion with Konrad Adenauer (German Chancellor, middle) and on his left is Heinrich Nordhoff (CEO of Volkswagen)

Stammbaum der Familie Porsche

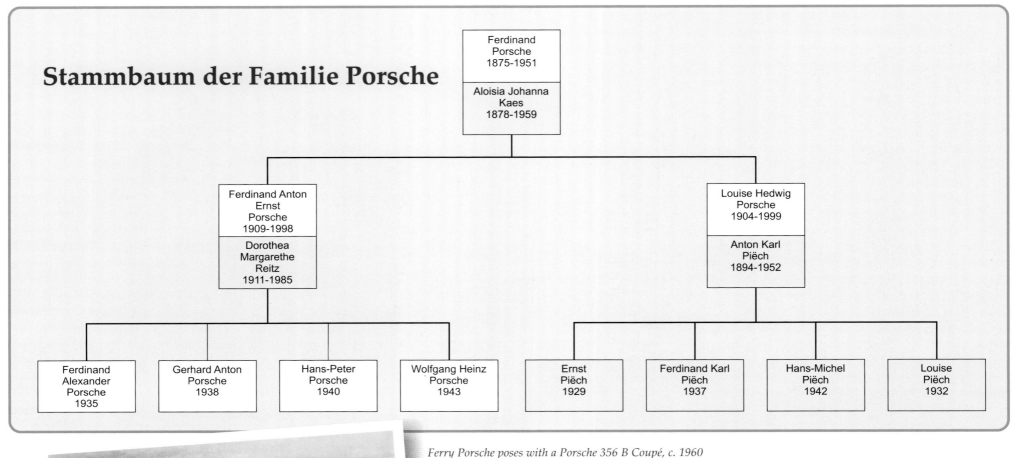

Ferdinand Porsche
1875-1951

Aloisia Johanna Kaes
1878-1959

Ferdinand Anton Ernst Porsche
1909-1998

Dorothea Margarethe Reitz
1911-1985

Louise Hedwig Porsche
1904-1999

Anton Karl Piëch
1894-1952

Ferdinand Alexander Porsche
1935

Gerhard Anton Porsche
1938

Hans-Peter Porsche
1940

Wolfgang Heinz Porsche
1943

Ernst Piëch
1929

Ferdinand Karl Piëch
1937

Hans-Michel Piëch
1942

Louise Piëch
1932

Ferry Porsche poses with a Porsche 356 B Coupé, c. 1960

Reutter 1963

When the Karosseriewerk Reutter & Co. GmbH was given the task of fabricating the bodywork for the proposed Typ 901, they baulked at the tooling investment needed for this new car. Porsche management responded in July of that year by buying the Reutter company for DM 6.0-million.

On March 1, 1964, Reutter was renamed Karosseriewerk Porsche GmbH and the approximately 1000-strong workforce was kept on by Porsche in its entirety. This was a really good move for Porsche and the Reutter workers who knew the Porsche operation inside-out anyway.

Long-time Porsche engineer and racing driver, Herbert Linge, told me in 2005, "They came all to Porsche. Ja, they built the body shop just like they had at Reutter, and you know, today there are still some of the old people from Reutter in the factory. They had very good people working there for Reutter."

Taken in 1956, this aerial photo of Stuttgart-Zuffenhausen shows the original Reutter building in the centre (with the dark roof). Immediately to the right of the Reutter building is the Porsche building Werk II, finished in November 1952, which in itself is quite amazing considering that Porsche only relocated to Stuttgart from Gmünd in 1950. The architect of the Porsche building, Rolf Gutbrod, was famous for having designed the concert hall, or Liederhalle, in Stuttgart. The larger group of buildings to the left of the photograph across the road is Werk I. Built in 1938, this building was confiscated by the American armed forces during the War and only returned to Porsche on December 1, 1955. Against the extreme left edge of the photo, where the two roads converge, is the small shed-like building in which the first 356s were built in Stuttgart in 1950 after returning from Gmünd. These were the old offices belonging to Dr. Ferdinand Porsche

This 1960 356 B Coupé shows off the car's sweeping design that had captivated Porsche drivers since its introduction in 1948. Even the model's dress was crafted during an era of design elegance

Typ 901 Prototype

Prototype 901 Typ 754 T9 developed by Erwin Komenda, January 1962

For any manufacturer, developing a replacement model is an anxious and uncertain time, especially when the model being replaced is the only vehicle you produce and it just happens to be a favourite with the public. However, at the helm was Ferry Porsche and he knew exactly what he wanted. Together with his son Butzi and the 356 designer Erwin Komenda, they set about developing the 356's replacement.

Ferry's son, 'Butzi' Porsche, who was emerging as a very competent design engineer, rose to the challenge. Born on December 11, 1935, in Stuttgart, Ferdinand Alexander Porsche was given the nickname of 'Butzi' by his family, a name that stuck with him all his life.

Adhering strictly to the 356's original design parameters, that is, a 2+2 body shell of fastback shape, a mid-1950s model was developed around the 356 chassis but this early design was quickly discarded as it lacked the flowing simplicity of the 356. Although initial sentiment within the design team was for a 4-seater car of fastback shape, a clear direction did not exist. Butzi Porsche developed an early prototype under the Typ 754 T7 designation and based on a 2400mm wheelbase, but Ferry Porsche did not like the direction in which this design was heading.

Ferry then decided to take back control and he set up two teams to tackle the design. The Typ 644 T8 project was to be spearheaded by Butzi Porsche, while the Typ 754 T9 was Komenda's design. This move was instigated by Ferry to study the two alternative designs in order to focus the direction the new model should ultimately follow. Ferry Porsche was insistent that the new model should not deviate too far from the outgoing 356 model, while still offering 2+2, rather than 4-seater accommodation.

As can be seen from the accompanying images, the T9 of Komenda shows more rounded lines, perhaps borrowing more from its 356 ancestry than the T8 of Butzi Porsche, which was a cleaner and simpler design. Interestingly, though, both of these prototypes featured a forward sloping B-pillar which in the final production car became a rearward sloping pillar.

The direction that Komenda's T9 design was taking displeased Ferry as he persisted in pursuing a model clearly offering full seating for four, instead of the 2+2 as Ferry had decreed. On the other hand, the T8 design model of Butzi was much closer to the vision which Ferry had in mind. Initial plans were for an engine fitted beneath a rear floor cover but this was changed to behind the seats due to excessive noise. In addition, Porsche engineer Ing Hans Tomala was charged with the responsibility of building a new, and quieter, overhead camshaft boxer engine for the T8 but with six cylinders rather than four, as in the 356.

The result of Butzi's work was a 2-seater body of fastback shape on a shorter wheelbase (around 2100mm), which even in its early stages was in fact very similar to the final Typ 901 shape. He then added a further 100mm to the wheelbase in order to allow for the 2+2 configuration his father wanted.

The development of the Typ 901 was a watershed for the company in several different ways, as more than with any other model, the development of this newcomer was responsible for opening up areas for potential friction within the company that had previously not existed. Where Komenda had previously designed the legendary 356, overall design responsibility for the new Typ 901 was ultimately given to Butzi Porsche who was leading the pack of younger generation Porsche family members who were taking responsibility within the firm. Ferry went so far as to place Butzi in overall control of the model department, whereas Erwin Komenda, chief of body development and who had been with the company since 1931, certainly lost some ground as a result of his stubbornness.

Ferry and Ferdinand Alexander 'Butzi' Porsche discussing a design issue in the Porsche Design Studio (c. 1959)

Typ 901 Prototype

Porsche Typ 901 T8 is being tested here by Herbert Linge at Weissach in 1963

Porsche Type 754 T7, 4-seater design for Typ 901/911 with 2.0-litre 130bhp engine. This prototype version was kept by the factory

Porsche Typ 901 prototype undergoing tests around Stuttgart on July 10, 1963. With the Frankfurt Motor Show launch only two months away, this car was in its final stages of development. Although the quite creative disguise is intended to throw off any snooping spies, the new body shape is plainly visible

(April 6, 1904 - August 22, 1966) Designer – Porsche 356, 911 And The VW Beetle

Although Ferry Porsche is, understandably, most often associated with the Porsche sports cars, the name of Erwin Komenda is frequently, and unjustly, omitted from such discussions.

The lesser-known name of Erwin Komenda was associated with some of the world's most significant motor cars. Born in Jauern am Semmering in Austria, Komenda spent most of his schooling, and certainly all of his post-school training, in the field of metalwork and design.

After successfully completing his studies at the Technical Institute for Iron and Steel Work in Steyr, Austria, Komenda attended the coach–building course at the Technological Trade Museum in Vienna, being taught by the renowned Viennese coachbuilder Johann Feldwabel.

In 1926 Komenda married his Viennese sweetheart, Auguste Eugenie Hauptmann. In the same year, Komenda moved to the automobile manufacturer, Steyr (located in the Austrian town of Steyr), where he met Ferdinand Porsche who had also joined the company to take up the position of technical director after leaving Daimler-Benz AG.

Four years later, aged just 26, Komenda was appointed deputy head of the Production Department at Daimler-Benz AG. Pioneering work under his direction included components such as independent suspension, spring axle suspension and countless variations on weight-saving and self-supporting bodywork construction which were established at the firm by Komenda, forming the basis of many generations of successful Daimler-Benz vehicles.

In November 1931 Komenda left his highly paid job at Daimler-Benz to join Ferdinand Porsche's newly-founded design office as the manager of its bodywork construction department. At that stage Porsche also carried out design and engineering work for other motor manufacturers, and during this time Komenda worked on designs for Auto Union, Zundapp and NSU. When Ferdinand Porsche was awarded the commission by Adolf Hitler to design a German 'people's car' or Volkswagen, the task was given to Komenda. Basing his design on an earlier NSU project, Komenda's brief included the development of both a saloon and a convertible Volkswagen. In addition to the Volkswagen Beetle, Komenda designed the Porsche 356, the first sports car to display the classic Porsche lines.

By the end of 1944, when the loss of the war was already inevitable and the Volkswagen plant lay largely in ruins, Porsche's first-class development team was evacuated to Gmünd in Carinthia, Austria, while Porsche himself went to Zell am See. Life in Gmünd was dominated by poverty and isolation as the engineers only had wooden huts for accommodation, but it was here, in November 1946, that Erwin Komenda's ideas for a sports car were committed to paper.

Officially, the Porsche 356 project began in June 1947 and the following month saw various bodywork structures and frames being completed, followed by the entire aluminium body which was hand-beaten over a wooden buck in these very basic conditions. During the winter of 1948/49, production in Gmünd was slow and irregular as manufacturing conditions in the wooden huts were far from convenient and so the whole operation was moved to Stuttgart in 1950.

The Stuttgart-based body manufacturer, Reutter Karosserie, was located alongside the Porsche factory in the suburb of Zuffenhausen. Importantly for Porsche, Reutter had large premises at their disposal which Porsche could rent if required, a development that was to materialise sooner than most expected. In 1950, with the beginning of Porsche 356 production in Stuttgart, the first pale grey example left the Reutter plant.

In 1953 Komenda designed the bodywork for the 'giant-killing' Porsche 550 Spyder, which beat so many much larger-engined cars on the race track. Komenda was also later responsible for styling the bodywork of the 'American Roadster', also known as the Porsche 540 Speedster, which made its debut in September 1954 on the recommendation of American Porsche importer Max Hoffman and Porsche racer John von Neumann.

In autumn 1955 Komenda's bodywork variations for the Porsche 356 A superseded the original 356 to be followed by the 356 B which was launched at the 1959 Frankfurt Motor Show. At this stage preliminary design work on the 356 replacement was already underway with the development of the T7 (1959) and T8 (1961) programmes.

Komenda envisaged Porsche's next sports car model as a 4-seater, seeing the advent of family travel as being the way forward. His argument was that those customers who had purchased a 356 as their first sports car had by now probably married and may even have a small family, and this new model would allow those existing customers to remain loyal to the marque with the increased interior accommodation that his 4-seater design offered. However, a full 4-seater sports car was not what Ferry Porsche had in mind.

Komenda faced being sidelined in the 901 design process because he wanted the car to follow his styling, but when this dawned on him he became more flexible in his approach and fell in with Butzi's plan. However, like most talented and professional designers, Komenda remained loyal to his own ideas while also understanding how to work with his colleagues to resolve most design challenges.

The significance of his contribution to global automobile design cannot be overestimated. Erwin Komenda lived to see the fulfilment of his earlier dreams; in August 1955 the one millionth Beetle was produced and the model was by then being exported to more than 100 countries. During 1965 the number of Beetles produced in that year exceeded the one million barrier for the first time.

The final years of Komenda's life were marked by conflicts with members of the Porsche family within the company over the development of the Porsche 904 and 911. Privately he was a modest, unselfish man and never spoke of his own success. He was an active worker right up to his unexpected and sudden death on August 22, 1966. Erwin Komenda's final resting place is in the family grave in Weyer an der Enns.

This photo shows the entrance to the Holzgrossindustrie which housed the Porsche works in Gmünd in the early days (1948-1950)

Ferry Porsche (right) pictured discussing an engineering issue in 1956 with long-standing colleagues, Karl Rabe (wearing spectacles) and Erwin Komenda. Karl Rabe (1895-1968) joined the Austrian engine company owned by Daimler (Austro-Daimler in Wiener Neustadt) in 1913 while Ferdinand Porsche (1875-1951) was its Technical Director. In 1931, when the Dr. Ing. h.c. F. Porsche GmbH company was established in Stuttgart, Rabe was offered the post of Chief Designer, which he retained until he retired in 1965. After this he continued to act as Ferry Porsche's personal technical adviser. Erwin Komenda (1904-1966) was Body Designer at Porsche from 1931

Part of the wooden shed complex in which Porsche developed its first 356 model

Taken in 1948, this photo shows Erwin Komenda (left) and Production Manager Otto Husslein discussing an engineering issue relating to the bodywork of the Porsche Typ 356 Coupé. These early cars are not unexpectedly referred to as Gmünd Coupés, the significance being not only where they were manufactured, but also the fact that these first 356s had aluminium hand-beaten bodywork

Dr. Ernst Fuhrmann
(October 21, 1918 – February 6, 1995)
The Carrera Legend

Born in Vienna, Austria, Fuhrmann attended the Technical College in his home town from 1936-1941. These were difficult times and in 1943 he worked at the AEG Research Institute in Berlin but by 1947 he found himself back in Austria as part of the founding team of Porsche in Gmünd. Together with Professor Eberan von Eberhorst, Fuhrmann worked on the 12-cylinder supercharged Cisitalia race car that year, but moved to Stuttgart when Porsche relocated there in 1950, the same year that he married his girlfriend, Elfriede.

Following his doctoral thesis on engine timing in high-speed internal combustion engines, Fuhrmann was responsible for developing the revolutionary four-cam Porsche Carrera engine, as featured in the 550 racer and the 356 Carrera range. More than any other, the Typ 547 engine put Porsche on the motor sport map of the world as it became a "giant killer" to quote Ferry Porsche's words.

Fuhrmann left Porsche in 1956 to become Head of Technical Development at Goetze AG in Burscheid, an automotive components manufacturer in the administrative region of Cologne. He was made a board member in 1962 and stayed with this company until Dr. Ferry Porsche successfully enticed Fuhrmann back to the Stuttgart firm in September 1971. He moved up the ladder quickly, becoming Management Speaker (Managing Director of the Management Board) in March 1972. He moved up again in November 1976 when he was appointed Chairman of the Board of Porsche AG, a position he held until December 31, 1980 when he left the company following a disagreement with Ferry over the future of the 911.

During his time with Porsche, Fuhrmann was awarded the Austrian Cross of Honour and he was also granted a Professorship by the Technical College in Vienna for his contribution to the field of engineering.

Professor Ernst Fuhrmann died on February 6, 1995, at the age of 76 in his home at Teuenbach in Styria, Austria. He was survived by his wife and two sons.

Replaced by the 356 C in 1963, this is a late model 356 B Coupé from 1962

Ferdinand Porsche with family in Untertauern in 1938. From left to right: Louise Piëch (née Porsche), Ferry Porsche, Aloisia Porsche (née Kaes), Anton Piëch, Ferdinand Porsche, Louise Piëch and Ernst Piëch

A Family Reorganisation

The onset of the 1960s witnessed a change of control within Porsche's family management team as the younger generation sought to exert its ideas on how the future of the company should look. The Porsche 901 first appeared during this difficult period of change, just as the long-established family hierarchy and organisational structures within this Stuttgart company were all but turned on their heads.

As we have seen, Professor Porsche's grown-up grandson, Butzi, had joined the company, and would take charge of managing development projects and occupy leading positions in the company. Confusingly, he was the third male descendant of the Porsche family to bear the name Ferdinand. One of the most important things he did on assuming management of the company was to establish a new design studio. In 1963, Hans-Peter Porsche joined the company, becoming Production Manager in 1965. Ferdinand Piëch, son of Louise Porsche and Dr Anton Piëch, had gained his engineering diploma at the ETH (Swiss Federal Institute of Technology) in Zurich and began his professional career at Porsche in 1965 as the manager of the testing and development department.

It is fair to say that these changes significantly influenced the development of the Typ 901 as Butzi Porsche brought his design and styling skills to the table. It was difficult for any non-family member to stand up to this strong family unit during these years.

Ferry Porsche and his sister Louise Piëch are pictured here with their mother Aloisia Porsche on the occasion of her 80th birthday on January 19, 1958 at the family estate, Schüttgut, in Zell am See, Austria

Ferry Porsche (seated on the wing of the Porsche 904) with Porsche dealers from the USA during their visit to Stuttgart-Zuffenhausen in 1963. Otto Erich Filius (4th from left), Executive Vice-President of the Porsche of America Corporation, the company's subsidiary and wholly owned importer of Porsche cars to the USA, Edgar Barth (8th from left), the successful Porsche works team driver and European hill climb champion in 1959, 1963 and 1964, Fritz Huschke von Hanstein (at right, behind Ferry Porsche), Porsche competition and PR manager, and Wolfgang Raether (far right), the Porsche KG sales manager. At the front left is the Porsche Type 901 presented for the first time at the German Motor Show in Frankfurt in September 1963. Butzi Porsche (1935), Ferry Porsche's eldest son, styled not only the 901 but also the Porsche Type 904 Carrera GTS (centre of picture). The 904 was the first Porsche to have a body made from glass fibre-reinforced plastic

Butzi Porsche sits proudly on the fender of an early Porsche 901, a car that he played a big part in designing and which helped to shape the company's future

Porsche Typ 901 Launch – IAA, September 1963

The official launch of the Porsche Typ 901 was set for the Internationale Automobil-Ausstellung (IAA), Frankfurt in September 1963 and, as one would expect, the Porsche stand was buzzing with eager onlookers as well as some sceptics. A successful launch for the new Porsche at the Frankfurt Show was a must for the Stuttgart manufacturer, as this was their home territory and at that time Frankfurt was the largest motor show in Europe, attended by the biggest contingent of international media.

The Frankfurt Motor Show was an important one for Porsche. This IAA promotional poster from 1963 captures the event for eternity

The back-end of the car received as much attention as any other aspect of the car, as journalists and other members of the media jostled for a view of the new 6-cylinder boxer motor

The introduction of Porsche's new sports car attracts a scrum of interested onlookers at the Frankfurt Show

On the left is the outgoing Porsche 356 C, while the new 901 on the right only gets half of the photographer's attention. This photograph was obviously taken during a quieter moment at the show. A successful launch was vitally important for the 901, not only because the new car had a hard act to follow, but the very future of the Stuttgart-Zuffenhausen company rested on just this one model

6-Cylinder Power

Up until the introduction of the Typ 901 in 1963, Porsche had preferred 4-cylinder power for its road cars, believing that a modestly-sized engine in a smaller but streamlined body could give startling performance. As usual, Porsche was right, except that the rest of the world was now producing ever-bigger cars with performance that the little 356 simply could not match. On the racing front they experimented with a flat-8 cylinder engine which was fine for the track, but could not be adapted for their road cars. Furthermore, it was also prohibitively expensive for normal production use.

The solution was to produce a new 6-cylinder boxer engine with overhead camshafts that ran quieter and more smoothly than the 4-cylinder Carrera engine, while still allowing plenty of scope for development in the future. In true Porsche style, the new power unit developed a rather conservative 130bhp which was up from the 95bhp of the standard 356 C but only equal to the mighty 2000 GS Carrera 2 Coupé.

The engine that set Porsche on the road to many motor sport victories. This 6-cylinder 1991cc engine, the Typ 901/01, formed the basis for Porsche's air-cooled engines for all 911 road cars right up until Porsche switched to water-cooling after the 1998 model year

This introductory sales brochure shows the newcomer's model designation prior to being changed to 911. It also tells the prospective buyer about the new 2.0-litre 6-cylinder boxer motor, developed especially for this model

Porsche 901 Or Porsche 911?

This car is a very early Typ 901 T8 photographed outside the Porsche plant, Werk I, in 1963

A problem surfaced with the introduction of the new model at the Frankfurt Motor Show when Peugeot objected to the use of Porsche's three-digit model description with a zero in the middle. The French manufacturer had secured the naming rights to such a three-digit numerical sequence and so the '901' had to go. The simple solution was to replace the offending '0' with a '1' ensuring plenty of room for the expansion of numerical model identification before reaching four digit model numbers.

Frankly, 'nine eleven' rolls off the tongue more easily than 'nine-0-one' or 'nine-zero-one' and so, with the benefit of hindsight, the French manufacturer did Porsche a favour by objecting to this early 901 nomenclature. When the vehicle arrived, it was well received by most and in time it grew on those sceptics who had initially said it was not fit to be a 356 replacement.

The phasing out of the Porsche 356 coincided with a decision to develop two separate lines of sports cars – specialist cars for racing and a line of more comfortable but still high performance, road-going sports cars for the general market. Research had shown that car buyers were becoming more sophisticated in their choices and this trend was reflected in their desire for quieter cars although many still desired the sensation of performance.

This market development required the introduction of a new engine, one that would give the same or greater performance, but importantly, one that was quieter in its delivery of power. These factors led to the development of the famous air-cooled six-cylinder boxer engine. However, a great amount of uncertainty surrounded the introduction of the new car itself as loyal Porschephiles questioned the need for a 356 replacement when they regarded the original model as a perfectly good vehicle

Porsche Typ 901/911 specs:

Model	Typ 901
Engine	6-cylinder horizontally opposed boxer type
Capacity	1,991cc
Maximum output	130bhp (96kW) @ 6,100rpm
Maximum torque	174Nm @ 4,200rpm
Compression ratio	9.0:1
Acceleration (0-100km/h or 62mph)	9.1 seconds
Top speed	210km/h or 131mph
Price	DM 21,900

Source: Porsche

Some journalists and industry observers questioned why Porsche introduced what looked like a fully-developed model at the 1963 IAA when it was, in fact, the one and only 901 available. No examples could be provided for testing by the press but, as this newcomer was not being promoted as a concept model, it was clearly intended for production. This was actually planned to commence the following autumn, a full 12 months away. Many felt that the company should have delayed the introduction until the 1964 Show, with cars being available for sale to the public immediately thereafter.

Once production commenced, just 82 examples of this early Typ 901 were manufactured before the company changed the model designation to '911' in October 1964, and so these very early cars are highly sought after today. Some Porschephiles claimed the new model was too luxurious for a Porsche, while others were disappointed with the phasing out of the 911's predecessor as the Carrera engine in the 356 C developed the same power output from just four cylinders. They felt the 356 C Carrera was a much more lively car than its successor, being both smaller and lighter. However, the Typ 901/911 was the product of a younger mind and intended for a new generation. What the market did not know at the time was that Ferry Porsche had plans to expand the 911's engine capacity in the future, something that could no longer be achieved with the old 356 motor.

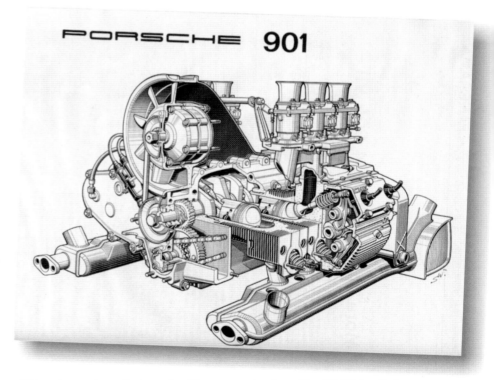

This cutaway shows the innards of the new overhead cam Typ 901/01 6-cylinder boxer engine

PORSCHE PANORAMA

OCTOBER 1963   Vol. VIII, No. 10

PRODUCTION SLATED FOR 1964

Porsche announces new Type 901

The long-rumored 6-cylinder 2 liter Porsche engine powering the new Type 901 car was announced by the Porsche factory late in August.

In a voluminous but vague announcement the new car was said to be not a 4 seater but a 2 + 2. On the cover, below, and on page 4 you will find all available photos sent to PANORAMA. Pictures of the engine evidently are not available.

Following are excerpts from the Factory's announcement, with some of the subjectiveness and translation peculiarities edited out:

Body and chassis

The body is even more aerodynamically smooth in form than the 356 Type. By increasing the wheelbase 120mm it became possible to enlarge the seating area, especially in the rear.

The overall width was reduced by 70mm, an advantage in today's traffic. In addition, the previous inside width has not only been retained but has been increased. The doors have been designed in such a manner that their greater width enables passengers to get in and out of the rear seats with greater ease.

The front fenders are fastened to the body by screws to facilitate front-end repair. The ventilation has been improved.

Engine

An opposed, 6 cylinder, air-cooled 2 liter engine is used since it is possible to reach higher RPM, and therefore higher power more economically than with a 4 cylinder engine. Both the Grand Prix and sports car experience were put to use in the design of this engine which has 1 overhead cam per cylinder bank. The cams, for the first time at Porsche, are driven by double row roller chains, while the forged crankshaft has 8 main bearings.

Transmission, axle, steering

A new 5-speed transmission was designed for this new engine.

The front suspension unit consists of a lower wishbone and shock absorber while the springing action is taken up by longitudinal torsion bars.

The rear suspension has trailing links which are supported by means of transverse torsion bars.

The rack and pinion steering is set up in the middle of the car. The steering column is divided

October 1963

3

It seems as though the writer of this article in Porsche Panorama was not entirely enthusiastic about the company's announcement of the new Typ 901 as a replacement for the much-loved 356

Porsche Statistics 1964

At the end of 1964, the combined workforce at Porsche (including the newly acquired Reutter company) totalled 2415 personnel. Annual production was 10,368 vehicles (including the 356 model) and the company achieved a turnover of DM 156m.

This is a very early publicity shot of the Typ 901 2.0 Coupé, 1963

Mindful of the company's limited resources (both financial and manpower) and the unthinkable consequences of not getting the 356's replacement right, the gestation period of the 911 was understandably a long one. On sale in the autumn of 1964 as a 1965-year model, 12 months after being shown at the IAA in Frankfurt, the first 911s were produced in Coupé form only.

Just like many of its European competitors, the Porsche 911 was a high-tech, high-spec sports car. Where many sporting cars still ran on solid rear axles with leaf springs, like the recently launched (April 1964) and much hyped Ford Mustang, the 911 had a new and sophisticated semi-trailing link rear suspension. Most performance cars of the time were equipped with a 3- or 4-speed gearbox, but the 911 came with a 5-speed 'box. The 911 was not a large car, as Ferry Porsche deemed that high speed was not necessarily a factor of large engines but was more a factor of a small and streamlined body. Ironically, the USA turned out

to be Porsche's chief market where speed and power were traditionally only achieved by big engines in even bigger cars. Size and noise meant everything in the States and, on this score, the new Porsche's success could be seen as a surprise because the 911 was smaller and quieter than anything around, but the little sports car from Stuttgart-Zuffenhausen had sophistication and motor sport breeding on its side.

Ferry Porsche was not big on decoration, and chrome embellishments were kept to a minimum for three reasons; cost, weight and he wanted the car's design to do the talking, not excessive ornamentation.

Ferry Porsche always felt that the car should communicate effectively with the driver and that an adequate set of instruments was essential for this purpose. Furthermore, it just looked sporty. On the very early 901 prototype model, the car only had two dials as in the 356 model, but this soon changed on Ferry's insistence.

This early 1965 brochure expounds the company's slogan, 'Driving in its finest form', which is just as applicable for the 911 in the 1960s as it is today

The Panorama magazine cover announces the arrival of the 1965 models

This interior shot shows that the five-dial dashboard was established as an early feature of the 911. In fact, this has become a permanent fixture in 911 design lore, as this cue has been carried forward into the current models

Christmas Gift Suggestions

PCA CAR BADGE $6.00
In 4 colors, enameled and chrome. 3 ½ in. dia.

PCA CUFF LINKS $2.75
Four colors, enamel and gold metal, ½ in. dia. Gift boxed.

PCA DECALS . . . . $1.00 doz.
PCA emblem in 4 colors, 2 in. dia. Display on drinking glasses, luggage, etc.

PCA EMBLEM (1 in. dia.) $1.75
(½ in. dia.) $1.00
Four colors and chrome. Makes a fine dash plaque or display on trophy. Epoxy cement (not supplied) will make it stick most anywhere.

PCA EMBLEM PIN $2.00
Same as emblem (above) but with pin and safety clasp.

PCA EMBLEM PATCH $1.00
PCA emblem embroidered in silk, 4 colors.

PCA LAPEL PIN $1.75
In 4 colors, enamel and gold metal, ½ in. dia. Safety clasp.

PANORAMA BINDERS $3.00
Durable blue plastic with PCA gold seal on cover. 'Porsche Panorama' on backbone. Holds 18 issues of 'Panorama' . . . without punching.

PCA TIE BAR $2.25
Emblem in 4 colors, enamel and gold metal.

PORSCHE HANDBOOK $1.50
By O'Cee Ritch.

RAND McNALLY ROAD ATLAS . . $2.00
120 pages, overall size 11 x 15 in. Maps in 4 colors. All US states plus Canada and Mexico. PCA seal and "Porsche Club of America" imprinted on cover.

PORSCHE TECHNICAL MANUAL . $3.00
By Henry Elfrink. All models through 356C.

PCA BANNER $6.00

PCA INTRODUCTION SLIPS . . . . . 1¢
Two-color flyer, 3 ¾ x 8 ½ in. Use to introduce Porsche owners to your PCA Region.

9th PORSCHE PARADE MUGS . . . 50¢

PORSCHE PRINT MATERIAL . . $4 per yd.
Material is 36 in. wide, protected by Scotchguard. Make your own skirts and shirts.

PCA LIGHTER $1.75
Lightweight lighter in Silvermist finish with PCA emblem etched in single color on front.

Regions should write for quantity discounts
Above items are all postpaid

ORDER FROM . . .

PCA EXECUTIVE OFFICE
5616 Clermont Drive   Alexandria, Va. 22310
Make checks and money orders payable to:
"Porsche Club of America, Inc."
Sorry, no C.O.D.

PORSCHE PANORAMA

Not sure what Christmas gift to buy the Porsche owner who has everything? Take a look at these suggestions, although the 1965 prices may no longer apply

1965 FRANKFURT Auto Show

Preview from GORDON WILKINS

Porsche

SINCE the last Frankfurt Show in 1963, Porsche has undergone the most significant changes in its sixteen years of automotive production by replacing the successful 356 programme with the new 911 and 912 series.

The presentation of the 911 prototype

MOTOR SHOWS

two years ago signalled the start of this new programme. Production of this all-new 6 cylinder model with a completely new body, designed to meet high motoring standards, began in October 1964. Its comfort, the safe handling, its powerful engine, the five-speed gearbox, and its top speed of more than 130 m.p.h., make the 911 a car of the international luxury class, which got world-wide acclaim.

Besides this high performance GT car, Porsche has recently presented the model 912. This car, equipped with the time-tested 90 h.p. flat-four engine, has also a 5-speed transmission and corresponds to the 911 in body style and handling characteristics. Both models will be shown in Frankfurt and will

Exciting newcomer is the Porsche Targa, which uses a roll-bar as a styling feature and comes as spyder, hardtop and soft-top.

Florio, the famous long distance race in the Highlands of Sicily, the car has a safety roll bar incorporated in its body.

Roll bars so far have been solely used in Grand Prix cars and prototypes, like disc brakes and independent suspension some years ago. In fact, in competition they have been a must, for on many occasions they have proven excellent safety devices. Porsche now is the first automobile manufacturer in the world to take up the idea and make it a production feature.

The safety roll bar concept may be con-

Section drawing of the Porsche Type 911.

feature a total of 18 detail refinements in coachwork and interior appointments.

Also on display at the Porsche stand will be the Porsche Carrera GTS 904, which has proved the world's most successful production sports car, during the last two years, as it won the GT Manufacturer's World-Championship (up to 2 litres) twice.

Porsche Targa

"Targa" is the name of the latest Porsche model, which was introduced to the public at Frankfurt. The "Targa" is neither convertible nor coupé, neither hardtop nor sedan, but a unique combination of the four. With the "Targa", Porsche not only presents a new car, but a new idea:

Called "Targa", in memory of the Targa

sidered as pace-setting in convertible body design for two reasons: it assures a so far unknown deal of safety in open car driving, and it offers various exciting new ways of open and closed driving in exceptional comfort.

The Targa models on show were:
● **Targa Spyder** convertible version, with the top and rear window open, gets its special appearance from the roll bar. The robust box-type construction of the roll bar

with a stainless steel finish will reduce open car driving hazards.
● **Targa Hardtop**, with detachable synthetic leather roof, which converts the car into a hardtop; with easy-to-operate snap fasteners, attached to the roll bar and windshield.
● **Targa Voyage**, the soft top version, is very convenient on long trips.
● **Targa Bel Air**, with the rear window closed and the top down — "topless" so to speak, giving the sensation of driving under a giant-size sunroof.

The Targa will be available in the 911 and 912 versions, and will be delivered around May, 1966. The price has not been fixed.

Renault

A RESTYLED version of the Renault 8-1100, designated the Renault 10, was announced before the show and featured on the Renault stand. Renault has stated that this will be an addition to the Renault range, and will not replace the 8-1100. It will sell at a higher price than the existing 1100 model.

(For South Africa, Renault Africa has pointed out, the Renault 10 will be introduced as a locally-manufactured model early in 1966.)

The Renault 10 has basic 8-1100 styling, but has been lengthened 8·5 inches mainly through a longer and more streamlined nose, which increases the capacity of the luggage compartment by 25 per cent. The trunk lid itself becomes flattened and lower, and the headlamp clusters incorporate indicator and sidelights. Headlamp diameter is increased.

There are minor changes to the interior,

The new six-cylinder, 2-litre Porsche 912 is top of the range.

CAR October 1965

34

Even in South Africa, the launch of the new Porsche models was keenly watched. Although little coverage has been given to Porsche's activities in that country, this image shows the well-respected local magazine, CAR, reporting on the 1965 Frankfurt Motor Show. British journalist Gordon Wilkins was describing the new models for the 1966 model year. CAR magazine was the first local motoring magazine in South Africa, being founded in 1957, and has developed an enviable reputation for accuracy over the years and is today one of the best-selling magazines of its type in the world

This is the first photo of a 911 that appeared in the summer 1965 edition of Porsche Post and is believed to be the first 911 in the UK. The car is a LHD, imported by a Sorjo Ranta and the alert photographer shot the car at the Porsche Club event at the Prescott hill climb on May 2, 1965. Porsche Post is still the official magazine of the Porsche Club of Great Britain

Comparisons

In 1964, the 4.2-litre Jaguar E-type had an alleged top speed of 150mph and cost £1992 while America's Chevrolet Corvette, fitted with a 3-speed manual 'box and a 327inch, 250bhp V8 engine would cost $4252. The 375bhp fuel-injected engine and 4-speed 'box would set you back a further $726.30. In the same year, a 2.0-litre Porsche 911 pushing out just 130bhp and fitted with a 5-speed manual gearbox cost its owner DM 21,900.

P-O-R-S-C-H-E Scripting

The styling and scriptology of the name, P-O-R-S-C-H-E, was down to one man in Porsche Design, Mr. Ploch. For three decades Ploch, the graphics man, was responsible for the promotional style or scriptology on all marketing and sales literature, working diligently on his own and certainly without the fully-staffed PR departments of today.

Said Tony Lapine, head of Porsche Design from 1969-1989, "He was our graphics man, and he was also our fabric man. Fabrics, colours, exterior and interior trim - one-man show. That was Mr. Ploch." He continued, "Then of course there was the Porsche logo. That was the elongated, very stout Porsche spelling, with the 'P' being longer [rather] than tall. The 'Spyder' and 'Carrera' script, I think also came from Mr. Ploch's desk."

Lapine explained that Mr. Ploch would sit down at his desk and begin to "sort of intuitively write it out, viewing it at arm's length and then putting it away. Taking it out again the next morning, he would say, 'Ja, I think it needs a little bit more work here on the 'O' or the 'Y' or something'. But," Lapine continued, "it was also handled in the flavour of the day, of the early 1950s. You know, a script like that you could very easily see over a drug store, saying 'Drogerie' or something." And so the style of the P-O-R-S-C-H-E lettering, with which we are so familiar today, was created over a period of time by one man at Porsche - Mr. Ploch.

Today we look back at the styling and design of these cars and hold them up as icons, but in their day the designers, draughtsmen, engineers and body craftsmen were all just doing their jobs to the best of their abilities.

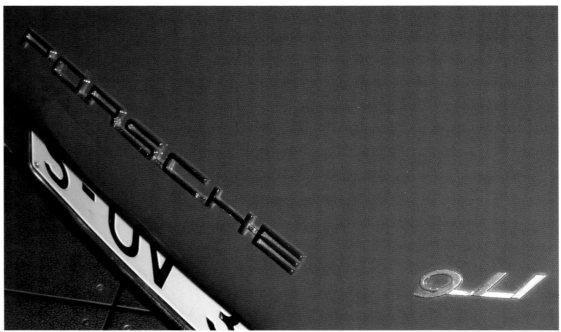

This early 911 engine cover clearly shows the elongated style of the Porsche name

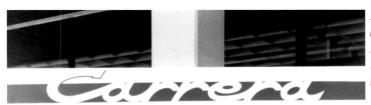

An example of the artwork produced by Mr. Ploch on display in the Porsche Design studio, c. 1972

CAR	MODEL	NATIONAL PRICE IN 1964	AVERAGE EXCHANGE RATE FOR 1964*	PRICE IN £-STERLING
Porsche 911	Coupé 1991cc	DM 21,900	11,100	£1972
Jaguar E-type	4235cc	£1992	N/A	£1992
Chevrolet	Corvette V8	$4252	4000	£1063

*The above table shows comparative sports car prices in £-Sterling in their respective countries of origin at the average annual exchange rate for the year. These figures exclude any import duties or other taxes as they are priced in their home markets. (*Note: historic exchange rates supplied by a leading international bank)*

With the lettering still in a longer, rather than tall style, the Carrera scripting was nevertheless distinctive and, although modernised on today's cars, it still follows the same basic style

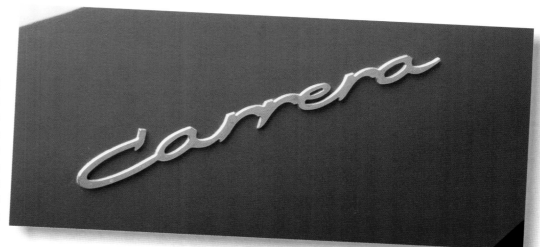

Porsche 912 – 1966 Model Year

In the first two years of production, there were few changes to the basic 911, the first big one coming with the introduction in April 1965 of an additional model, the Porsche 912. The car was introduced to the media at the Solitude race track near Stuttgart in what was that circuit's last year of active racing, rather a sad end to what was a very popular track in the early days.

The 912 was produced in response to a request from the Porsche Sales Department for a low cost, entry-level model to be added to the Porsche range. Luckily, the rather sombre mood hanging over the future of the Solitude circuit did not have a dampening effect on the sales of the 912 which went on to become one of the company's best-selling models. The 100,000th Porsche produced was in fact a 912 Targa produced for the Baden-Württemberg state for highway patrol duties, and was handed over at a ceremony on December 21, 1966.

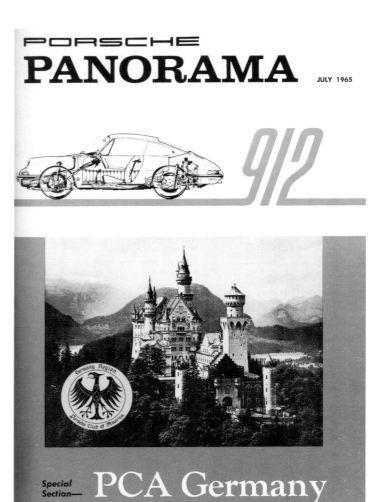

PORSCHE PANORAMA JULY 1965

Panorama magazine announces the new Porsche 912

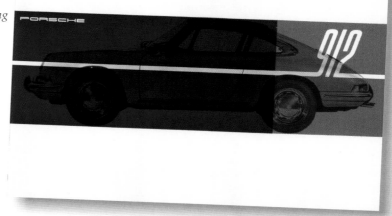

Both this brochure and the one opposite show the 912 in side profile, an angle which in itself confirms the car's strong 911 roots

The Porsche 912 was an attempt to provide a 911-lookalike for those buyers in the market who could not quite afford to make the step up to a fully-loaded 911. The 912 was fitted with a 1582cc 4-cylinder boxer engine straight out of the old 356 and cost as little as DM 16,250. This engine developed a meek and mild 90bhp giving the 912 a top speed of 185km/h or 115mph. Porsche reasoned that this model would provide the stepping stone for those folk who would hopefully one day make it into the big league, and between 1965-1969 they sold around 30,000 examples of this (at the time) much maligned and somewhat unloved model

This promotional poster produced by Porsche informs the prospective buyer that the new 912 is unmistakably a traditional Porsche in profile, character and elegance, complementing the lifestyle of the successful and the informed. Presumably that means that all Porsche-buyers are well informed – about what, the poster does not elaborate!

ENGINE			
Number of cylinders	4	Transmission gear ratios	1st gear = 11:34 / 11:34
Bore	82.5 mm (3.25 in.)		2nd gear = 18:34 / 19:32
Stroke	74.0 mm (2.91 in.)		3rd gear = 22:29 / 24:27
Displacement, actual	1582 cc (96.5 cu.in.)		4th gear = 25:26 / 28:24
Compression ratio	9.3 : 1		5th gear = 28:24
Horsepower	90 DIN HP (102 SAE HP) at 5800 RPM		Reverse = 11:16
Maximum torque	12.4 mkp (90 lbs/ft)		20:43
Horsepower / displacement ratio	57 DIN HP/liter (1.07 SAE HP/cu.in.)		

ENGINE DESIGN		CHASSIS	
Type	Opposed, four stroke cycle	Chassis type	Monocoque, unitized with frame
Cooling	Air cooled	Service brake	Hydraulic, single circuit
Crankcase	Light alloy	Effective friction area	185 cm² (28.7 sq.in.)
Cylinders	Cast iron liner in finned light alloy jacket	Wheels	Perforated, steel disc
Cylinder heads	Light alloy	Tires	6.95 H 15 (165 HR 15 optional)
Valves per cylinder	2	Steering	Rack and pinion
Valve arrangement	Overhead	Steering ratio	1 : 16.5
Valve timing	Pushrods	DIMENSIONS	
Camshaft drive	Gear-type	Wheelbase	2211 mm (87.05 in.)
Camshaft bearings	Plain journals	Track, front	1337 mm (52.63 in.)
Crankshaft	Forged, 4 plain journal main bearings	Track, rear	1317 mm (51.85 in.)
Connecting rod bearings	Plain journals	Overall length	4163 mm (163.90 in.)
Air blower drive	V-belt through generator	Overall width	1610 mm (63.39 in.)
Crankshaft / air blower ratio	approx. 1 : 1.8	Height (unladen)	1320 mm (51.97 in.)
Lubrication	Forced feed, gear-type	Ground clearance	150 mm (5.91 in.)
Fuel pump	Mechanical, diaphragm	WEIGHTS	
Carburetors	2 dual-throat downdraft, Solex 40 P II-4	Dry weight (DIN)	970 kp (2134 lbs)
ELECTRICAL SYSTEM		Maximum permissible weight	1290 kp (2838 lbs)
Battery voltage	12 V	Maximum axle load, front	570 kp (1254 lbs)
Battery capacity	45 Ah	rear	750 kp (1650 lbs)
Generator output	300 W max.	CAPACITIES	
Ignition	Battery coil	Fuel tank	62 liters (16.4 U.S. gals)
Distributor	Centrifugal advance	Oil sump	approx. 5 liters (5.3 qts)
Firing order	1-4-3-2	Transmission and differential	2.5 liters (2.65 qts)
Ignition timing	3° BTC	Hydraulic fluid reservoir	0.2 liters (7 fl.oz.)
POWER TRAIN		PERFORMANCE	
Number gears	4 or 5 speed option, 1 reverse	Range w/o refueling	approx. 450-500 km (280-310 mi.)
Synchronized gears	All forward speeds	Top speed	approx. 185 km/h (115 mph)
Final drive	Spiral bevel	Fuel consumption (DIN)	8.5 liters/100 km (29.5 mpg)
Rear axle ratio	7:31		

E · W 223 e · Dr.-Ing. h. c. F. Porsche KG, Stuttgart-Zuffenhausen · Printed in Germany · Subject to change without notice

PORSCHE HISTORISCHES ARCHIV

Porsche AG · Hist. Archiv
Porsche 912

englisch   BK 573
Exempl. 1 / 4   KBK 8

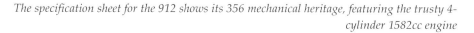
The specification sheet for the 912 shows its 356 mechanical heritage, featuring the trusty 4-cylinder 1582cc engine

Ferry Porsche Honoured

On November 9, 1965 Ferry Porsche was awarded an honorary doctorate by the Technical University in Vienna in recognition of his service to the automobile industry. This entitled him to use the title 'Dr. tech. E.h'.

Export Sales Growth

Foreign imports into America were growing year-on-year and the industry was beginning to notice these numbers by 1965. Although the numbers were still miniscule by overall US industry production levels, they were nevertheless on the increase and this caught the attention of the domestic manufacturers and industry analysts.

Although there had been a slump in foreign imports into the USA during 1961 and 1962, following an all-time high of over 614,000 units in 1959, the numbers were once again beginning to rise and, more than anything else, this told the industry that the market, as a whole, was beginning to move once again.

At this point an analysis of the figures only listed the top 10 manufacturers, such as Volkswagen, Mercedes, Renault, Volvo, MG and others, with Porsche only being included in 'others' due to their relatively small sales figures.

At the end of 1964, industry analysts predicted (correctly) that sales looked set to increase the following year again. Two main reasons were cited for the growth; firstly, that foreign manufacturers were finally giving greater attention to providing better service facilities for their cars sold in America and, secondly, those manufacturers had stepped up their advertising in national American publications, ensuring greater market exposure for their products.

Imports of foreign cars into the USA, 1959-1964:

Year	Quantity of foreign cars imported
1959	614,131
1960	498,785
1961	378,622
1962	339,160
1963	385,624
1964	484,131
1965	563,673

Source: Wardsauto.com

PORSCHE POST

CHRISTMAS 1966

vice facilities.—Winchester Hill, Romsey, Hants. Romsey 3185. [5917
F. W. KERRIDGE (NORMANDY STREET), Ltd., Peugeot distributors, offer the finest sales, spares, service facilities.—Normandy St., Alton, Hants. Alton 2224. [N3009

PONTIAC
LENDRUM & HARTMAN, Ltd., Flood St. (off King's Rd.). Chelsea, London. S.W.3. Flaxman 5774 and 4801. [0950/R

PORSCHE
PORSCHE CARS GREAT BRITAIN, Ltd., invite prospective purchasers to visit their works to see and try the latest 911 and 912 models, illustrated literature on request.—Falcon Works, London Rd., Isleworth, Middlesex. Isleworth 1011. [N1003
WHYKE MOTORS, Ltd., distributors for Sussex.—Bognor Rd., Chichester. (Tel. Chichester 3888.) [0861/R

The Autocar magazine carried an advertisement in the Classified section inviting prospective buyers to visit the Porsche showrooms to view the new models and take a test drive (August 19, 1966)

Go ahead. Drive it.   You'll never forget it.

Even the Porsche sales brochures became rather suggestive in the 1960s, inviting one in to indulge in the pleasure to be derived

911 Enters The World Of Motor Sport

Porsche's first factory entry in a major sporting event with the new 911 was in the 1965 Rallye Monte Carlo where the car's reputation was entrusted to factory development driver/engineers, Herbert Linge and Peter Falk. As the accompanying promotional poster shows, the pair finished second in class and a creditable fifth overall.

Since Porsche first ventured into motor sport, Le Mans had always been a favourite hunting ground for them. Although there was no hope of overall honours for the factory at this stage, the 911 certainly held its own in the field. It was on motor racing circuits such as this one that Porsche would learn valuable lessons in how to produce more power and extract greater performance from their race cars.

The advantage in entering a production-based car in tough endurance races such as Le Mans, is that the experience gained would later be developed and applied to their production models, toughening the breed in the process.

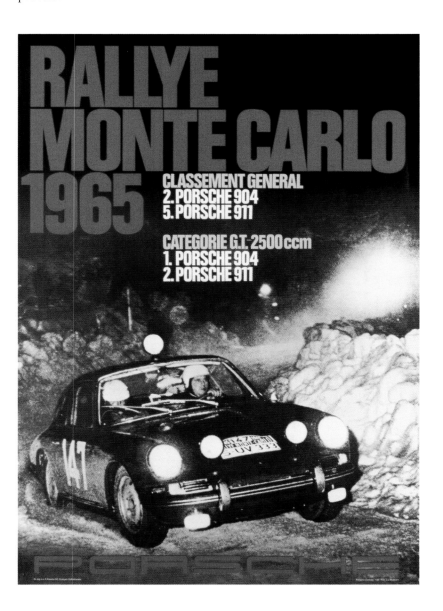

Changing Times – The 1960s

There was a lot happening in the world that influenced designers in 1966. Society was becoming a lot more liberal in its thinking as Leslie Hornby, a 17-year-old student from West London, burst onto the fashion scene. 'Twiggy' to the rest of the world, she was to help make the mini-skirt famous and so begin a whole new fashion revolution. In August 1966, The Beatles released two new singles, *Yellow Submarine* and *Eleanor Rigby* (Capitol Records) and the group began recording work on *Sergeant Pepper's Lonely Hearts Club Band* later that year. On the other side of the pond, singer/song writer Bob Dylan released his *Just Like A Woman*, as he continued to weave his magical music skills for millions around the world.

Every year following the annual shutdown in the summer, Porsche would return to the market with their new model, usually around August, for the next year and, in this time-honoured tradition, Porsche presented their 1967 models in the autumn of 1966. The new 911 S had a more powerful engine, now producing 160bhp, thanks to an encouraging result in the 1965 Rallye Monte Carlo, where such a model had finished a creditable fifth overall in the hands of works drivers, Herbert Linge and Peter Falk.

But 1966 was a time when the British motor industry was busy imploding. In July of that year, the British Motor Corporation merged with Jaguar to form British Motor Holdings, which at this time produced over 20,000 cars per week. Through the 1950s and 1960s, the British motor industry produced more sports cars than any other nation on earth, but that was all about to change. The following year, Chrysler purchased a majority shareholding in the Rootes Group and Leyland took over Rover. Throughout this time, Porsche continued to work away quietly and efficiently in the suburb of Zuffenhausen, manufacturing just one single model type – the 911.

Porsche 911 and 912 production statistics

Model Year	Introduced	911 Production	912 Production
1965	October 1964	3300	5000
1966	August 1965	1708	6692

Source: Porsche

IMPROVING THE ACT

By the second half of the 1960s, Porsche was beginning to move into the big league as a manufacturer of sports cars with sales showing signs of strong growth. Although the numbers were small, they were impressive in Porsche terms. Buyers were now also looking at the 911 as an altogether different animal from the lively but simple 356 with its minimalist interior.

The 911 had by now matured and established itself as a serious, comfortable and high quality contender in the grand touring market. No longer could you refer to the Porsche sports car as an "upside down bath tub", as some had dubbed the 356, since the 911 had pleasing looks and styling, and above all, excellent driveability.

With each successive model since its introduction in 1963, the 911, now four years old, had matured and developed with more power and a variety of new models. Rolf Sprenger had joined Porsche in 1967 and was responsible for developing the fuel injection system for the boxer engine, as no such system existed for such a power unit anywhere in the world. Sprenger later became head of the 'Sonderwunsch' programme, a separate department set up to cater for the increasing demand from customers who wanted more power from their Porsche, or simply to personalise their 911 in some way. This became affectionately known as the Special Wishes Department.

Billed as a 'safety convertible', Porsche presented its new Targa at the Frankfurt Motor Show in autumn 1965. This was Stuttgart's reaction to the impending stricter safety requirements for open-top cars in the American market, where an all-out ban on convertibles in the future seemed a strong possibility. The Targa offered convertible-style motoring through its removable roof panel, but with the security of a fixed roll-over bar.

Following Porsche's successful exploits in the 1965 Monte Carlo Rally, the company introduced the more powerful 911 S (160bhp) a year later. Marketed as a 1967 model, the 911 S was available in both Coupé and Targa forms. The following year saw the introduction of the 911 T (Touring) which was now being offered as the entry-level 6-cylinder model while the previous standard model was now called the 911 L. From this year on, all models could be purchased with the optional Sportomatic gearbox.

The absence of a Carrera model was perhaps less of an issue within the company than it was for customers. Porsche, at the time, was pursuing a strategy of building cars for the road, with a separate line of race cars for the track. Where previously the 356 had been adapted for competition in the early days, Porsche had benefited from the unmistakable advantage of having the 550 as a dedicated racer, and not a converted road car, and they had the results to support this policy.

From the outset, the 911 had been designed first and foremost as a road car and was therefore too heavy to be considered as a serious competition vehicle. During the mid-1960s, this had enabled the competitions department to develop the 904 (Carrera GTS) and 906 (Carrera 6) as the company's dedicated racers. These two cars had proven to be more than capable of carrying the baton for Porsche in competition.

This policy allowed the engineers on the production car side to develop the 911, making it into a fully-fledged, world-beating sports car. During this period, 1967-1969, annual production of the 911 more than doubled.

TIMELINE (1967-1969):

1967	1968	1969
Sportomatic introduced.	911 S with more power.	912 phased out.
Targa body style introduced.	911 T replaces 912.	Last year for 2.0-litre engine.

Everybody liked the new 911. January, 1967 heralded the start of a great year for Porsche

The Porsche 911 2.0 Targa (1967) was a hit with many Porsche drivers, but one has to ask if the excited onlookers behind this model were just very enthusiastic holidaymakers roped in for a bit of fun, or were they from Rent-A-Crowd?

This contemporary shot of the new 911 S 2.0 Coupé (1967) shows a girl whose affections, if her pose is anything to go by, are clearly torn between the statue of the lion on the left and the new Porsche

PORSCHE

EXTRABLATT
SPECIAL EDITION
EDITION SPECIALE

FÜR DIE INTERNATIONALE
MOTORPRESSE

FOR THE INTERNATIONAL
MOTORING PRESS

POUR LA PRESSE
D'AUTOMOBILE

1

DER NEUE
THE NEW
LA NOUVELLE **911S**

28. JULI 1966

New for 1968 was the Porsche Typ 911 L 2.0 Coupé. This was the decade of colour, so it is very appropriate to have such a spray of orange and red in this publicity shot

David Stone navigated for Vic Elford when the pair won the Monte Carlo Rally in 1968 driving a Porsche 911. Stone is seen here holding their trophies outside AFN Motors, originally manufacturers of Frazer Nashes and later Porsche importers

The in-house newspaper, Porsche, announces the arrival of the new 911 S for 1967

911 Targa (1967)
Where Does The Name 'Targa' Come From?

In many ways, the 911 Targa was an amazing vehicle, offering its owner a variety of options to suit his, or her, motoring style. The name *Targa*, meaning plaque or shield in Italian, was given to the legendary road race, the Targa Florio, which was run every year on the twisty, and sometimes treacherous, mountainous public roads on the island of Sicily. Created in 1906 by wealthy Italian pioneer racing driver and automobile enthusiast, Vincenzo Florio, the event ran until 1977 (last international was in 1973) when it was discontinued because of safety concerns.

Head of Sales at Porsche, Harald Wagner, observed that several other motor manufacturers used the names of famous race circuits for their sports cars, and decided that Porsche should adopt such a name. Due to Porsche's strong showing in the Sicilian event over the years, the Targa name was adopted in 1965 for their new convertible model with its built-in safety roll-over bar.

At first, the Targa model came equipped with a flexible plastic rear window, usually referred to as a 'soft window', and early models with this feature are extremely rare today. There were several ways in which this 911 Targa model could be enjoyed, the first, known as the Targa Hardtop, being all enclosed with roof panels in place and the rear window zipped up for all-weather protection. By removing the hard roof panels, you created the Targa Voyage as these covers could be stored in the trunk for convenient reattachment during your journey. By unzipping and opening the plastic rear window and removing the top panels, you created the Targa Spyder, while the Targa Bel-Air position consisted of the top in place with the rear window rolled down. Later the Targa was offered with a solid rear glass equipped with a demister and this model was called the 'hard window' Targa.

The Targa was really a model for all seasons, as with the roof panel off you could enjoy fast motoring in the open air without the normal wind buffeting often associated with full convertibles at the time. By lowering the soft rear window as well, you could then fully enjoy the open-air driving experience, and even in winter with the roof panel in place and rear window lowered, occupants were protected from the cold and any light rain, while still enjoying the brusque, chill air during a blast through the countryside. It was a car for all driving styles too, as there was no difference in performance between the Coupé and Targa models.

In reality, the Targa was actually something of a compromise. Chassis rigidity dictated that a full convertible body would have required re-engineering as an additional model but this would have been too costly. Indeed, this has always presented a challenge to engineers when a Coupé body has been converted to a Cabriolet, rather than the other way around.

Early prototype Targas explored the use of a flexible roof cover that could be rolled back and stored behind the seats. This option would certainly have been easier to remove or replace without even getting out of the car, and Porsche went so far as to print this in their sales and promotional literature before the car's launch. However, the flexible roof panel did not go into production. So popular was the Targa model in Germany, that as much as 55% of the 911s sold there consisted of this new body style in its early years.

The German police liked to have a few 911s in their fleet of cars, and it is not hard to understand why. Who would not relish the opportunity of driving a Porsche belonging to someone else who also kindly pays for the petrol and gives you a licence to drive as fast as you like, whenever you like (well almost)? This 'Polizeifahrzeug' is a Typ 911 2.0 Targa

The first Targas were delivered to the German police in December 1966 while the first Targas available for the general market were only delivered to customers in January 1967. Here, a Porsche 911 2.0 Targa highway patrol car is on duty in the Düsseldorf area (c. 1967)

chri sto pho rus

Nr. 89 / November 1967

The *Christophorus* magazine was founded by journalist Richard von Frankenberg and graphic artist, Erich Strenger. First published in 1953, this magazine has become a favourite with Porschephiles and is very collectible as a set. The first few issues of this magazine can fetch up to US$1000 each at auction

Below Left: Herbert Linge drives a Porsche Typ 911 2.0 Targa at a press presentation at the Hockenheim Motodrom, 1967

The versatile Targa was an ingenious way of satisfying the driving requirements of Porsche owners in differing weather conditions. It offered four different roof positions as described in this sales brochure below

PORSCHE **targa** *4* IN ONE

For many reasons, the unique, new Porsche **targa** is a truly significant innovation in open touring-car design. Even the name has special significance, for it's a fitting tribute to the world-famous Targa Florio, the annual "race of a thousand curves" through the sun-drenched mountain streets and roads of Sicily. In this most revealing road race, the remarkable stamina of Porsche-built cars has been dramatically and publicly demonstrated year after year. To enthusiasts around the world, there is a very close and logical association between the names Targa Florio and Porsche. The designation **"targa"** is also well chosen because the word means "shield" in Italian, and the new Porsche cabriolet adds an extremely functional measure of open-car protection to the rugged reliability that is characteristic of all Porsches.

In the **targa**, the House of Porsche has again combined functional originality with the great art of automotive engineering — the creative combination that has repeatedly enabled Porsche to achieve new breakthroughs in the design and construction of high-performance grand tourisme cars.

The distinguished stainless steel bar, an integral part of the **targa's** monocoque construction, gives the car more than just a distinctive appearance. It provides a high degree of safety for the **targa's** occupants, adds valuable strength and rigidity to the car, and it allows the unique topside changes to be made with a minimum of effort.

Should you decide to drive with the **targa** fully open, you can remove the roof section quickly and easily — and it can be neatly stored in the luggage compartment or under the passenger seats.

In all, there are four basic variations possible in the openness of this racing-inspired high-performance convertible. Whatever the weather, you

can adapt the **targa** for maximum comfort — from the fully closed protection of a coupe, to the unrestricted enjoyment of a fully open car.

Even at highway speeds, with the **targa** fully opened to the sky, disturbing wind noises and air currents are largely eliminated by the built-in roll bar and the car's aerodynamically designed exterior surfaces.

This happy meeting of form and function should satisfy even the most demanding individualist by the kind of personal environmental control it gives him.

To suit different personal styles of driving, the **targa** is available with the engines and equipment offered in the three Porsche coupes: the 912, the 911, and the 911 S. Whichever of these **targa** models you select, you can be sure that the exclusive design and advanced-engineering features — common to all Porsches — have made the car you choose both extremely safe and years-ahead in quality of performance.

targa

FOUR CARS IN ONE

"Someday All Convertibles Will Have A Roll-bar"

Perhaps this was just a bit of sales talk, but even if it was, the Targa was an attractive model and destined to be a huge success for the company. Remember, this slogan was written at a time when American safety regulations were at their most stringent, with even the Chevy Camaro discontinued in convertible form as from 1970 due to the actions of certain pressure groups. It is rather amazing that the authorities there did not find some way of outlawing even the Targa roof!

At this time it was believed that legislation would be introduced in the States that would have ruled out a full convertible body. Although the Targa would have passed such rules due to the inherent strength of its roll-bar, this perceived threat in the USA threw the cat among the pigeons in the design world. As a result, a whole decade of car design was influenced by this legislation which was apparently pending in the US but which was never actually made law.

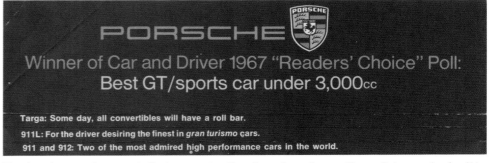

PORSCHE
Winner of Car and Driver 1967 "Readers' Choice" Poll:
Best GT/sports car under 3,000cc

Targa: Some day, all convertibles will have a roll bar.

911L: For the driver desiring the finest in *gran turismo* cars.

911 and 912: Two of the most admired high performance cars in the world.

The American market was vitally important to Porsche and so a favourable result in a readers' poll in one of the most influential enthusiasts' magazines in the States, Car And Driver, *was good news for the company. The Readers' Choice Poll voted the 911 as 'Best GT/Sports Car under 3000cc' as well as the 911/912 being voted two of the most admired high performance cars in the world. Stuttgart could hardly remain silent about this and promptly produced this handy little fold-out brochure in recognition of the achievement*

This page of the brochure tells you how even back in 1967, you could arrange to collect your new 911 or 912 from the factory in Stuttgart in person. This would also entitle the buyer to enjoy a guided tour of the factory as part of the deal

Porsche 911 S 2.0 Targa on display at a motor show in 1966. This car is fitted with Fuchs alloy wheels which were available on the 911 S (model year 1967) and had the all-aluminium look, without paint

Erwin Kremer corners hard in his 911 S 2.0 during the 1968 Touring Car Championships held at the Nürburgring circuit

Early 911 Competition Success

It wasn't only Porsche who wanted to win races with the 911, it was also privateer teams who saw the potential of the new sports car. The term 'new' is used here as the 911 was not rushed into competition because Porsche had other weapons with which to win championships, such as the dedicated 904 and 906 race cars.

An important early result for a 911 came in the 1966 Daytona 24-Hour race, three years after the car's launch, where a 16th place finish was achieved. This encouraging result was bettered the following year when two 911s finished in 9th and 10th spots overall against some tough opposition which included Ferraris, Ford GT40s and Porsche's own 906 and 910 racers. This successful exposure on American soil was enormously significant in Porsche's quest for market growth there. Further encouraging results that year were achieved at Sebring, Spa and also in the treacherous Targa Florio. A significant 14th place finish in the hands of Robert Buchet and Herbert Linge in the 1967 Le Mans 24-Hour race further signalled the 911's potential as a racer.

Kremer Racing, a private Porsche vehicle repair and race preparation workshop based in Cologne, Germany, had built up quite a reputation through racing their 356 B in the early 1960s, and so turned their attention to the 911. Erwin Kremer, together with his brother Manfred, purchased a 911 from Porsche and with this vehicle, which they prepared in their workshops, proceeded to dominate the European Touring Car Championship in 1968.

Erwin claimed his first big title that year with an overall win in the 24-Hours of Spa and, in the process, helped Porsche to win the Manufacturers' Championship.

Factory drivers Robert Buchet and Herbert Linge drove their 911 to an overall 14th place in the 1967 Le Mans 24-Hour race. Here the 911 can be seen on the right at the finish

911 Targa Marketing
And Promotional Material

Model year 1967 (in reality August 1966) was to prove a big one for the Porsche 911 with the introduction of its revolutionary new roof style, the Targa.

Open-top motoring had never been this safe and Porsche were quick to emphasise in the motoring press the many practical and aesthetic advantages. Several American and British motor manufacturers would follow suit with their own variations of the Targa roof (Triumph Stag in 1970 and Camaro/Firebird in 1978), an option which is still offered by Porsche today.

targa 911

Sicherheits-gepolstertes Armaturenbrett, Transistordrehzahlmesser, Gesamt- und Tageskilometerzähler, elektrische Benzinuhr, Öl-Thermometer, Ölstandanzeiger, Öldruckmesser. Kontrolleuchten für Batterieledestrom, Fernlicht, Begrenzungslicht, Blinker, Handbremse. Elektrische Zeituhr, 3stufiger Scheibenwischer, Zigarrenanzünder, Lichthupe. Handschuhkasten mit Magnetverschluß und verschließbar. 4-Speichen-Holzlenkrad, Armstützen, Haltegriff für Beifahrer, verstellbare Vordersitze als Liegesitze ausgebildet, 2 Hecksitze im Fond als Gepäckauflage umklappbar, Lenkradschloß, 2 gepolsterte Sonnenblenden. Türtaschen beidseitig, benzinelektrische Zusatz- und Standheizung, Kofferraum 200 Liter. Luftgekühlter Boxer-Heck-Motor, Hubraum 1991 ccm, 6 Zylinder, 8fach gelagerte Kurbelwelle. 130 PS bei 6100 U/min. Einzelzylinderköpfe, hängende Ventile, obenliegende Nockenwelle, Nockenwellenantrieb durch Ketten, automatische Kettenspannung, 6 Vergaser mit 2 gemeinsamen Schwimmergehäusen, Trockensumpf-Schmiersystem. Ölkühler mit thermostatischer Regulierung, 12-Volt-Drehstrom-Lichtmaschine. 5 Vorwärtsgänge, Porsche-Synchronisierung, wartungsfreie Hinter- und Vorderachse durch Federstäbe abgefedert, hohe Kurvenfestigkeit durch zusätzlichen Stabilisator, Zahnstangenlenkung, Sicherheitslenksäule, Scheibenbremsen wartungsfrei, automatische Nachstellung. Handbremse als Trommelbremse mit hohem Wirkungsgrad. Gürtelreifen 165 HR 15.

Safety cushioned dashboard · transistorized tachometer · speedometer incorporating total and trip distance recorder · electric fuel gauge · oil gauge · oil temperature gauge · oil pressure gauge · pilot lamp for generator, high beam, parking lights, turn signal, handbrake · electric clock · 3-speed windshield wiper · cigarette lighter · headlight signal · lockable glove compartment with magnet · 4-spoked wood rim steering wheel · arm rests · passenger grab handle · adjustable front seats are fully reclining · two occasional rear seats changeable into luggage space · steering column lock · 2 cushioned sun visors · map pocket in each door · engine heating system and gasoline-electric heater · luggage compartment 7 cu. ft. Air-cooled horizontally opposed six cylinder engine at rear of car · displacement 1991 ccm · eight-bearing crankshaft · 148 HP (SAE) at 6100 rpm · individual cylinder heads · overhead valves · overhead camshafts · camshaft drive through chains · automatic chain tensioning · 6 carburetors with 2 common float housings · dry sump lubrication · thermostat-controlled oil cooler · 12 volt three-phase generator with integral axial fan drive · single plate dry clutch · 5 forward speeds · Porsche synchronization · maintenance-free front and rear axle, suspension by torsion bars · high cornering stability through additional anti-roll bar · rack and pinion steering · safety steering column · maintenance-free disk brakes · self-adjusting devices · handbrake designed as drum brake · braced tread tires 165 HR 15.

targa 912

Sicherheitsgepolstertes Armaturenbrett, Transistordrehzahlmesser, Gesamt- und Tageskilometerzähler, elektrische Benzinuhr, Öl-Thermometer, elektrische Benzinuhr, Kontrolleuchten für Öldruck, Batterieladestrom, Fernlicht, Begrenzungslicht, Blinker und Handbremse. 3stufiger Scheibenwischer mit elektrischer Scheibenwaschanlage kombiniert, Lichthupe, Zigarrenanzünder, Aschenbecher, 4-Speichen-Kunststofflenkrad, Haltegriff für Beifahrer, Handschuhkasten mit Magnetverschluß, verstellbare Einzelsitze als Liegesitze ausgebildet, 2 Hecksitze im Fond als Kofferablage umklappbar, Lenkradschloß, 2 gepolsterte Sonnenblenden. Türtaschen beidseitig, Frischluftregulierung, stufenlos regulierbare Motorheizung. 4 Zylinder Boxer-Heck-Motor, luftgekühlt, 1582 ccm Hubraum, 90 PS bei 5800 U/min., 4fach gelagerte Kurbelwelle, hängende Ventile, über Stoßstangen angetrieben, Druckumlaufschmierung, 2 Doppelfallstromvergaser, 12-Volt-Lichtmaschine, 300 Watt max., 45 Ah. Batteriezündung. 5 Vorwärtsgänge, zwangssynchronisiert, 1 Rückwärtsgang. Knüppelschalthebel. Selbsttragender, gepreßter und geschweißter Stahlblech-Kastenrahmen, Zahnstangenlenkung mit abgewinkelter Sicherheitslenksäule, Einzelradaufhängung an Vorder- und Hinterachse, drehstabgefedert, alle Gelenke an Lenkung, Vorder- und Hinterachse wartungsfrei. Scheibenbremsen an allen vier Rädern, zusätzliche Trommelbremse als Handbremse an den Hinterrädern, Good Year 6.95 H 15 High-Speed-Reifen für alle fünf Räder auf silbermetall-lackierten Stahlfelgen montiert.

Air-cooled flat four engine at rear of car, displacement 1582 cc, 102 HP/SAE at 5800 rpm, four-bearing crankshaft, pushrod operated overhead valves, forced-feed lubrication, 2 dual-throat downdraft carburetors. 12-volt generator, 300 W — 45 Ah battery, coil ignition. Optional 5 speed transmission, ring synchromesh, central floor change, 1 reverse gear. Unit-construction chassis, rack and pinion steering with double universal-jointed steering shaft, independent suspension front and rear, torsion bar springing, steering joints and rear axle universal joints maintenance-free, disc brakes on all four wheels, parking brake of the drum-type incorporated in the rear brake discs, Good Year 6.95 H 15 high-speed tires on all five wheels, fitted on silver painted steel rims. Dashboard padded on top and bottom, transistorized tachometer, speedometer with total and trip mileage recorder, oil temperature gauge, electric fuel gauge, indicator lights for generator, oil pressure, high beam, parking lights, turn signals, handbrake. 3-speed windshield wipers combined with electric washers, headlight flasher, cigarette lighter, ashtray, 4-spoked steering wheel, arm rests, courtesy grip for passenger, lockable glove compartment with magnet, individual front seats fully reclining, 2 occasional rear seats changeable into luggage space, 2 padded sun visors, map pocket in each door, fresh air vents, infinitely variable heater.

This sales brochure inner page gives the comparative specifications and safety data for both the 911 and 912 Targa models

"Inspired by racing", claims this advertisement. The roll-bar is an adaptation of the roll-bar found on racing cars, enabling the owner to enjoy the full benefits of the Targa's performance in greater safety

roll-bar
convertible
safe as
a coupe

This promotional poster for the 1967 Porsche 911 Targa emphasises the four roof combinations available as well as the robust nature of the roll-over bar, "Safe As A Coupé", making a virtue of a necessity

NOVEMBER 1965   Vol. X, No. 11

PORSCHE
PANORAMA

AVAILABLE FOR THE 1967 MODEL YEAR IN THE UNITED STATES

'Targa' debuts at Frankfurt Show

The convertible version of the 911 and 912 series was unveiled by Porsche at the Frankfurt Auto Show, Sept. 18-26.

The new "Targa", according to the Factory, "is neither convertible nor coupe, neither hardtop nor sedan, but a unique combination of the four."

A novel feature is a safety roll bar, the first time such a feature has been built into a convertible design of a series production car.

The new car is named after the famous Targa Florio road race held each year in Sicily. Porsche cars have been competing successfully in this race for the past 10 years.

The Factory says that the safety roll bar concept not only offers safety in an open car, but also offers a series of variations on open and closed driving.

Targa Spyder—The convertible version, with the top and rear window open (see cover photo) gets its special appearance from the roll bar. The box-type construction of the roll bar has a stainless steel finish.

Targa Hardtop—A detachable synthetic leather roof converts the car into a hardtop. The "roof" is attached to the windshield and hardtop by means of snap fasteners. The wide-view, plastic rear window offers excellent rear vision. (See photo.)

Targa Voyage—The soft top version is convenient on long trips because the rolled up top may stay in the car, and is easily put into place between roll bar and windshield.

Targa Bel Air—Options here are rear window closed, and top down; or top up, and rear window zipped open.

Delivery to the USA will begin with the 1967 model year; units should be available in August or September, 1966. The USA price was not announced. Although Cabriolets (with padded tops) have been more expensive than Coupes, the long-type Roadster was less expensive. Because the new Targa is somewhat of a hybrid, the price is unpredictable at this time.

November 1965

3

Panorama magazine quoted the factory literature referring to the Targa as follows: "Neither convertible nor Coupé, neither hardtop nor sedan, but a unique combination of the four"

Erich Strenger – 1922 To 1993

Colleagues, Erich Strenger and Richard von Frankenberg, in discussion (c 1956)

Well known graphic artist and designer, Erich Strenger, was responsible for Porsche's racing posters and promotional brochures from 1950 up until 1982. His work went on to become famous around the world for its very explicit and striking style. Strenger's unique approach employed a technique that not only effectively portrayed the speed and dominance of Porsche in motor sport, but which also captured the attractive styling of the car while at rest.

Many people feel that this period of graphic illustration in automotive art is far more expressive as a communications medium than the ensuing photographic era. Such striking artwork enabled Strenger to introduce movement and speed, a style that was years ahead of other artists in this field.

Who was Erich Strenger? Born in December 1922, Strenger was a late returnee from Russian imprisonment following the cessation of hostilities, only making it back to Germany in 1949. Co-incidence brought him and race photographer Julius Weitmann together and it was whilst attending a modelling shoot for *Miss Cover Girl* at the Stuttgart movie theatre, that Strenger found himself seated next to journalist Richard von Frankenberg, then doing part-time work for Porsche.

Von Frankenberg struck up conversation and soon Strenger found himself with a graphics commission for Porsche. In the beginning there was no money involved as not even Porsche had money with which to pay the young journalist or the artist at that stage. Both men could see Porsche sports cars had a future and were happy enough just to have the opportunity to work, confident that such commitment would bring rewards later.

In 1953 von Frankenberg and Strenger jointly founded the *Christophorus* magazine which Strenger said later, "just sort of came together". Similarly, the famous Porsche strap line, 'Driving In Its Most Beautiful Form', was the result of casually discussing advertising ideas with his colleagues rather than sitting down with the aim of devising a world-beating marketing slogan. That is the way it was done back then.

When asked how the name *Christophorus* came about, Strenger explained that he and Richard von Frankenberg felt that most Porsche owners would be driving their cars much faster than most other motorists on the road. Due to this inevitability, the two felt that Porsche drivers would most likely need the protection of a patron saint, and so the magazine was named after Saint Christopher!

Much of Strenger's creative work came about through requests from Huschke von Hanstein, Porsche's PR supremo. Following a weekend race win, Von Hanstein would phone up Strenger on the Sunday night and ask him to produce a poster by the Monday, which he invariably managed to do. Later, Strenger got wise and prepared poster designs ahead of the weekend races, fully expecting Porsche to win, and, when Von Hanstein's call came through, Strenger could say in all honesty that it was already done.

Strenger admits that his graphic illustrative style came from watching many motor races. In fact, he was no mere spectator, having competed personally in the gruelling Rome-Liège-Rome Rally, the Mille Miglia and the Corsica Rally. No doubt, such inside knowledge helped to inspire many ideas for his now famous artwork.

Initially all Strenger's work was done through the medium of art, but as pressure mounted to get more and more material produced for Porsche, the focus shifted to photography. There was no conscious push in this direction, it just came about naturally, although Strenger admits that it was not as expressive as the traditional graphics approach.

Erich Strenger worked with Porsche from 1950 to 1982. Just as the Porsche company was handed down from Ferry Porsche to his son Butzi, so too did Strenger pass the studio to his son Rolf on Erich's 60th birthday. Erich Strenger retired in 1982 to run *Christophorus* and to pursue his passion for painting. Sadly, he passed away on February 16, 1993 at the age of 71. With him went a generation of creative automotive artistry that will be admired and cherished for many years to come.

The strong links early on between Porsche, Erich Strenger and Richard von Frankenberg are all captured in this poster. Strenger's name can be seen in the top left corner of the poster which records a class victory by von Frankenberg and Wolfgang Count Berghe von Trips in a Porsche

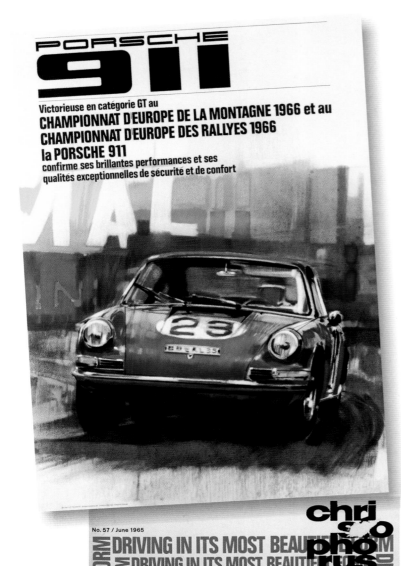

Conscious of the average American's desire for an automatic gearbox, Porsche introduced their own in the form of the Sportomatic. In order to give as much publicity to this forthcoming option as possible, and in the hope that the Americans would buy it in their droves, Porsche fitted a Sportomatic 'box to a factory-prepared 911 R and entered it in the 1967 Marathon de la Route at the Nürburgring. This gruelling, car-breaking 84-hour event was the ultimate test of endurance for both man and machine. Fortunately for Porsche, the gamble paid off as Vic Elford, Hans Herrmann and Jochen Neerpasch drove the car home to victory in this truly unique event.

Following this success, Porsche introduced the Sportomatic gearbox in their production cars the following year. Although the '67 Marathon de la Route victory had given Porsche the publicity they wanted, the Sportomatic 'box was not the success they had hoped for as most 911 drivers wanted to experience the thrill of a full-blooded sports car with a genuine floor shift.

The Sportomatic was a 4-speed semi-automatic gearbox in which the hydraulic torque converter took up the starting clutch function, and to all intents and purposes, driving a 911 Sportomatic was like driving any other automatic car. As the company literature said at the time, "This may render driving effortless, particularly in urban traffic, but driving enjoyment is not curtailed. One can shift gear, but one doesn't have to."

From model year 1976, the Sportomatic was available with only three gears and, with more stringent regulations coming into effect in several export markets, gear ratios were changed to reduce engine noise. The longer second gear in this three-speed gearbox resulted in a lower engine speed and thus a lower decibel level.

At the end of model year 1980, the Sportomatic transmission was discontinued as the torque of the new 3.0-litre engines was too high for this type of gearbox.

Strenger successfully captured the action and atmosphere in this depiction of Porsche's motor sport achievements for 1966

Strenger and von Frankenberg created the Porsche slogan, 'Driving In Its Most Beautiful Form', which the magazine Christophorus put to good use on the cover of their June 1965 issue

This Porsche sales brochure highlights the sunny, top-down style of driving that the 911 Targa offered

1967 Models – The Porsche 911 S

Realising that the market wanted more models to choose from than just the Coupé or Targa, Porsche set about providing buyers with additional alternatives. Introduced in 1967, the 911 S Sportomatic (Sportomatic was available on all models across the range) offered automatic motoring to those drivers who wanted the sporty image but without the hassle of gear changing. The uprated 911 S now boasted 160bhp thanks to further motor sport experience gained in the 1965 Monte Carlo Rally where Herbert Linge and Peter Falk finished fifth overall in a racing 911 S. This enabled the engineers in Stuttgart to confidently develop a reliable boost in power for the production engines.

Porsche introduced the 911 S to the press with a presentation at Hockenheim in 1966, a rather appropriate setting for the launch of their new, sportier model

Marathon de la Route

84 Stunden Nürburgring   22.-26.8.1967

Gesamtklassement: 1. Herrmann/Neerpasch/Elford auf Porsche 911 Sportomatic
(9900 km mit 117,8 km/h)

PORSCHE
siegt mit
Sportomatic

In theory the Sportomatic gearbox should have been a winner, but somehow an automatic gearbox for a sports car did not go down well with drivers, especially in the 1960s. This was the decade of the hairy-chested sports car and an auto 'box just did not give the right impression

A Porsche 911 2.0 Targa Sportomatic awaits delivery (1967)

The model standing in this contemporary 1967 publicity shot with the new 911 S 2.0 Coupé looks most uncomfortable as she poses for the photographer. Her Paisley-patterned slack suit is very pink and very period, contrasting strongly with the bright 911 and rather austere building in the background

The new 911 S now featured a more powerful 2.0-litre engine developing 160bhp

140 mph Porche 911 'S'

A new super-fast model has been added to the Porsche range of Gran Turismo coupes. Based on the six-cylinder 911 introduced late in 1963, it has a top speed of 140 miles an hour, an increase of about 10 m.p.h., and accelerates to 60 m.p.h. in 7.5 seconds. Magnesium wheels are employed in the interests of improved brake-heat dissipation and reduced unsprung weight. Cast hollow brake discs are used for the first time on a GT car.

Suspension has been improved by the use of adjustable units and an additional stabiliser enhances handling qualities.

The two-litre engine employs two triple-throat Webers and has an overhead camshaft for each bank of three cylinders. Output is 180 bhp at 6600 r.p.m. and 144 ft/lb at 5,200 r.p.m. Luxury trim includes a leather covered steering wheel. German Price of the 911 S is approximately $5,000.

elegante sportiva

sportiva *elegante*

PORSCHE

Due to the competition success of the 911 S, especially in rallying, Porsche produced this clever **elegante/sportiva** promotional poster showing the adaptable nature of the more powerful 911 S. Equally at home in competition, the new 911 S was also the motoring choice of the discerning business executive, or so we are led to believe

1967 SCCA Class C Production Champion Alan Johnson knows that Royal 76 is **powerful enough to make a difference**

Alan Johnson and Roger Bursch took no chances on gasoline for their Porsche 911 S in the 1967 American Road Race of Champions. They took Union Oil's Royal 76 premium with them — all the way from California to Daytona Beach.

Why Royal 76?

Winner Alan Johnson puts it this way: "Roger and I have experimented with a lot of gasolines in the years we've been racing together. We learned to experience that Royal 76 works better — delivers maximum power, mileage and performance."

Royal 76: a balanced blend of eight powerful fuels —

Exactly the same gasoline you get at any Union Oil station, that won the Can-Am series at Monterey . . . at Riverside . . . at Stardust.

Why not try a tankful of championship performance in your car?

UNION 76

Winning Stateside always presented an ideal opportunity to tell the market there that Porsche had beaten the local opposition. It gave Stuttgart much pleasure to rub it in with the opposition

Fuchs Alloys

As from 1967 the famous Fuchs (the German word for 'fox') alloy wheels, manufactured by the well-known German industrial giant, Otto Fuchs KG, became a fixture on the 911 models and remained the standard wheel of choice until they were replaced 22 years later, in 1989. In its first year of manufacture, the Fuchs forged aluminium wheel was a rather narrow 4.5J x 15 and was shod with 165 VR 15 rubber. The following year the wheel was widened to 5.5J for better handling.

These famous Fuchs alloys have become so much a part of Porsche's history

Exhaust Emissions

Porsche was the first European manufacturer to comply with American exhaust emission control regulations. So proficient were the Porsche test facilities in Weissach, that the company was requested by the US Environmental Protection Agency (EPA) to perform emissions tests on the export models of other European car manufacturers destined for America. It is rather ironic that the Americans were so strict with their emission regulations on the small number of foreign imports when it was the American car with its big V8 engine that produced more exhaust emissions than most other cars.

British super spy, James Bond, will always be identified with Aston Martins in his movies, as traditionally this car was perceived to represent the pinnacle of the UK sports car industry. Porsche saw this as a market that they would like to muscle in on with the 911 which was fast becoming a competitor to the bigger sports car manufacturers in Europe and the UK. The Porsche seen in this sales brochure coming out of the centre of the wheel hub is reminiscent of the introduction to the James Bond movies of the 1960s. In the well-known introductory scenes to his films, Bond would walk across the screen, stop, turn towards the camera and fire his gun. The bullet travelling towards the camera would then change into the next image, forming the following frame to this introductory sequence. In the same way, the central hub of this new Fuchs alloy resembles the barrel of a gun and the new 911 S, the bullet – it's very Bond, it's very 1960s

1968 Models – A-Series

911 T Coupé/Targa

The 911 T (Touring) was introduced as the entry level 6-cylinder model in 1968. The 911 T offered the same 1991cc 6-cylinder boxer engine that appeared in the other 911 models, but in a de-tuned state (110bhp). At almost DM 6000 cheaper than its more powerful 911 S sibling (DM 24,970), the 911 T was initially only offered with a 4-speed 'box, the 5-speed unit being introduced the following year.

Over the years, Porsche engineers have never been comfortable with building a model down to a fixed price as, at the very heart of a Porsche is its engine, representing speed and performance. Rather, Porsche engineers had become very good at building cars that went fast and won races. So, to build an entry-level or economical model did not sit comfortably with them. However, the 4-cylinder 912 had done what it set out to do, and that was to attract customers at the lower end of the market.

Although the Porsche 912 had outsold the more powerful 911, it nevertheless was not what Porsche had in mind for a fast sports car and the 4-cylinder 356 engine, used in the 912, was phased out of production.

911 L Coupé/Targa

The 911 L had taken over as the 'normal' or 'standard' model as Porsche sought to provide greater choice for its growing number of customers. The engine and running gear, however, were similar to the rest of the 911 range, being equipped with a 6-cylinder boxer engine producing 130bhp and it was also available with a 5-speed or optional Sportomatic 'box.

The 1968, or A-Series, model was the last of the short wheelbase cars, being 2211mm. The 911 (and 912) had retained the same original body dimensions since introduction at Frankfurt in September 1963: length 4163mm, width 1610mm, height 1320mm, with a wheelbase of 2211mm.

A new Porsche 911 T 2.0-litre Targa (1968)
is seen here in a factory pre-delivery car park, ready for shipment

Highlighting the executive profile of the Porsche sports car, this 911 Targa is parked up alongside a Boeing 707. International travel was very much a part of the Porsche driver's lifestyle and here the Targa's occupants are ready to board their flight to some exotic destination. Not only was the 911 Targa a modern concept in 1968, but so was the Boeing 707

This is the new Porsche.

We've been thinking about it for 17 years.
Ever since the classic Porsche was introduced in 1948, many have thought of it as the ultimate car for getting from here to there in the fastest, safest, most enjoyable manner possible.
But time is a great teacher.
All we have learned in a generation of racing and testing has gone into the new Porsche.
It is faster. More nimble. More beautiful. Far roomier.
Even the famous Porsche ride—one of life's great pleasures—has been improved.
A new generation of Porsche has been born.
Go ahead. Drive it. You'll never forget it.

The high-performance, unusually well-instrumented Porsche 911 has new 6-cylinder, air-cooled, 148-hp rear engine, new 5-speed gearbox. Top speed 130 mph. The lower-priced Porsche 912, sister to the 911, has famous SC, 4-cylinder engine, new 4 or 5-speed gearbox. Top speed 115 mph. New Porsche fastback design offers 75% more field of vision, even better suspension, far more elbow room and under-the-hood luggage space. Superb 4-wheel disc brakes, precise handling, welded body make Porsche one of world's safest cars. Complete interior safety package is standard. For domestic or overseas delivery, see dealer or write Porsche of America Corp., 107 Tryon Avenue West, Teaneck, New Jersey 07666.

Advertising in American car magazines was important for Porsche. This ad announces the arrival of the new models for 1968

Pictured from left to right: Ferdinand Piëch, Ferry Porsche, Peter Porsche and Ferdinand Alexander Porsche standing beside a 1968 Porsche 911 S 2.0 Targa

What was 1968 all about if was not about 'flower power'? The model posing with this 911 L 2.0 Coupé seems lost in her own little world of flowers and vibrant colours

This Porsche 911 L 2.0-litre Coupé (1968) is registered and ready for collection by its owner from the Stuttgart plant

911 E Coupé/Targa

While retaining the same overall body dimensions, the 1969 models had the wheelbase extended by 57mm (from 2211mm to 2268mm), thereby improving roadholding and ride. For the 1969 model year, the 912 entered its last period of production and it was also the final year that the 911 was powered by the 2.0-litre engine.

In the summer of 1968, Porsche introduced the 911 E which replaced the 911 L of the previous year. The E, with its mechanical twin-row Bosch fuel injection pump, now produced 140bhp and was listed at DM 21,645 (Coupé).

911 T and S Coupé/Targa

Although the 911 T still produced the same power output as the previous year's model, the 911 S was now rated at 170bhp, 10bhp up from the year before.

With the benefit of hindsight, the S was an early indicator that Porsche was gearing up to produce something more powerful in the future and which offered greater performance. As we shall see later, the S was an important model in Porsche's rise to almost total dominance in sports car racing over the years that followed, its influence being felt right up to the popular Carrera Cup and Supercup events today.

The 1969 Targa model now had a heated, fixed rear window instead of the 'soft' window with which it was introduced four years earlier.

Again it is all about flowers, as this 1968 model 911 L 2.0 Coupé is framed by blooms

Anyone looking for a used Porsche in 1968 needed to look no further than the Classified section of Autocar, where Porsches of all manner and description could be found (July 18, 1968)

1966 911 de luxe Porsche with radio, one owner, specimen motor car, £2,500. (C2000)
JOHN ALCOCK, Walley St., Biddulph, Stoke-on-Trent, Phone, Biddulph 3174. (8607)
1966 Series Porsche 912, red with black interior, genuine 13,000 miles only, a superb example in absolutely spotless condition.
PLOUGH MOTORS (STROUD VALLEY) LTD., Stonehouse, Gloucestershire. Phone, Stonehouse 2382. (C3137)
JACK ROSE LTD. offer: 911S, 1967, super condition, 7,000 miles only, accept £3,350. Stafford Rd., Wallington, Surrey. Phone, Wallington 4473. (C4016)
PORSCHE Super 90, 1961 model in super condition, a specimen for year, attractive cream colour, £695. Phone, M. and W. Autos, Loughborough 3920. (8432)
1966 Porsche 912, fixed-head coupe, 2+2, 5-speed box, dark grey, red interior, fitted safety belts, immaculate condition, 13,850, £1,875.
F. ENGLISH LTD., Poole Rd., Bournemouth. Phone, Bournemouth 20731. (7751)
1966 (Sept.) Porsche 911S, blue with black interior, very good condition, radio, belts, fog-lamps, etc., 17,000 miles, £2,950. Phone, Byfleet 43463. (7865)
912, 1966, guranteed, 9,280 miles, dark blue with tan, latest engine mounting, positively congruous condition throughout, finest used Porsche we have known for sale.
GLEN HENDERSON MOTORS, Porsche distributors, Ayr, Scotland. 67608-9. (8591)
1966 Porsche 912, white-black upholstery, 14,000 miles, one owner, radio, seat belts, iodine quartz driving lamps, £1,895. Part-exchange and H.P. available. Phone, Keswick 386 and 845. (7865)
Porsche Cars Wanted

Graphic artist, Erich Strenger, produced all Porsche's calendars, often doing the photography himself as well. This December 1968 image shows Santa Claus delivering presents to a group of children – the 911 was no doubt intended for their father

A 1969 model 911 T 2.0 Targa looks pretty in this town setting

Porsche 911 E 2.0-litre Coupé (1969), now with extended wheelbase

As covered in the company newspaper,
Porsche News, *the 911 T (1969) now
offered more speed and improved safety*

*Greater performance for the Porsche 911 S 2.0-
litre Coupé (1969) now dictated even wider 6J x
15 Fuchs alloys*

*A customer could still order his Porsche 911 T 2.0-litre
Coupé (1969) with standard wheels*

The announcement in Porsche News *at
the top of this page reads – "SAFETY = A
Car Designed For Function + A Trained
Responsible Driver"*

PORSCHE

The 911 R was a limited-run competition car which built on the earlier successes of the 911 S. With only 24 cars produced, the 911 R was highly sought after and for good reason because Brit Vic Elford and Dutchman Gijs van Lennep brought their R home in third place in the 1967 Mugello round of the Sports Car Championship, behind two factory 910s.

The Porsche 911 R attracted further international attention when it set several new world records at the Monza circuit for the 20,000 and 25,000km distances as well as for the 72 and 96

hour time trials. The 911 R used in this record run was fitted with a Sportomatic transmission which had already proved reliable in the 84-Hour Marathon de la Route at the Nürburgring.

It is hardly surprising that the R was such a lethal weapon, as the Porsche engineers had fitted the 2.0-litre 906 engine into the 911 body. This 1991cc 6-cylinder engine produced a whopping 210bhp. The 911 R would later form the basis for the legendary Carrera RS 2.7 model which in itself was a vital link in the chain which culminated in the all-conquering, 935 Le Mans winner of 1979.

It can be seen how the lightweight trunk lid is compressed at speed as the 911 R speeds along the Monza banking during its record attempt

The 911 R looks every bit the race car at its media introduction at the Hockenheim circuit in December 1967. Note the vented rear windows and lightweight front indicator lights

SCHUCO, the legendary German toy manufacturer, which was founded in 1912 by Heinrich Müller and Heinrich Schreyer, produced a scale model of the 911 S in 1969. This pack of twelve models, found in the depths of the Porsche Museum, is still shrink-wrapped, just as it was on the day it left the factory

Porsche Cars In Great Britain

AFN Limited, the manufacturers of Frazer Nash cars in England, began importing Porsches to Britain in 1952, when the German sports cars were still relatively unknown. When, in 1958, Frazer Nash stopped production, AFN concentrated on building up the business of importing and selling Porsches.

At this time, Colonel H.J. 'Aldy' Aldington ran the Frazer Nash company at the Falcon Works in Isleworth, and when son John had completed his apprenticeship at Porsche's repair department in Stuttgart, he returned to the family business. John initially worked in AFN's repair department, but soon began developing the business side, finally taking control of the company in 1965 after his father had suffered a stroke. Eight months later, at the age of 30, John Aldington formed Porsche Cars Great Britain Limited to import and distribute Porsche cars.

Volkswagen tried to muscle in on the act in the early 1970s, wanting to take over the importation and distribution of Porsches in the UK, but John put up a strong defence. Ferry Porsche backed Aldington, but in the process took control of the company. In 1972, PCGB Ltd was reconstituted with Ferry Porsche as chairman, John Aldington and Dr Ernst Fuhrmann as Joint Managing Directors, and Heinz Branitzki as Finance Director.

John Aldington supervised the company's expansion with considerable skill, making Britain the second largest export market behind the United States, and in order to expand PCGB moved to purpose-built headquarters in Richfield Avenue, Reading in February 1977. Within 10 years, they moved again to a still larger headquarters in Calcot.

After presiding over a golden period of growth between 1976 and 1987, John decided to relinquish his directorship and his remaining 40% shareholding to the Porsche factory. Porsche Cars GB is now wholly-owned by Porsche AG in Stuttgart, while the UK and Ireland are now the third largest market for Porsche in the world, after Germany and the US.

John Taylor Aldington passed away on November 17, 2006.

Ferry Porsche is pictured making a presentation to H.J. 'Aldy' Aldington in 1975 on his retirement. Inset left, Aldy's brother W.H. Aldington and right, Aldy's son John, or J.T. Aldington

This was the scene in the busy Sales Department of AFN Motors in 1977

W.H. Aldington chats with journalist and Porsche racing driver, Paul Frère, at an AFN Motors social function in 1978

Rampant Porsche Growth

While the Stuttgart manufacturer was going from strength to strength in the 1960s, the British sports car industry had contracted a rather serious case of the wobbles, thanks to some poor management decisions taken in the upper echelons of British Leyland. In December 1967, the last Austin Healey 3000 Mk III (BJ8) left the plant after British Leyland decided to discontinue the model. The Austin Healey Sprite was also axed around this time. Britain was at one stage considered by many to be the sports car capital of the world and represented strong competition for Porsche in the market. But with the British sports car industry all but melting away before their eyes, one could just imagine the glee in Stuttgart.

The Swinging Sixties

Looking back at the 1960s, the market place had become a much more liberal, demanding and sophisticated place by the end of the decade, and manufacturers had to adapt to customer requirements in order to keep pace with car buyer's expectations. To be considered 'cool' during this era, one had to project the right image to remain accepted within one's social circle, and the Porsche 911 quickly became an icon of 'cool' in this modern society.

The Swinging Sixties had witnessed Woodstock, Jimi Hendrix, the mini skirt, the Vietnam War and flower power. More Rolls-Royces than ever before were being driven by long-haired, denim-clad new millionaires scarcely out of their 20s, and this development turned the whole establishment on its head. If the motor manufacturers did not take note of this evolution of traditional social structures and the explosion of wealth amongst the younger generation, then they were surely doomed to obscurity.

Perhaps this is one of the reasons why the British sports car industry evaporated so quickly as they believed their traditional values would pull them through this 'temporary' phase. There was an expectation that this growth in new wealth amongst the young would soon pass away and that all would return to normal. However, history shows us that it did not and Porsche, being a smaller, more flexible firm, was able to adapt more easily to these changes.

A trendy young couple arrive in the city for an evening's entertainment at the theatre. Their transport, naturally, is a 1969 Porsche 911 E 2.0 Targa

AFN, the official Porsche distributors for Britain, was established as far back as the early 1950s. In the late 1960s, H.J. Aldington and his son John set up Porsche Cars Great Britain Limited together with Porsche in Stuttgart, and this arrangement allowed the UK office to appoint local distributors as they saw fit. These two period advertisements appeared in Autocar during May 1969 and were still permitted to reflect the independent names of each distributing dealership. Today, all of these independent names have been replaced by the words 'Porsche Centre'

In this poster from 1969, Porsche make good use of their sporting success through the clever use of a speed comparison between the racing and roadgoing 911 sports car. In the top half of the image, speed is emphasised by this fast moving US racing 911, while the roadgoing 911 below, which is actually standing still, uses the fast moving train behind the car to create the sense of speed

It is interesting to see the combination of Porsche vehicles on the stand at this motor show in Britain in 1970. Obviously the company wanted to promote its new models and the purpose of a racing car on the stand is to highlight the connection between Porsche's racing heritage and their road cars. However, it is interesting to note that they have chosen in this case to display a 908 KH, or short tail, as this car was used by the factory in the 1968 season only. The 908 Spyder and LH (long tail) were raced in the 1969 season, while the 917 was raced in the year of this show. As Porsche have confirmed that this 908 racer was not one of their own museum cars, it was probably provided locally by a private owner to bolster the visual impact of the stand

Publication May 23, 1969

329 PORSCHE: The Man and his Cars, by Richard von Frankenberg. Porsche, designer of the victorious pre-World War II Mercedes S-series Sports and Auto-Union GP cars, the Volkswagen (in 1933), and the early versions of the magnificent Porsche sports and racing cars, is the last great design engineer to visualize and create a car in its entirety. Von Frankenberg, author, former Porsche factory team driver, and editor of **Christophorous**, the Porsche magazine, sets forth Porsche's career, the successes of his cars in competition, and the recent progress of the marque under the direction of his son, Ferry. This lavishly produced new edition brings the remarkable history of the man and his cars up to 1969 and includes the latest models and their outstanding successes. "Well worth the price ... A scholarly and complete work ... An excellent job, which we recommend without reserve." — **Sports Car**, organ of SCCA. Price $9.95 before publication. Afterwards $10.95.

● $1 with book purchase of $25 or more at reg. prices

The multi-talented Richard von Frankenberg, co-founder of the Christophorus *magazine, author and journalist, was also a Porsche team driver.* Road & Track *magazine carried this book ad for Robert Bentley Publishers in America, promoting the book:* Porsche - The Man and his Cars *written by von Frankenberg himself*

Porsche 911 and 912 production statistics

Model Year	Description	911 Production	912 Production*
1967		4152	7791
1968	A-Series	6957	8459
1969	B-Series	10118	5515

Source: Porsche

THE 911 FLEXES ITS MUSCLES

Porsche entered the new decade, having dropped the 912 from their range and introduced a new, bigger engine. With regard to this increase in engine capacity, many would have said, "about time", because it was now six years since the introduction of the Typ 901 at the 1963 IAA, during which time the 911 had been powered by the same 1991cc engine. But things do not happen quickly in the depths of the Stuttgart-Zuffenhausen workshops, nor is it very likely that there will ever be a hastily cobbled together new model to come from Porsche. Things are done in a measured way in Stuttgart as this was the way of Ferry Porsche, and this work culture has become ingrained in each successive generation of engineers to begin work there.

Having taken six years to introduce its first increase in engine capacity, from 2.0-litres to 2.2-litres, it took Porsche just two years to introduce their next engine increase from 2.2-litres to 2.4-litres (1972), with a further significant engine increase later that same year in the form of the 2.7-litre engine. With hindsight, that amounts to a single increase in six years followed by a further three increases in the next two years, which was rather out of character.

Clearly the Porsche engineers had reached a point at which they all concurred, almost impulsively, that they had a bullet-proof engine that could handle a lot more power than was initially thought. This new-found confidence led them to take these rather dramatic steps, in Porsche terms at least, enabling the company with its wider product range to make sizeable in-roads into the sports car market at a rate and magnitude previously not thought possible.

The Porsche 2.2-litre range signalled the start of the 911's recognition by the market that this really was a reliable performance car with practicality to match. Expensive, yes, but if you were in this league then a Porsche 911 was the car to be seen in. Some competitors in the sports car market produced either sporty versions of their mainstream model, or an off-shoot model using the same engine with perhaps modified suspension. Porsche, on the other hand, only made the 911 and the mid-engined 914 (a joint venture with Volkswagen) at this stage, and so sports cars were their business.

On the corporate front, Porsche of America Corporation (POAC) was wound up at the end of 1969 and its activities taken over by the Porsche-Audi Division of the giant Volkswagen of America Inc. This gave Porsche a much bigger distribution network and substantially extended the Stuttgart manufacturer's repair and servicing capability in the States.

Backed by years of motor sport experience, the 911 was by now a mature all-rounder that had been developed to the point of being a comfortable Grand Tourer for all manner of drivers, including women. Traditionally, some men did not mind the odd bit of tinkering with the carbs or adjusting the windscreen of the Morgan to keep out the chill for a quick blast down the motorway. This is not to be disparaging to the female segment of the market, but in the early 1970s sports cars were only just becoming a reasonably-priced and practical accessory for some women. Previously, sports cars had been mainly the domain of men.

With the advent of 'equality of rights' for all and 'women's lib' in the 1970s, more and more women were able to consider a more expensive car and all of a sudden the 911 became an attractive proposition. Apart from impressive performance, a further benefit of owning a Porsche 911 was that entry to, and exit from, the car was as easy as any normal saloon car. Retaining one's dignity while getting in and out of a Lotus Elan, Austin Healey or similar such car in a mini-skirt or short dress required some rather clever cross-legged manoeuvres!

Porsche, however, followed a policy of not aiming the 911 specifically at either men or women, and thus, effectively, had the sports car slotting into a 'gender neutral' position, ensuring that the 911 appealed equally to all customers. The company had observed that some women drivers were attracted to the 911 because they perceived it as a masculine type of car and they did not want to be seen as 'girly'. In that context, a feminine positioning would have discouraged these customers. And, as all these things are in the eye of the beholder, the reverse position would also have held true for male drivers.

TIMELINE (1970-1972):

1970	1971	1972
Introduction of 2.2-litre engine.	Weissach Development Centre opened.	Introduction of 2.4-litre engine.
Introduction of 911 E.		Carrera RS 2.7 shown at Paris Salon in October.

The Porsche 911 E 2.2 Coupé was the middle of the range model, fitting in between the T and S models in 1970

The 911 was intended as a versatile sports car, and customers included those with sporting pursuits. This model is a 911 E 2.4 Coupé (1973)

Way back in 1948 when the first 356 was conceived, Ferry Porsche insisted that his sports cars would have a rear engine layout as this would help the car to grip better in the snow and muddy conditions of many parts of Europe. It is a good thing that he stuck to his original plan, as the additional weight over the rear axle of this 911 2.2 Coupé (December 1970) would certainly have been needed for traction after this photo shoot was finished

Even the mighty Porsche 911 with its powerful new 2.2-litre engine was forced to slow down for some rather special pedestrians on this European country road

Being put through its paces on Porsche's recently opened test track at Weissach in 1972, this new 911 S 2.4 Coupé is being readied for production

The 1970 model 911 had rubber strips on the bumper overriders. This proud Italian customer takes delivery of his new 911 from a salesman at a VW/Porsche dealership. Interestingly, this customer chose a Porsche over a Ferrari, often the domestic sports car of choice for well-to-do Italian males of the era

Executive transport on the ground and in the air. A new 2.2-litre 911 S sits waiting in front of a private aircraft, but this is no ordinary set of wings or wheels. The 911 S would have been the road transport of choice for Ferry Porsche and his sister, Louise Piëch, and as the identifying lettering on the plane shows, it was their own private company aircraft. With 'D' for Deutschland referring to a German registered plane, the last three letters of the combination 'D-IFLP' stood for 'Ferdinand-Louise-Porsche'. This aircraft was used by Ferry and his sister Louise for their long distance business trips and it even flew them to Africa on one corporate excursion

What The Media Had To Say About The New 2.2-litre 911

Dudley Noble, of The *Financial Times*, said that the justification for an enthusiast buying a 911 was that it represented one of the fastest and most sophisticated sports cars on the market. The writer could only cite a bit of engine noise as a possible downside to the car, but then the sound was 'music' to the ears of the average Porsche driver.

With eight models between the price of £2261-£5574 (depending on options), there was something to suit most requirements, but with an average house price in Britain in 1970 of £4975, it is not hard to see why there were not a lot of 911s on the roads there. The cost of this 911 E on test was £4585 (including UK purchase tax). Despite this, the 911 was still given a positive review by the writer.

Appropriately, Noble gave the 911 a rather novel description – instead of VW, with reference to its forebears, Noble called this car the SW, which in his book stood for 'Schnell-Wagen' rather than 'Volks-Wagen'.

Porsche 911 T 2.2 Targa 1971 driving through the countryside. Close inspection of this image will show that the 911 can certainly carry two adults up front, with two children and the dog in the back. A sticker in the rear window draws attention to the new 2.2-litre engine

Motoring

A powerful Porsche

BY DUDLEY NOBLE

THE People's Car which Dr. Ferdinand Porsche created at Hitler's behest could have been acquired for nothing by the Allies at the end of the war. But, after both U.S. and U.K. motor bigwigs had pronounced it devoid of any commercial future, it was left to the Germans to do with it what they could—with the British Army's aid. We all know the outcome.

The first car actually to be known by Dr. Porsche's name was built from Volkswagen components, and since his death his son Ferry has ably carried it from strength to strength along its basic conception of a compact and aerodynamic sports model.

Eight versions

Porsches come in eight versions, at prices ranging from £2,261 to £5,574 and are now all six-cylinder engined. The one sent for test was a 911E, which is very near the top of the list, and I noticed that it could be fitted out with optional extras that in all would total £485, exclusive of radio.

Such prices may seem high for an occasional four-seater of only 2.2 litres engine capacity. The justification, from the enthusiast's point of view, is that the Porsche is one of the fastest and most sophisticated sports cars on the market.

On all the 911 types (there are a "T," an "E" and an "S," with maximum speeds varying from 127 mph to 143 mph) the air-cooled "flat" engine is mounted rearward of the back wheels. On a new 914 produced jointly by Porsche and VW, it will be centrally located—as, indeed, it was on Dr. Ferdinand's very first Porsche about 20 years ago. Fuel injection is fitted to both the 911E and the "S" (the

highest-priced model). This brings 30 bhp more from the engine as compared with the dual 3-choke carburetters fitted to the less costly "T" versions.

The power unit certainly runs smoothly, but it is noisy, with clatter from the drive to the cam-

SPECIFICATION

ENGINE.—Horizontally-opposed six-cylinder, capacity 2,195 cc, compression ratio 9.1:1. Maximum power 175 bhp gross (155 bhp net) at 6,200 rpm. Fuel injection (mechanical).

TRANSMISSION.—Five-speed all-synchromesh, central gearlever. "Sportomatic" (automatic) transmission available as extra (£170).

DIMENSIONS.—Length 13 feet 8 inches, width 5 feet 3½ inches, height 4 feet 4 inches. Weight 20 cwt. Tank capacity 13½ Imperial gallons.

PRICE.—Basic £3,510. Including purchase tax £4,584 15s 10d. Importers: Porsche Cars, Falcon Works, London Road, Isleworth, Middlesex.

shafts in the cylinder heads, whirr from the cooling fan and, of course, no water jacketing around the cylinders to act as a sound insulator. But noise (as I have remarked before) is music to the average Continental's ears. It never became unbearable, but those accustomed to, say, Rolls-Royce's ideas of sound levels might not approve of it.

Compensation lies in the Porsche's performance, which matches that of most cars with twice the engine capacity. Relatively speaking, flexibility is not its strong point, and one should keep the revs up; the flywheel is light and suits acceleration rather than slow pulling; certainly the slightest touch on the

accelerator pedal brings an instantaneous response.

Much of this stems from the body's highly streamlined shape, which also helps to keep fuel consumption within bounds: when I drove gently 20 mpg was possible, but a heavy foot raised this to perhaps 15 mpg, so I would say 18 mpg is a fair average, and on four-star petrol.

The manual gearbox has five forward speeds and both fourth and fifth are higher ratios than direct drive. Gear changing is delightful, with the proviso that bottom brings the lever up against the passenger's legs.

All four wheels are disc-braked; no undue pressure is required to operate them, even in emergency.

Suspension has been improved and, combined with a lengthened wheelbase, makes for extremely high cornering power. At the rear there are trailing arms and torsion bars; at the front hydro-pneumatic self-levelling struts are a major factor in the Porsche riding quality which, for a sports car, is very good indeed.

Light steering

Steering is light, responsive and quite high-geared, so a delicate touch on the padded-rim steering wheel is advisable.

The front seats are comfortable, adjustable over a wide range, fully reclining and with provision for attaching headrests. Instrumentation is comprehensive, and three gauges convey information about lubrication—very important on an air-cooled engine, where the oil is largely used as a coolant.

In every way it is the sports car par excellence. I would term it an "SW" (Schnell Wagen) in contradistinction to the overdone "GT."

Saturday, February 14, 1970 was St. Valentine's Day, when motoring matters were perhaps less of a priority in some people's minds, but nevertheless the Financial Times *carried a very positive review on the new 2.2-litre 911*

Porsche in a field – this Porsche 911 E 2.2 Coupé (1970) looks as pretty as a picture, which in the 'Flower Power' days of the late '60s, early '70s was rather appropriate

The driver of this 1970 Porsche 911 S 2.2 Coupé interrupts his journey to consult a map before continuing on his way. Careful examination of this photograph will reveal two adults sitting in the back seats – hopefully for them this journey was not a long one!

Comparative table of 911 prices in Porsche's major markets

Model Year 1969 (introduced October, 1969)	Germany	Great Britain	America
911T	DM 19,969	£ 2295	$ 5508
911E	DM 24,975	£ 2870	$ 6888
911S	DM 27,139	£ 3119	$ 7485

The vehicle prices in Great Britain and the USA exclude any import duty and tariffs in order to provide an accurate comparison with the home nation, Germany. Exchange rates supplied by a leading international bank

● PORSCHE ask us to point out that the 3,000-mile service interval mentioned in our review on June 8 refers to another model and not the 911E, for which the figure should be 6,000 miles.

6-7-70.

Porsche were quick to point out that the Guardian's review on June 8, 1970, contained an error in the reported oil change interval, and the newspaper subsequently printed this correction the following month

What Should It Be, An E-type Or A Porsche?

Ian Breach, motoring writer at *The Guardian*, pointed out in his Monday morning motoring column that most buyers considering a Porsche 911 in Britain might also have considered an E-type Jaguar or a Lotus in their purchase decision. Although all three cars offered roughly equal performance, that is where the similarities ended. In Britain, the Porsche cost considerably more than the two alternatives mentioned in the report, but this was just one factor that any prospective buyers of the German sports car had to consider.

Breach makes more than just a passing reference to Rolls-Royce cars in matters pertaining to service costs, as he, obviously along with many others, was pretty impressed by Porsche's quality of finish and attention to detail. This observation is supported by the reliability of Porsche sports cars which was, by comparison, well above that of other cars in the same segment. In fact, so impressed was the writer, that he was prepared to go to extraordinary lengths to retain the test car for himself after his 10-day and 1100-mile turn behind the wheel, much to the dismay of the press office!

The small but very important lengthening of the wheelbase had reduced the car's early tendency to become tail-happy in the wet, and overall driveability was nothing short of excellent. There were some minor niggles, but these were forgotten when the overall package was considered.

The writer pointed out that Porsche 911 buyers tended to be people who knew, or wanted to know, more about their cars than the average motorist. Breach finished his report with a classic observation – 'The 911 makes a driver out of a motorist'. He could not have been more right.

MOTORING GUARDIAN

Below, the Porsche 911E: flat-6 aircooled engine, Bosch six-element injection, five-speed gearbox, rack and pinion steering (2½ turns, 34 feet), ATE discs, 15in. wheels on 6in. rims, 12v. alternator electrical system, Sportomatic gears available.

8·6·70

Scorch in a Porsche

IAN BREACH tests the Porsche 911E

COMPARISONS are not only odious but painfully difficult to make between the Porsche 911E and the other two 2+2 cars we tested in recent weeks (Lotus, April 27, and Jaguar E-type, May 18). All three are concerned with a similar driver in mind, offer—with some gives and takes—comparable performance and quality, and differ in cost by amounts unlikely to separate ownership by wealth. Indeed, if one takes the price of an E-type in Germany (£3,500 for the manual-gear model), one finds the home-ground Porsches on competitive terms. The 911 comes in three basic versions—the T, the E, and the S (145, 175, and 200 bhp): in Britain the coupés cost £3,670, £4,584, and £5,211 respectively.

What you get for the extra money (E-type, £2,708; Lotus, £2,515) is not easy to define. True, Porsche are beautifully rugged in a way that perhaps only the designer of Auto-Union and, later, the Beetle would make them: brass nuts are used where another manufacturer would be happy to use mild steel, ratings and tolerances are scrupulously adhered to, underbody parts are heavily protected against rust and damage. But then no one expects a Lotus or a Jaguar to fall to bits, do they?

Nevertheless, I am informed that a great many owners have come to Porsche eager to make the comparison, and the figure that speaks loudest for itself is that more than 70 per cent of the Stuttgart production is sold to previous Porsche owners.

There are enough 356 models left on the roads to prove Porsche's claim to longer-than-usual life, and second-hand prices tell their own story: a 1965 912 (now discontinued to make room for the 914 range) was sold in December by a garage I know for nearly £1,600—only £800 less than its original price. So much for durability. Reliability in service depends on what must be the most exhaustive (and expensive) quality control procedure outside Rolls-Royce.

Every engine is run on an individual test bench for fuel consumption readings, power output (the engine is rebuilt if it does not deliver at least the quoted rating), and dozens of other measurements. The car, once assembled, is run on a test course for 22 miles (which compares with a 10-minute roller test for most production cars).

A driver's car

Like Rolls, Porsche aren't too keen for the novice to go poking around in their engine. Settings are fixed with lock-nuts and painted over, components are arranged and designed to yield only to the most delicate of special tools, wielded by the most carefully trained mechanics. In any event, the fuel-injection system fitted to the 911 requires not only mechanical nous and dexterity, but a fair knowledge of microelectronics. Even the electrics are unorthodox: two 12v batteries, fail-safe light circuits, three-speed wipers.

For all that, the 911E is a driver's car. The central, and largest, dial on the instrument panel is the engine-speed indicator, a more relevant guide for the man who properly uses all five of the 911's forward gears than the speedometer. The gearshift takes some time to master, and in spite of a cheery wave of the hand as I left the Porsche establishment at the old Frazer Nash works in Isleworth, it required more confidence than I thought I possessed to filter straight into a West London rush hour.

The following day it was easier. The day after it was natural. And by the time 1,100 miles had been put on the clock I was ready to have the car replated and sprayed, change my name to Furtwängler, and move to a very remote part of Scotland.

It's a car which gives hardly any indication—in dry weather at least—of its limits. Corners on roads, good, bad, or indifferent, can be taken at speeds which would lift most other cars off their wheels (on the 911E these are 6in. light alloy, shod with magnificently tubby Michelins). Front-end wag—expected from a car with a 40/60 weight distribution—is practically nonexistent, partly through a minor lengthening of the chassis since the first 911s made their appearance, but mainly because of a low centre of gravity (the car sits only 6in. off the ground) and a taut suspension. But although our tests — on long motorway stretches and Fylde coast roads —were in dry conditions, the 911's rally successes in ice, snow, and water, underline its exceptional roadholding.

Some motoring magazines now seem to boast their indifference to the 70 limit when driving cars like the Porsche. But it is asking for trouble to test the car's top speed on a public highway: our model, with only 1,000 miles on the clock at the start of the test, would not achieve the full rated speed of 137 mph, but even at the 132½ mph we squeezed (with full encouragement from Porsche) on a closed airfield, one is only too well aware that—on a motorway—one would be bearing down on cars doing 70 as if one were driving at a concrete wall at more than 60 mph. Our test of a sustained high speed came in a fast but comfortable journey from London to Wigan.

Indeed the comfort seems to be enhanced at high speeds. The noise level drops markedly after acceleration through the gears—the 911 needs plenty of stick to pull away in low gears at town speeds. After that, levels rise slowly from a low-70dBA mark at 30 to just over 80dBA at 70 miles an hour. Opening the (electric) windows raises the level by about 1dBA; the side windows produce a little whistle, but nothing to complain about.

The acceleration figures are not so good as Porsche's factory provided, possibly because I feared a burnt clutch more than I need to have done. Our 0-50 time was a constant one second behind their time of 5.9 seconds. But it seemed fast enough for anyone, and the acceleration at high speeds is really quite astonishing.

Steering is neutral. Absolutely. I now believe the tale of a Porsche salesman who clinched a sale by taking the car up to 100 mph or so, putting his hands in his pockets, and then braking to rest. Safety, in fact, is engineered all the way through the 911, from its massively armoured body shell (the car weighs just over a ton), to its very powerful hand and foot disc-operated brakes (cooled through open fins and seemingly fadeless under repeated crash-stop tests). Inside the car, comfort is matched with safety in easy-to-read instruments, accessible controls, and restful seats.

Minor cavils

One or two little niggles. The boot and engine compartment release catches (that for the petrol tank too) are on the left-hand side of the body. Porsche tell me that it would cost a great deal to change them over for the right-hand market, and I accept this, but it's still an inconvenient stretch to get at them. The gearshift, too, is for German drivers: first is engaged by pushing against your passenger's knee. The oil-level indicator is, doubtless, a useful instrument, but it fluctuates alarmingly when the car is in motion and calls unnecessarily for a top-up. Lights are not much more than adequate for a car of this potential speed, though an extra pair are to be seen on most Porsches as optional accessories. Wing mirrors, too, would seem a desirable original.

Porsche fit Irvine seat belts, but not the inertia-reel variety, which they claim made too much noise (Irvine are now developing a quieter one). The present one leaves something of an annoying spaghetti hooked around the seat-adjustment control unless it is thrown over the seat—in which case it is likely to be stepped on or caught when the little ones (up to 12 years) get into the back seats. A thought that occurs among these minor cavils is that service intervals are short for the sort of driving one would expect an owner to indulge in: 3,000 miles isn't very far in a 911E.

Fuel consumption varies a lot between drivers and roads, but our ten-day test returned something over 19 m.p.g., which appears to be a moderately good figure (the tank holds 13½ gallons, including a "reserve" of 1½ gallons). We liked driving it: unlike the E-type, the Porsche produced a sense of admiration among other drivers, and not a few comradely headlight blips from 911 owners coming in the other direction. It also brings about those peculiar roadside conversations with men who want to know what the mean piston speed is. It's about 2,400 feet per minute. The 911 makes a driver out of a motorist.

The Motoring Guardian *report by Ian Breach – June 8, 1970*

Motoring

Expensive but good

BY JAMES ENSOR

NOT MANY Porsches are sold in Britain and for a good reason. The cheapest true Porsche, the mid-engined VW-Porsche 914/6, costs almost £3,500 and not many people are prepared to spend that much for a two-seater, which is only available in left-hand drive.

A more practicable, if still expensive proposition is the Porsche 911, which starts at £3,600 and runs all the way up to £5,600. The 911 T, the cheapest, has most of the Porsche features, including its 2.2-litre six-cylinder engine, but without the extras such as electronic fuel injection and a removable roof which push both the price and performance up so remarkably.

The 911 T is, however, a very refined sports car with enough performance from its 125-b.h.p. version of the Porsche engine to satisfy all but the most determined drivers. Although it can only be described as a sports car, the Porsche comes as something of a revelation for those brought up in the British tradition of the MGB and TR sports cars. For Dr. Ferdinand Porsche, who designed the forerunner of the 911 at the end of the last war, saw no reason why sports cars should have the traditional hard suspension and heavy steering which most British sports cars still exhibit.

The Porsche, within the limitations of its two seats (the two rear ones really are for emergency use only) is as comfortable as most saloon cars in its class. The steering is accurate and direct but not at all heavy so that the Porsche can be swung along twisting country lanes at remarkable speeds without any sensation of stiffness.

Town driving too is very easy, partly because of the excellent Porsche Sportomatic gearbox. It has the advantage of an exceptionally flexible and powerful engine, so that even in heavy town traffic, one hardly needs to change gear. Porsche sales staff even advised me to treat it like a full automatic, selecting an intermediate gear and leaving it there while in town.

SPECIFICATION

ENGINE: Six cylinder horizontally opposed twin overhead camshaft unit of 2.2 litres producing 125 b.h.p. net.

DIMENSIONS: Length 13 feet 8 inches. Width 5 feet 3 inches. Height 4 feet 4 inches. Weight 22¼ cwt.

PERFORMANCE: Maximum speed 125 m.p.h. Acceleration to 60 m.p.h. in 9 secs.

PRICE: 911 T Lux with Sportomatic £4,154. Cheapest 911 T £3,671.

This is certainly possible, because the engine has such good torque at low speeds, but I preferred to use the easy gear change to achieve a slightly quieter and livelier performance. The Sportomatic has a clutch which is electronically operated from the gear lever, so that gears can be changed simply by moving the gear lever.

One cannot drive the Porsche for long without being thoroughly impressed by the thoughtfulness of its engineering. Even the 911 T is no boulevard sports car. It is designed for high speeds and quite capable of achieving them safely. The low bucket seats, for instance, provide the accurate well-braced support which one needs when driving fast but which is so often lacking.

The instrumentation and upholstery are as well designed and finished as you would expect for the price. The interior of the car I drove was finished throughout in black leather, with basketweave leather seats and a padded leather dashboard, which produced a pleasingly integrated effect.

The instruments, which Porsche supplies liberally, are all well positioned in front of the driver, where they can be safely read. Most of the controls are operated from steering column switches, so that one can wash and wipe the windscreen without taking one's hands off the wheel. The heater, too, is easily reached; the controls on the dashboard are easy to operate and provide individually controlled hot or cold air.

The 911 T is in some ways similar to the Triumph Stag. It is too refined to be classed as an ordinary sports car, yet it can outshine most true sports cars in roadholding and performance. The 911 T is, of course, almost twice as expensive as the Stag, whose arrival may well reduce the demand for cars like the Mercedes 280 SL and Porsche in Britain. But for some, a Porsche will still be the only answer and I can appreciate their reasons.

Well Sprung

James Ensor, the motoring writer for The *Financial Times*, gave the 911 T a very glowing report, but unlike the other motoring journalists of the day, he focussed on the 911's all-round package as a comfortable sports car. Of course he referred to the car's effortless power and speed, but he spent a good deal of his review praising the elements of comfort and ergonomic integrity.

Ensor sought to compare the 911 T to the MGB and Triumph sports cars, explaining that most British sports cars had hard suspension, but that Ferry Porsche had succeeded in producing a fast sports car with acceptable suspension for both town and country driving.

Privateer Racing

Following some encouraging results in their previous two seasons, in 1970 Kremer Racing purchased from the factory a red 911 ST which was built up in the Kremer workshops according to Erwin's requirements. For the Kremer race team, this car represented their first real big-time racing project. The 911 ST was fitted with a slightly larger 2.3-litre version (2247cc with 1mm larger bores, developing 240bhp) of the 2195cc standard production engine.

Perhaps significantly for Kremer Racing, the start of a new decade was also their first outing at Le Mans. The Kremer Racing 911 was entered under the team name of Ecurie Luxembourg, and far from being overawed by the importance of the event, Erwin Kremer and partner Nicolas Koob brought their car home in a very credible seventh place overall. This represented a first place finish in the GT Class 2000-2500cc in this, the most classic of endurance races.

You would be right to point out that there were only seven classified finishers out of 51 starters that year, two of which were Ferraris, but for the Kremer Racing team this result represented an exceptional achievement considering their limited experience in the big league with a very meagre racing budget.

Erwin Kremer is seen here driving his 911 ST in the 1971 ADAC 1000 km race at the legendary Nürburgring in which he finished 12th overall with Jürgen Neuhaus. The Kremer Racing number 82 car was the top-finishing 911 team in the field

Kremer and Koob drove a fast but steady race to bring their 2.3-litre Kremer Racing 911 ST home in 7th place in the 1970 Le Mans 24-Hour race

The Kremer pit garage was a busy place during their scheduled stops but the Cologne crew kept the number 47 car running like clockwork throughout the 24 hours

Financial Matters

In September 1970, the two principal shareholders of Dr. Ing. h.c.F. Porsche KG, namely Ferry Porsche and his sister, Louise Piëch, increased the company's equity from DM 3.0-million to DM 20.0-million. At this stage, Porsche was generating sales of DM 430-million and had a staff of 3891.

From Humble Beginnings

Started in 1952, the *Christophorus* magazine had become popular amongst Porsche owners and circulation had grown impressively. The year 1972 signalled the 20th anniversary and the popular in-house publication was by now distributed worldwide to Porsche customers.

A press release issued by the Porsche press department in 1972 recognised this important milestone and explained, "Christophorus, well known in the Christian world since his first mention in writing in 1293 in the Leganda Aurea, martyr, one of the fourteen 'helpers in need' against unexpected death and dangerous situations, popular saint in the Orient and Occidental countries, patron of waggoners, and since the start of the 20th century, Patron Saint of motorists".

Erich Strenger and Richard von Frankenberg worked their magic in creating what has today become an iconic publication. Not content with merely displaying the various Porsche models in simple settings, they sought to illustrate these cars in a truly artistic and eye-catching manner. The magazine cover with the girl and the red 911 is from May 1971, while the golden 911 with the US Army helicopter is from the July 1972 issue of Christophorus

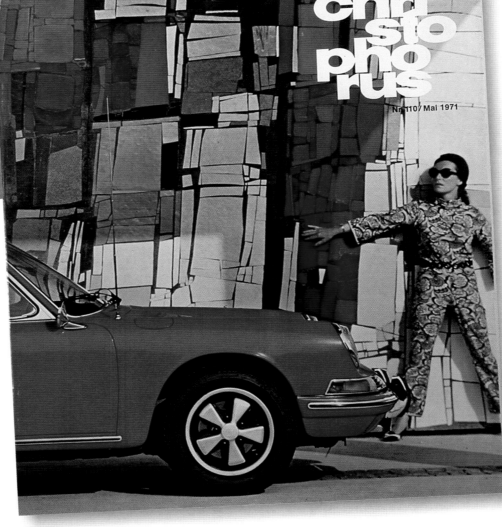

Porsche drivers start young, as the July 1973 cover of Christophorus *shows*

PRESSE-MITTEILUNG

Pr 72/72 (Es.E)

PORSCHE

"CHRISTOPHORUS," PORSCHE HOUSE MAGAZINE FOR 20 YEARS

Two years ago he was excommunicated by the Pope, but Paul VI emphatically reinstated him in his capacity as a Patron Saint: Christophorus, well known in the Christian world since his first mention in writing in 1293 in the Legenda Aurea, martyr, one of the 14 "helpers in need" against unexpected death and dangerous situations, popular saint in the Orient and Occidental countries, patron of waggoners, and since the start of the 20th century, Patron Saint of motorists.

Twenty years ago, when Dr. Ferdinand Porsche and Professor Albert Prinzig, then general manager of the young firm in Stuttgart-Zuffenhausen, sired the idea of their own magazine for the friends of the House of Porsche, with the well known motor journalist Richard von Frankenberg to be commissioned as editor, the idea of "Christophorus" as a title was suggested. Because more than anywhere else, a Patron Saint is needed for fast cars and races ...

As the first issue of this magazine was published in February 1952, now is the time to look back on these twenty years. From the beginning, subscriptions were handled not with the publisher, but directly with the House of Porsche; from the beginning, front and rear covers and the two-sided center spread were printed in four colors; from the beginning, Richard von Frankenberg has worked with the same graphic artist for copy and layout: Erich Strenger, who has later become responsible for nearly all the racing posters and is still on the Christophorus team today. A permanent contact for printing was even established back in 1952: the Bechtle firm in Esslingen.

At the beginning of the year 1952, the standard Porsche model was the Type 356. With its 1300 cc engine and 44 horsepower, it attained a top speed of 145 KM/h (90 mph) – at that time the fastest production car in Germany! Rumors were already going around, however, about a 1500 cc Porsche. In October 1951 Huschke von Hanstein, Richard von Frankenberg, and the then German sports car champions Petermax Müller, Walter Glöckler, and Hermann Ramelow drove a 1500 cc coupe to a string of world records in 72 hours of racing Montlhéry.

At its inception Christophorus was published in a mini-edition of 3500 copies. Today, more than 20.000 copies are sold to the whole (Porsche) world, and there is an English edition translated by the American motor journalist Jerry E. Sloniger.

7 STUTTGART 40   PORSCHESTRASSE 42   TELEFON 0711/8203(1)   TELEX PORSCHEAUTO 07-21817

Issued on September 2, 1972, this Porsche press release details the impressive growth of the Christophorus *magazine not only in circulation numbers, but also in terms of product quality and respectability in the market*

The magazine reports on Sport, technical information, and travel; in addition all famous Porsche customers pass in revue for the reader: whether it be Olympic medalist Erhard Keller, French film star Mylène Demongeot, or Astronaut Walt Cunningham.

As a bicentennial commemoration a special 72 page issue is presented, which includes among other things a glance back over the three International Manufacturers Championships for Porsche cars.

Quite frequently Christophorus has been a motif for presentation of pictorial art, as in the copper etchings of Dürer and von Martin, or the Christophorus from the south tower of the 1442 Sebaldsu Church in Nürnberg, now on display in the German Museum. The modern masters have also paid their respects, and Germany's most famous woodcarver, HAP Grieshaber, produced a Christophorus woodcut especially for the magazine of the House of Porsche.

Whether a Saint, or "only" a Patron Saint, Christophorus is a willing and true helper in need for all drivers.

OP
No.3b
2/9/1972

The Weissach Story
The Jewel In Porsche's Crown

If you build sports cars for sale to the public, it stands to reason that you will want to test your product on the road, under realistic conditions, before selling any cars. In Porsche's own words, production in 1949 was 'modest'. However, therein lay their strength as Porsche was able to ensure top quality in terms of both finish and engineering.

During these early years, the autobahns between Stuttgart and Heilbronn, as well as the roads around Stuttgart itself, served as the proving grounds for Porsche's engineers on which to test their cars. With traffic being relatively sparse at the time, the Porsche engineers had every opportunity to try out the cars and components they had designed and built at the Zuffenhausen plant. But, as traffic became denser, extreme driving tests on public roads became increasingly difficult and as a result, in 1953, a small aerodrome near Malmsheim was made available to Porsche for them to conduct specific tests and trials. But even this temporary solution was hardly satisfactory since the facility was not large enough and, being an airfield, it did not offer the variety of road conditions and gradients required for proper testing.

By the mid-fifties, it became obvious that the only way to solve the problem was for Porsche to establish their own dedicated test facility which would provide all possible driving conditions, away from the prying eyes of the press and public. Suitably convinced that this was the way forward, Porsche test engineer, Helmuth Bott, presented a document to management on January 29, 1960, formally referring to the 'Weissach Project' for the first time.

However, the origins of the Weissach Development Centre actually date back to 1931, when Ferdinand Porsche established his own company in Kronenstrasse in Stuttgart. Known as Dr. Ing. h.c. F. Porsche GmbH, Konstruktion und Beratung für Motoren und Fahrzeuge, this company formed the original core from which the Weissach Development Centre grew. Initially, this was in response to their own internal need for vehicle testing and improvement, although in time other manufacturers would commission Porsche to test their products too.

The process of developing a dedicated test centre began when Porsche acquired a piece of land in 1960 in the Weissach region, 25 kilometres north west of Stuttgart-Zuffenhausen. A skid pad was constructed at first, together with a wide range of road surface testing options, but the facility would grow to include a full test track by the end of the decade.

With their eyes on an even bigger goal, the Development division of Porsche together with its Construction, Testing and Design departments moved to the new Weissach Development Centre in the summer of 1971. In addition to the large test track, Weissach also became the home of further elaborate installations such as a wind tunnel, crash test facility, exhaust emissions test centre and a wide range of drivetrain test booths serving both in-house development work and customer assignments.

The importance of the test facility at Weissach cannot be overemphasised in Porsche's history. Not only did this give the company the ability to test their own vehicles thoroughly, but it also presented them with an additional income stream through providing engineering solutions for other manufacturers. This in itself gave Porsche the ability to understand what other manufacturers were getting up to in the market by such companies bringing their engineering problems to Porsche for them to solve. This 'think tank' was perhaps one of their more important development projects, one which sustained Porsche when new car sales were flagging. This was Porsche's 'jewel in the crown'.

Weissach timeline

1960	November 18, Porsche buys 94 acres of pasture in the Weissach and Flacht communities.
1961	October 16, ground is broken by Dr. h.c. Ferry Porsche for the development of Weissach.
1962	October 15, approval is given for the construction of the skid pad and dynamic driving test facilities.
1969	July – test track completed.
1971	October 1 saw the opening of the Development Centre (Stage 1). Acceleration sled developed for testing of seating and restraint systems.
1972	Official international presentation of the Development Centre to the press. Roll-over tests with Porsche 911. Side impact tests. December 21, Porsche KG becomes a joint-stock company (AG) shortly after moving to the Weissach Development Centre.
1973	First crash test facility in Weissach. Long-life car research project seeking to save materials and resources developed at Weissach and presented at Frankfurt Motor Show.

Source: Porsche

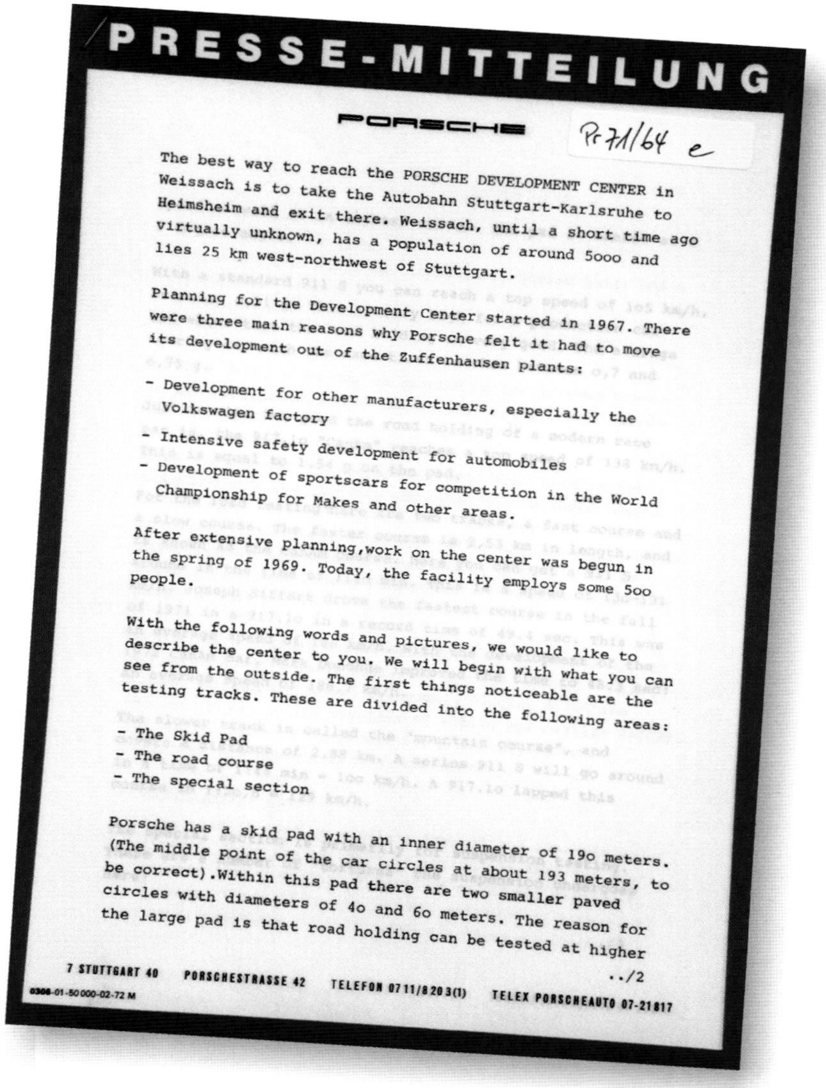

/PRESSE-MITTEILUNG

PORSCHE   Pr 71/64 e

The best way to reach the PORSCHE DEVELOPMENT CENTER in Weissach is to take the Autobahn Stuttgart-Karlsruhe to Heimsheim and exit there. Weissach, until a short time ago virtually unknown, has a population of around 5000 and lies 25 km west-northwest of Stuttgart.

Planning for the Development Center started in 1967. There were three main reasons why Porsche felt it had to move its development out of the Zuffenhausen plants:

- Development for other manufacturers, especially the Volkswagen factory
- Intensive safety development for automobiles
- Development of sportscars for competition in the World Championship for Makes and other areas.

After extensive planning, work on the center was begun in the spring of 1969. Today, the facility employs some 500 people.

With the following words and pictures, we would like to describe the center to you. We will begin with what you can see from the outside. The first things noticeable are the testing tracks. These are divided into the following areas:

- The Skid Pad
- The road course
- The special section

Porsche has a skid pad with an inner diameter of 190 meters. (The middle point of the car circles at about 193 meters, to be correct). Within this pad there are two smaller paved circles with diameters of 40 and 60 meters. The reason for the large pad is that road holding can be tested at higher

7 STUTTGART 40   PORSCHESTRASSE 42   TELEFON 0711/8203(1)   TELEX PORSCHEAUTO 07-21817
0308-01-50000-02-72 M   ../2

Announcing the opening of the Weissach Development Centre, Porsche issued this eight-page press document explaining how the media could find their way to the new plant 25km north west of Stuttgart. It went on to give details of how important the new facility was for the company and what technical resources were available there

Several City dignitaries, officials and senior Porsche personnel had been present at the inauguration of the test facility in Weissach on October 15, 1962. Among those attending the opening ceremony of the new Weissach facilities were: Ferry Porsche, Mr Kempf (Mayor of Weissach) and Mr Wurz (Mayor of Flacht). Porsche personnel included Wilhelm Hild (race engineer), Helmuth Bott, Johann Kern (Finance Director), Hans Tomala (Technical Director), Herbert Linge, Ghislaine Kaes, Peter Falk and Helmut Rombold. Various different Porsche 356 B Coupés can be seen here during the demonstration drive – the first car being a 356 B (T5) Coupé, followed by a new 356 B Carrera 2 Coupé

An early aerial photograph shows a birds eye view of Weissach (also called Porsche Werk 8), taken in 1969

Construction continued with further test facilities being built at Weissach in 1970 and 1971

In 1973, Werk 8 still looked much like a building site with new test facilities being added regularly as this aerial view shows

Another aerial view of Werk 8 in Weissach, c. 1973

This aerial view of Weissach taken in 1976, shows how the test facility had matured into a massively important piece of the greater Porsche puzzle. No longer looking like a building site but a professional and world-class test facility, Weissach was the envy of many, much larger manufacturers around the world

Changes At The Top

Effective from April 1, 1971, there were several significant appointments to the Board of Management of Dr. Ing. h.c.F. Porsche KG. Joining Dr. Ferry Porsche on the Board was Heinz Branitzki (Finance), Karlernst Kalkbrenner (Human Resources), Ferdinand Piëch (Technology and Contract Development), F.A. 'Butzi' Porsche (Design) and Dr. Michel Piëch (Administration). In October of the same year, development engineer of the famous 4-cam Carrera engine, Dr. Ernst Fuhrmann, rejoined the company after a 15-year absence, taking over the Technology Department.

The Family Steps Aside

At the beginning of 1972, the Porsche and Piëch dynasties decided that family members would no longer be appointed to executive management positions within the company. This had previously led to some unhappiness when certain high-ranking family members were seen to be creating their own little empires within the organisation.

At this time a resolution was passed by the partners of Dr. Ing. h.c. F. Porsche KG converting the limited partnership into a joint-stock corporation with a share capital of DM 50-million. In August of that year, Dr. Ferry Porsche took over as Chairman of the Supervisory Board, and Dr. Ernst Fuhrmann was appointed as Spokesman (Managing Director) of Porsche's Board of Management.

Following the company's conversion to a joint-stock company, the name 'Dr. Ing. h.c. F. Porsche AG' was entered in the national trade register on March 1, 1973.

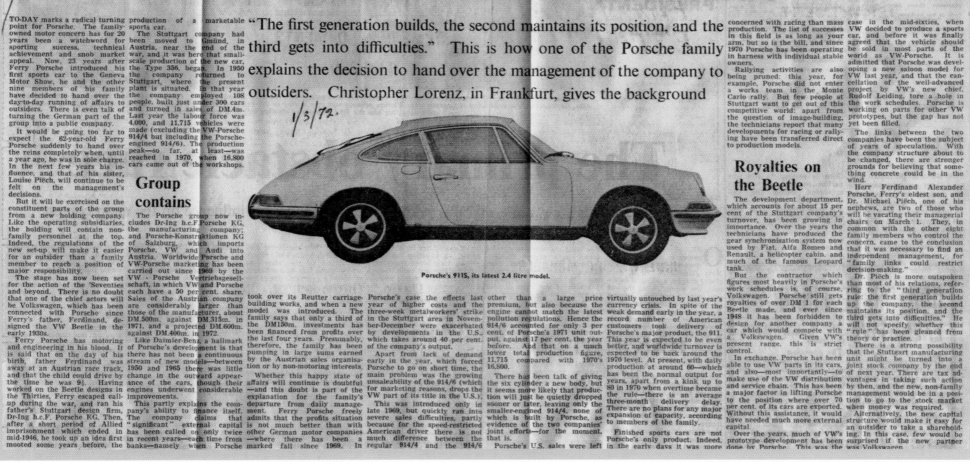

The Executive's World EDITED BY DAVID PALMER

Porsche at the crossroads

"The first generation builds, the second maintains its position, and the third gets into difficulties." This is how one of the Porsche family explains the decision to hand over the management of the company to outsiders. Christopher Lorenz, in Frankfurt, gives the background

1/3/72.

TO-DAY marks a radical turning point for Porsche. The family-owned motor concern has for 20 years been a watchword for sporting success, technical achievement and snob market appeal. Now, 23 years after Ferry Porsche introduced his first sports car to the Geneva Motor Show, he and the other nine members of his family have decided to hand over the day-to-day running of affairs to outsiders. There is even talk of turning the German part of the group into a public company.

It would be going too far to expect the 62-year-old Ferry Porsche suddenly to hand over the reins completely when, until a year ago, he was in sole charge. In the next few years his influence, and that of his sister, Louise Piëch, will continue to be felt on the management's decisions.

But it will be exercised on the constituent parts of the group from a new holding company. Like the operating subsidiaries, the holding will contain non-family personnel at the top. Indeed, the regulations of the new set-up will make it easier for an outsider than a family member to reach a position of major responsibility.

The stage has now been set for the action of the 'Seventies and beyond. There is no doubt that one of the chief actors will be Volkswagen, which has been connected with Porsche since Ferry's father, Ferdinand, designed the VW Beetle in the early 1930s.

Ferry Porsche has motoring and engineering in his blood. It is said that on the day of his birth, father Ferdinand was away at an Austrian race track, and that the child could drive by the time he was 9½. Having worked on the Beetle designs in the Thirties, Ferry escaped call-up during the war, and ran his father's Stuttgart design firm, Dr-Ing h.c.F. Porsche KG. Then, after a short period of Allied imprisonment which ended in mid-1946, he took up an idea first mooted some years before, the production of a marketable sports car.

The Stuttgart company had been moved to Gmünd, in Austria, near the end of the war, and it was here that small-scale production of the new car, the Type 356, began. In 1950 the company returned to Stuttgart, where the present plant is situated. In that year the company employed 108 people, built just under 300 cars and turned in sales of DM.4m. Last year the labour force was 4,000, and 11,715 vehicles were made (excluding the VW-Porsche 914/4 but including the Porsche-engined 914/6). The production peak—so far, at least—was reached in 1970, when 16,800 cars came out of the workshops.

Group contains

The Porsche group now includes Dr-Ing h.c.F. Porsche KG, the manufacturing company; and Porsche-Konstruktionen KG of Salzburg, which imports Porsche, VW and Audi into Austria. Worldwide Porsche and VW-Porsche marketing has been carried out since 1969 by the VW - Porsche Vertriebsgesellschaft, in which VW and Porsche each have a 50 per cent. share. Sales of the Austrian company are considerably larger than those of the manufacturer, about DM.500m. against DM.315m. in 1971, and a projected DM.600m. against DM.400m. in 1972.

Like Daimler-Benz, a hallmark of Porsche's development is that there has not been a continuous stream of new models—between 1950 and 1965 there was little change in the outward appearance of the cars, though their engines underwent considerable improvements.

This partly explains the company's ability to finance itself. The company claims that "significant" external capital has been called on only twice in recent years—each time from banks—namely when Porsche took over its Reutter carriage-building works, and when a new model was introduced. The family says that only a third of the DM150m. investments has been financed from profits over the last four years. Presumably, therefore, the family has been pumping in large sums earned by the Austrian sales organisation or by non-motoring interests.

Whether this happy state of affairs will continue is doubtful—and this doubt is part of the explanation for the family's departure from daily management. Ferry Porsche freely admits that the profits situation is not much better than with other German motor companies—where there has been a marked fall since 1969. In Porsche's case the effects last year of higher costs and the three-week metalworkers' strike in the Stuttgart area in November-December were exacerbated by developments in the U.S., which takes around 40 per cent. of the company's output.

Apart from lack of demand early in the year, which forced Porsche to go on short time, the main problem was the growing unsaleability of the 914/6 (which for marketing reasons, drops the VW part of its title in the U.S.).

This was introduced only in late 1969, but quickly ran into severe sales difficulties, partly because for the speed-restricted American driver there is not much difference between the regular 914/4 and the 914/6 other than a large price premium, but also because the engine cannot match the latest pollution regulations. Hence the 914/6 accounted for only 3 per cent. of Porsche's 1971 unit output, against 17 per cent. the year before. And that on a much lower total production figure, 11,715 compared with 1970's 16,800.

There has been talk of giving the six cylinder a new body, but it seems more likely that production will just be quietly dropped sooner or later, leaving only the smaller-engined 914/4, none of which is built by Porsche, as evidence of the two companies' joint efforts—for the moment, that is.

Porsche's U.S. sales were left virtually untouched by last year's currency crisis. In spite of the weak demand early in the year, a record number of American customers took delivery of Porsche's major product, the 911. This year is expected to be even better, and worldwide turnover is expected to be back around the 1970 level. At present, with daily production at around 60—which has been the normal output for years, apart from a kink up to 80 in 1970 when overtime became the rule—there is an average three-month delivery delay. There are no plans for any major expansion of capacity, according to members of the family.

Finished sports cars are not Porsche's only product. Indeed, in the early days it was more concerned with racing than mass production. The list of successes in this field is as long as your arm, but so is the bill, and since 1970 Porsche has been operating in harness with individual stable owners.

Rallying activities are also being pruned: this year, for example, Porsche did not enter a works team in the Monte Carlo rally. But few people at Stuttgart want to get out of this competitive world: apart from the question of image-building, the technicians report that many developments for racing or rallying have been transferred direct to production models.

Porsche's 911S, its latest 2.4 litre model.

Royalties on the Beetle

The development department, which accounts for about 15 per cent of the Stuttgart company's turnover, has been growing in importance. Over the years the technicians have produced the gear synchronisation system now used by Fiat, Alfa Romeo and Renault, a helicopter cabin, and much of the famous Leopard tank.

But the contractor which figures most heavily in Porsche's work schedules is, of course, Volkswagen. Porsche still gets royalties of over DM 1 for each Beetle made, and ever since 1948 it has been forbidden to design for another company a car which would compete with a Volkswagen. Given VW's present range, this is strict control.

In exchange, Porsche has been able to use VW parts in its cars, and also—most importantly—to make use of the VW distribution and service chain. This has been a major factor in lifting Porsche to the position where over 70 per cent. of its cars are exported. Without this assistance, it would have needed much more external capital.

Over the years, much of VW's prototype development has been done by Porsche. This was the case in the mid-sixties, when VW decided to produce a sports car, and before it was finally agreed that the vehicle should be sold in most parts of the world as VW-Porsche. It is admitted that Porsche was developing a new saloon model for VW last year, and that the cancellation of the well-advanced project by VW's new chief, Rudolf Leiding, tore a hole in the work schedules. Porsche is working on parts for other VW prototypes, but the gap has not yet been filled.

The links between the two companies have been the subject of years of speculation. With the company structure about to be changed, there are stronger grounds for believing that something concrete could be in the wind.

Herr Ferdinand Alexander Porsche, Ferry's eldest son, and Dr. Michael Piëch, one of his nephews, are two of those who will be vacating their managerial chairs on March 1. They, in common with the other eight family members who control the concern, came to the conclusion that it was necessary to find an independent management, for "family links could restrict decision-making."

Dr. Piëch is more outspoken than most of his relations, referring to the "third generation rule: the first generation builds up the company, the second maintains its position, and the third gets into difficulties." He will not specify whether this "rule" has been gleaned from theory or practice.

There is a strong possibility that the Stuttgart manufacturing unit might be turned into a joint stock company by the end of next year. There are tax advantages in taking such action by then, and the new, non-family management would be in a position to go to the stock market when money was required.

Alternatively, the new capital structure would make it easy for an outsider to take a shareholding. In this case, few would be surprised if the new partner was Volkswagen.

By the end of 1972, Porsche's workforce totalled 3950. Although sales were down on the 1970 numbers, production figures for 1971-72 had stabilised. Little did the motoring world know what lay ahead in 1973 with the oil price crisis, which is probably just as well, as most manufacturers would not have produced as many cars during that period for fear of ending up with parking lots full of expensive, unsold automobiles.

In a knee jerk-reaction, many motor manufacturers planned overnight to drop or significantly reduce the production of larger, performance-oriented vehicles in favour of smaller, more fuel efficient models, but Porsche stuck to their guns. Not surprisingly, luxury and specialist sports car manufacturers were the worst hit and in 1974 Aston Martin ceased production.

Sales of Porsche cars, on the other hand, followed a roller-coaster ride with 911 production increasing by almost 30% in 1973, but then settling back to earlier levels. These were uncertain times and 1975 saw a big fall in sales again. However, from 1976 onwards, 911 production began to climb to new heights.

Zöllner & Co was a Kiel-based company specialising in auto tracking systems. Pictured here at the Weissach test facility, an American-spec 911 T 2.4 Targa is put through a rolling road test – one can just make out the chains anchoring the front wheels to the ground (c. 1972)

Here a Porsche 911 S 2.4 Coupé (1972) is put through its paces in the sound test studio at the Weissach Research Centre

Low flying! A Porsche 911 S 2.4 gets airborne at the Weissach proving ground in 1972

THE 911 FLEXES ITS MUSCLES

A Porsche 911 T 2.4 Coupé (1972) is given the full treatment during a driving test on the punishing uneven surface track around Weissach (Werk 8)

A Porsche 911 undergoes emissions testing at Werk 8 in 1972. The emissions testing facility at Weissach was so comprehensive that other European manufacturers who exported their products to America first had to get them tested here, as the US emissions watchdog used this Porsche facility as its benchmark

Another rolling road test rig at Weissach. This time the test car is a 911 E 2.4 Coupé (1973)

The 911 2.4-litre

Down by the Riverside – the words to that well-known Southern gospel song come to mind here. This is a 911 E 2.4 Coupé (1973)

Hot on the heels (at least in Porsche terms) of the new 2.2-litre introduced for the 1970 model year came the announcement of an even bigger and better engine with which to power the 1972 models. The increase in engine capacity was driven by the need to meet new fuel requirements in several key export markets where a lower lead content petrol was being introduced. In order to run on the regular grade fuel, the Porsche engineers lowered the compression ratio but achieved greater power and speed by bumping up the engine capacity.

For the 1972 model year, engine capacity was increased from 2195cc to 2341cc, this increase being achieved by lengthening the stroke from 66mm to 70.4mm thanks to a redesigned crankshaft. The extra 146cc may not sound like a huge jump when stated in this manner, but power in the 911 S went from 180bhp to 190bhp, providing considerably better acceleration across the rev range.

As from model year 1972, the wheelbase was increased by 3mm to 2271mm. Dimensions were: length 4127mm, width 1610mm, height 1320mm. This was the only real change to the body dimensions of the 911 apart from the 1969 increase in which the rear axle and wheel arches had been moved back by 57mm in the body giving greater stability. In fact, the body length varied but these differences had to do with the different rubber fitments used on the bumpers and bumper overriders. These dimensions varied (4127mm to 4147mm) between model years and also between the 911 T, E and the S models.

One other small body change introduced as standard on the 1972 911 S but optional on the T and E (standard on all models from 1973), was in the sheet metal below the front bumper, which had been reshaped to provide an air dam for improved air flow. This almost insignificant change was surely the forerunner of the revolutionary air flow body package that accompanied the Carrera RS 2.7 two years later.

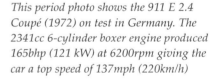

This period photo shows the 911 E 2.4 Coupé (1972) on test in Germany. The 2341cc 6-cylinder boxer engine produced 165bhp (121 kW) at 6200rpm giving the car a top speed of 137mph (220km/h)

This Porsche 911 T 2.4 Coupé (1972) is fitted with unusual all-blue Fuchs alloy wheels

A Porsche 911 2.4 Coupé poses in a typical forest setting under a blanket of freezing fog – Porsche calendar, January 1973

In the foreground is a 911 E 2.4 Targa, on the left is a yellow 911 S 2.4 Coupé, while on the right is a red Typ 914/6. These cars are all from the 1972 model range

The Long Arm Of The Law

It is not difficult to understand why the police in Germany wanted to have a fleet of Porsche patrol cars with which to carry out their duties. On the one hand, it ensured that they (almost) always caught any wannabe James Hunt-types who fancied their chances of outrunning the law. On the other hand, it also served as a useful talking point, if you were lucky enough to be the driver of one of these vehicles.

Quite how many fugitives one could get in the back seat of a Porsche 911 if the authorities did catch up with their miscreants was never disclosed in the Porsche literature, but it was not likely to be very many. If the 911 police car was anything like any other pursuit car belonging to the German authorities, then the back seat was no doubt crammed full of emergency highway equipment and speed ticket books, with little or no space for any 'baddies'.

These photos show an official 'Stuttgarter Polizeifahrzeug' in the form of a Porsche 911 T 2.4 Coupé (c. 1972). The Stuttgart traffic police have enjoyed the high speed capabilities of several generations of Porsche sports cars which started with the 356 in the late 1950s. Viewed from any angle, this car would certainly get your attention if it appeared unexpectedly next to you on the motorway or popped up in your rear-view mirror all of a sudden

This Porsche 911 E 2.4 Coupé is set against a fine example of traditional Bavarian architecture. The 1973 model pictured here is sporting the new 'cookie cutter' wheels introduced on this model year while the small front horn grilles which were chrome plated on the previous model are now black plastic

This Porsche 911 E 2.4 Coupé (1973) demonstrates the 'go anywhere' nature of the 911 sports car for a younger and more mobile generation

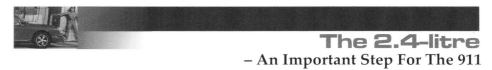

The 2.4-litre
– An Important Step For The 911

The 1973 2.4-litre 911 offered the Porsche driver a car that could be used for most motoring requirements, the best pursuit of all being able to head off into the sunset on some twisty and challenging country road.

An important modification, which enabled the 1973 F-series 911 to better meet the needs of an increasingly mobile car-buying public, was the increase in fuel tank capacity from 62 litres to 85 litres. This 37% increase in the fuel tank's capacity enabled the 911 to become an even more desirable touring car than it had been before.

This sporty 911 S 2.4 Coupé poses in front of a row of imposing but traditional German houses. This 1973 model features the new square-shaped rear-view mirrors which replaced the earlier round units and the 'Porsche' lettering along the rocker panel was an optional extra, while the old 356 in the background contrasts well with the modern shape of its younger sibling

In the 1970s, increased use of cars signalled a downturn in a more traditional form of transport, the train. This 911 E 2.4 Targa (1973) contrasts the old with the new, highlighting the flexibility of sports car travel and the independence it offered to the discerning motorist

What more could a sports car enthusiast want than to be behind the wheel of a 911 and to have an open motorway ahead? Here a trio of 911s enter a section of German autobahn, with a 911 S 2.4 Coupé at the rear. This car is a 1972 model as it still has the chrome tail light surrounds which were replaced with black plastic fittings the following year

How It All Comes Together

Photographing a sales brochure or advertising campaign is an expensive exercise, and very often the photos obtained at one such photo shoot will be used for a multitude of marketing and promotional campaigns. The accompanying photos show how the images have been incorporated into the final marketing brochure which the buyer would be handed when walking into a Porsche dealership to look at a 911.

In previous years, many of the images seen in sales brochures and advertisements would have been hand drawn by an illustrator, as photography was both expensive and not as advanced as in later years. Colour photography at that time was only used by companies with big ad budgets and besides, immediately post-War, there were many illustrators walking the streets looking for work. This is exactly how Erich Strenger and Richard von Frankenberg started with Porsche, as illustrators.

It was in the 1960/70s that photography was more widely used as creative reproduction processes became cheaper and more advanced. Even more importantly, motor manufacturers needed to turn a marketing campaign around in a shorter time than was possible with traditional illustrations. Lead times to market were constantly being shortened and with an increasing number of model launches being planned by manufacturers, the pressure was on to produce more work, more quickly. The accompanying photographs would not only have been used in promotional brochures but, as in this case, they were also given out to the press for use in magazine features.

Unfortunately though, much of the creative flair of artists is lost in photography as the artist's ability to capture the atmosphere of the setting is better achieved through the pen or paint brush of an illustrator.

Above is the finished product with both of the accompanying photographs reproduced in this 1973 catalogue ready for the prospective 911 customer

Grand Touring The Porsche Way

Ferry Porsche always insisted that the 911 should be able to carry an adequate amount of luggage, as a sports car was not just for posing; it was also for enjoying the open road and that meant long distance travelling. The accompanying photograph demonstrates the extraordinarily generous luggage compartment for a sports car the size of the 911.

Ferry also wisely insisted that his designers should ensure that the 911's trunk should be big enough to carry the obligatory set of golf clubs. His reasoning was, correctly as it turns out, that many of those fortunate enough to own a 911 would also have sufficient leisure time and funds to pursue the sporting desires of their choice. This requirement in fact dates back to the design of the early 356 model as well.

The 911's trunk was able to swallow an amazing amount of luggage for a sports car of this performance capability and comfort. This is a 1973 Porsche 911 E 2.4-litre

Motoring

Two views of a Porsche

THE PORSCHE 911 S is a difficult car to assess, because its price of £5,200 seems hard to justify except on the grounds of a performance which is illegal in Britain. This car sells for under £4,000 in Germany, but duties, purchase tax and transport costs jack it up in Britain into the exclusive £5,000-plus bracket.

Clearly there are people who will buy the 911 S purely because of its 150 mph top speed and amazing acceleration. But we suspect that there is a much larger class of buyer which cares less for the ultimate performance than for the Porsche's ability to provide comfortable, fast motoring for two people and perhaps a couple of children. Here Anthony Martin and James Ensor give their individual assessments.

Fine performance

Anthony Martin writes: The new, larger-engined Porsche is essentially an enthusiast's car. Although it is now old-fashioned in looks and passenger comfort, in terms of sheer acceleration and performance it represents the ultimate. Top speed is 150 mph and its acceleration to 60 mph will outpace a V12 Jaguar E Type or a Ferrari Dino. To better this type of performance one would have to spend several thousand pounds more for a marginal gain.

The driving position is an acquired taste as the pedals are offset. The seats are inclined to be a little too snug for some, and taller drivers will find they have very little head room. None the less the car is well tailored ergonomically for fast driving, with a range of large, clear instruments and switches easily available.

The clutch is not light, but is progressive and bites well on powered take-off. The brakes are fairly heavy, being unassisted by servo, but the all-disc system can take heavy punishment without fade.

A new gearbox pattern is easy and smooth to operate, Porsche having a legendary reputation for providing superb synchromesh.

The new 2.4-litre six-cylinder engine delivers far more torque than the previous, smaller Porsche engines, allowing one to drive the car in higher gears than before; the car pulls away fast and smoothly even in fifth gear at 30 mph, but frequent gear-changing is very much part of the joy of driving this car. Maximum revolutions for the engine are 7,200, and it is here that one is aware of the tremendous engineering that is contained in the vehicle.

A direct light and responsive steering matches the car's quick gait, and the Porsche feels as happy as 140 mph as it does at 40 mph. In skilled hands the 911S can be driven very quickly indeed with fantastic reserves of safety in braking and acceleration.

The ride is a magnificent combination of saloon-like comfort and sports-car firmness; all bumps and road striations are absorbed without shock or discomfort. Unlike many more delicate fast cars it can negotiate bad surfaces with a very great feeling of solidity.

Driving a Porsche produces an enthusiasm that results in fantic marque loyalty. The new 2.4 911S is an even greater improvement on its desirable predecessors and can be recommended to the wealthy enthusiast driver without qualification.

Some criticisms

James Ensor writes: Judged as a fast executive sports car rather than a racing machine, the Porsche does not score so well. I have no complaints about the handling, feel, roadholding or gearchange of the Porsche, all of which are justly renowned. But the seats are not what I would expect for upwards of £5,000, being rather hard and slippery.

The fresh air ventilation system is old fashioned and not very effective. But the heater is far worse. Its output depends entirely on the engine speed, so that I found I had to adjust the red vent lever almost as often as I changed gear in order to maintain an even temperature. Otherwise one is roasted on the motorway and chilled in traffic.

The fuel consumption is high —one cannot hope for much better than 13-15 mpg even if driving moderately. Luggage space in the front boot is very restricted because of the low boot line, though one can pile several cases into the rear seat space. These seats are too small for adults but they will carry smallish children in comfort.

The Porsche 911 T, £1,000 cheaper, and with a detuned version of the same 2.4 litre engine, is obviously a better buy for anyone not contemplating flat-out Continental motoring. But even this model seems expensive alongside rivals such as the Lotus Plus Two and the Jaguar E Type which can offer most of the Porsche virtues, except for the sheer performance.

I cannot claim to have been unmoved by the Porsche's delightful roadholding and superlatively smooth engine. Almost all the faults of the rear engined, air-cooled layout have been ironed out over the years, and one would have to be a very reckless driver to get into trouble in the Porsche. But I do feel that one should have more interior refinement at this price.

Two Journalists – Two Opinions

It has often been said that you can expect as many different opinions about a new car as you have journalists reviewing that car.

The *Financial Times* used not one, but two motoring journalists to pass comment on the new 911 S. Anthony Martin found, just like many other motoring journalists of the day, that the 911 dealt superbly with road imperfections and bumps, unlike many far more expensive and 'delicate' sports cars at that time.

James Ensor, on the other hand, reported the 911 S fell short in the areas of seat comfort and ventilation and heating, especially for a car costing the top side of £5,000. Although Ensor was somewhat critical of the cost of the 911 S, he was 'not unmoved' by the car's capability and performance.

And The Wheels
Go Round And Round

From 1972, there were three different wheel styles available - the standard steel wheel rim, the familiar Fuchs alloy and the new 'cookie cutter'. The last-named wheel was so called because of its resemblance to the kitchen utensil.

These wheels were available on 1973 model year cars, the last of the original 911 series before the new G-series cars. In fact the first model to wear the new 'cookie cutters' was the 911 2.4-litre of August 1972, just in time for the new 1973 season.

The wheel favoured by the vast majority of 911 drivers of this era was the Fuchs alloy wheel which appeared on this model for a marathon 22 years, between 1967 and 1989

Introduced as an option for the 1973 model year were the new 'cookie cutter' wheels as fitted to this Porsche 911 T 2.4. These wheels were shod with Dunlop SP 57, 185/70 VR 15 rubber

The 911 Was Moving Up In The World

Well-known motoring correspondent and author, Eric Dymock, wrote in *The Guardian* newspaper (May 1, 1972), that the 911 had to all intents and purposes moved up a notch in the market. No longer was the 911 competing with the likes of the Jaguar E-type or the Volvo P1800, but it was more likely to be matched against the Ferrari Dino, BMW 3.0-litre, Lamborghini Urraco and the Mercedes-Benz 350 SL.

This market re-alignment was based not so much on the car's greater performance capabilities, which were already impressive, but because of its higher purchase price. In Britain the entry level 911 T cost £3838 (US $9595) while the top of the line 911 S would set you back £5221 (US $13,052) or even over £5500 (US $13,750) for the Targa option, bringing it in line with other up-market grand tourers.

From the satisfying clunk of closing the door to the well lubricated click of the fuel filler mechanism, Dymock praised the car for its engineering build quality, pointing out that what might constitute noise to the casual observer, was music to the engineer. The only criticism the writer could level at the 911 was the higher fuel consumption due to the switch to unleaded fuel, and the lack of space for rear seat passengers and luggage.

This newspaper cutting appeared in The Guardian *(May 1, 1972), clearly highlighting what a sophisticated and high quality sports car the 911 had become*

G. 1.5.72.

£10,000 two-car family

ERIC DYMOCK tests the Porsche 911E and the Daimler Limousine

PORSCHE may not be one of the *grandes marques*: it is much too modern. But if it cannot match Alfa Romeo, Mercedes-Benz, or Rolls-Royce for pedigree, it has become a latter-day classic of a different sort. A car admired for qualities not many of the others have.

Dr Ferdinand Porsche designed cars for many years before one ever bore his own name. Among the creations of his tiny design office in Stuttgart were the Auto Union Grand Prix cars, the K d R car which Hitler adopted as the Volkswagen, and the Tiger tank.

The first proper Porsche was not made until 1948—a sort of sports Volkswagen, with many components derived from or inspired by the VW. It had an air-cooled engine at the back with four cylinders horizontally opposed, and was a small aerodynamic coupé. It was soon winning rallies and minor races, and by the time Dr Porsche died in 1951, turning the business over to his family, it was selling steadily.

Porsche cars evolved but have only undergone one major redesign in the past 25 years. Over several seasons in the mid-sixties, the four-cylinder range was gradually replaced by the six-cylinder series, now known as the 911, with a roomier, better-looking body.

Yet the conception of a small, fast sporting car, with room for two adults and two children remained unchanged. It was still air cooled, and handled well in spite of the rearward weight bias.

Porsche policy channelled most of the advertising budget into a racing programme. The family reasoned that for a relatively small firm, producing a specialist sports car in limited numbers, the money would be better spent convincing customers that Porsches were built to the standards of successful racing cars.

In sports car racing, Porsche became almost unbeatable. A brief attempt to enter Formula 1 was not encouraging, but Porsche cars won the Monte Carlo Rally three years in succession (1968-70) and their reputation in motor sport was assured.

When the 911 was introduced, not only was the design radically altered, but the price of the entire range rose dramatically. For a

time, the bottom end of the "real" (as opposed to the unsuccessful Type 914, or "VW-Porsche") range of Porsches competed with sports cars around £2,000.

But now the 911T costs £3,838, and the top of the range, the 911S is £5,221, or over £5,500 in open, left-hand drive form. The 911E as tested is £4,665. Instead of competing with the 6-cylinder Jaguars, or say the Volvo P1800, it is now matched against the Ferrari Dino, the 3-litre BMW, the Lamborghini Urraco, or even the Mercedes-Benz 350 SL.

The car's performance has increased. It now does 150 mph as near as makes no difference, and the acceleration would probably be alarming to the inexperienced or nervous.

It is not so much that it jerks the head back—you can do that by letting in the clutch suddenly. What takes

PORSCHE £4,665

you by surprise is the surge forward when you open the throttle and snick into fifth gear at about 120 mph.

Rear engines put most of the car's weight on the rear wheels—in the case of the Porsche, around 60 per cent with a near-empty fuel tank at the front. This helps the driving wheels to grip the road, but it can have unwanted effects when you drive round corners, or in cross-winds. The weight at the rear could tend to upset the balance on a corner.

There are two sorts of car with the engine behind the driver. There are those usually called "mid-engined," with the power unit where most cars have a rear seat. With the engine ahead of the rear axle, within the wheelbase, the weight distribution is nearly ideal.

With the engine behind the rear axle and overhanging the rear wheels—effectively in the boot—some effect on the handling is only to be expected. In the early days of the Porsche, the effect was to make it difficult on corners. The back would yaw out, and the car seemed perpetually on the threshold of a skid.

Happily, things have improved. The suspension now deals with the rear-engine position to give the Porsche strong but eminently safe characteristics. But

getting the best out of the car needs skill; you need to learn new tricks if you are going to drive it fast.

The steering is superbly sensitive, feeding information about the road back to the driver, and the car grips in a way that nearly everyone, except drivers of good vintage sports cars, has quite forgotten. With precision of this sort, you can feel the point where the front wheels are about to lose their grip on the corner; it is time to increase the power and take off a little steering lock as you dictate the point where understeer leaves off and oversteer takes over.

The interior is a little ascetic. Materials tend to be practical and hard-wearing rather than luxurious. Bristly carpet and matt black surrounds for the severe-looking instruments contribute to the austere look. Upholstery is firm, comfortable, and fully adjustable.

Everything works with efficient sorts of noises; those satisfying clunks you get from closing the doors, well greased clicks from the mechanism that works the fuel filler cap from inside, and an impressive subterranean rumble from the linkage to the five-speed gear-box. Clunks, clicks, and rumbles to everyone else, but music for engineers.

You carry children or luggage in Porsches; if you want both, you cannot have much of either. The front boot is shallow, and the small rear seats fold down to make a platform for suitcases.

This is an almost ideal car for touring—fast, quiet, and comfortable, with a level ride soaking up the bumps, and exemplary handling and road holding. It used to be even better before the Germans went on to unleaded petrol and Porsche reverted to an 8.5:1 compression and made other modifications to allow for low octane ratings.

They made the change because an enlightened Government has decided to reduce octanes until they can be raised by other means than adding lead to petrol.

Porsches now run on 91 octane (two star) fuel with no ill-effects whatever, except for considerably increased consumption. They now do 13 to 15 mpg instead of 18 to 20 mpg, justifying the alarmist warnings from the "lead lobby" that clean petrol would cost us all money.

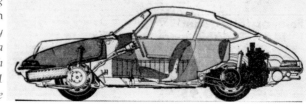

Racing Around The World

As the potential of the 911 began to impact in motor racing circles around the world, so more and more professional teams entered them. Just as Kremer Racing and Georg Loos Racing were well-known in Europe, so too was the formidable Brumos team of Hurley Haywood and Peter Gregg in American racing circles.

The European GT Championship in 1972 read like a Porsche 911 S benefit series, as the odd De Tomaso Pantera or Ferrari 365 GTB/4 punctured what can only be described as 911 S domination. Top European drivers such as Erwin Kremer, John Fitzpatrick, Clemens Schickentanz, Jürgen Neuhaus and Paul Keller headed the leader board regularly.

The formidable pairing of Haywood and Gregg took their 911 S to an impressive fifth place finish in the Sebring 12-Hour race on March 25, 1972

The number 41 Porsche 911 S 2.5-litre of Michael Keyser/Jürgen Barth/Sylvain Garand finished 13th overall in the 1972 Le Mans 24-Hour race, but the number 45 car of Fernand Sarapoulus/Dominique Bardini/Raymond Touroul failed to finish, retiring after 183 laps with engine trouble

In the Spa 1000kms race on May 7, 1972, Erwin Kremer/John Fitzpatrick finished in eighth place overall in their Porsche 911 S

Porsch-AH!

Many admirers of the German sports car brand the world over get the pronunciation of the famous P-O-R-S-C-H-E name wrong. Certainly, the vast majority of Porsche followers refer to the make as if there was no 'e' on the end of the name, the final 'e' being silent in the English language. However, real experts and Porschephiles all know that one must stress the last letter of the name to the extent that it is almost overemphasised – 'Porsch-AH'.

In fact, this matter received such attention in America, where this little-known Stuttgart firm had to fight really hard to have its voice heard, that one of the motoring magazines there decided to write a whole article on the subject. With the onset of a new baby in their household, *Road & Track* writer, William Moffat, explained how he made the transition from a Morgan sports car to a Porsch-ah. The move was prompted by a friend, naturally a Porsch-ah driver, who convinced Moffat on the positive attributes of the German car, not to mention the extra space for the baby in the back which the Morgan did not offer.

WHEN I WAS transferred from England to the United States we brought along our pet Morgan, the third member of our family for more than three years. Now, after a year of prosperity, the wholesale manufacturing of booties warned me our first pair of baby shoes would not hang beneath the mirror of the Morgan. We sadly had been telepathing Volkswagen to each other for a month when a long-unseen friend and new member, we learned, of the local Porsche Club dropped by.

I could not bear it, I confessed, in spite of how much I already loved that creature bulging beneath my dainty wife's tarpaulin-styled smock. I started to tell him of the nightmare I had had of the lace-hung Volks . . .

"Do you have any predisposition towards a Porsch-a?" he asked in his crisp German accent.

I gasped, eagerly.

"Porsch-as are proliferating presently," he declared with remarkable equanimity. "Why not purchase one."

"In fact, come with me to the meeting Friday night," he said slipping into a sort of knee-length leather flight coat. "Someone will most certainly know of a 'used one you could afford."

"And after you have obtained your Porsch-a, you may be permitted to join the rest of us in our club. Ve stick together, you know."

I told him that sounded pretty clubby as he left. Once out he stuck his head back in. "Porsch-as last perpetually, by the vey. Ask Kenneth Purdy. Guten abend."

He was gone and silence lingered Divinely in the room. I shivered. He seemed a different man.

"When did he start using a cigarette holder?" the skeptical side of my life asked.

I hadn't noticed. I told her I thought maybe he used it to signal other drivers. Dashing, anyway, didn't she think.

"Porsches don't wave at other cars, do they," she more or less stated, as one knowledgeable about such matters.

"I, uh, well, Hell," I joked. "Not in town anyway. I mean you're paying a devil of a lot of . . ."

"That means I can't wave Halloo at Helen anymore, then, doesn't it . . ."

Her favorite joy in driving the Morgan, besides slipping the clutch on hills, was waving to her dear friend who also drove one. Now she looked at me as though I had told her she couldn't have the baby.

Bill picked me up for the meeting on Friday. He was dressed in a narrow pin stripe suit and wore a chic black Homburg perched jauntily on his head. He contrasted strikingly with my baggy tweeds, always apropos to Morgan outings. I wondered for an instant how the rally and skiing pins attached to my tweed chapeau would look adorning a German Bowler.

"Auf Wiedersehen," my dear wife said closing the door.

Outside the touch of the Porsche's door handle felt like a chrome-plated invitation to a Stuttgart luxury ball, and I dropped, ungainly, into luxury's lap.

"You have a lot of room in here," I said, trying to find a familiar foothold for the ride ahead. We moved off, my knees flopping loosely and insecurely without the shoe-like fit of oneness the Morgan inspired, my body tensed in anticipation of wheel and coach bouncing in unison. It never happened, of course. I just sat there leaning slightly into the corners as Bill maneuvered in classic straight-arm fashion.

"This car rides amazingly well," I said, reveling in my comfort. "Is the suspension leaf or coil?"

"Uh," the pilot replied.

"The suspension," I repeated, louder. "What kind?"

No answer.

"Halloo, Bill!" I shouted, instinctively reaching for the steering wheel. "You awake, old man?"

It was a naive question. It was perfectly obvious that he was operating as close to automatically as I had ever seen. But for my impetuosity I earned a quick sidelong glance as though a bothersome but inconsequential stone had avoided the windscreen and stung his cheek.

"Okay. How are the brak-os, then?" I persisted. Now I didn't really mean to ask that question just at that time. Bill was pressing down into an intersection with his turn signal on and, operating the gearbox, obviously trying to out-do the light. Anyway, the little stone drew blood, he missed the shift down to second and, giving up all hope of recovery, mashed the brake pedal to the floorboards as the light turned red. The brakes were bloody good.

"Instruction book in der glove box," he growled, angrily pointing his hyper-rigid finger at a small brass plaque.

BY J. WILLIAM MOFFETT

ILLUSTRATIONS BY HOWARD SHOEMAKER

IST DAS NICHT EIN PORSCHE CLUB?

Although this is a more recent photograph, it shows another side to the Porschephile, and as the saying goes – "the difference between men and boys is the size and price of their toys". In the world of Porsche sports cars, a man's hobby almost certainly extends beyond the garage and into his home, as Porsche drivers are just as enthusiastic about little ones as they are about bigger examples

10 Years On (1963-1973)

The F-series 911 marked the 10th anniversary of the 911's introduction. A car that had started out as the replacement to the 356 model, and which supposedly had such a hard act to follow, had now become an iconic sports car in its own right. That is not to diminish the status of the legendary 356, but the 911 had met and surpassed all expectations imposed on it by the press and by Porsche themselves. But most importantly of all, it had created its own following of loyal Porschephiles, just as its predecessor did.

The 911 excelled both on the track and in the High Street, and this had helped Porsche to shift metal through the showrooms to such an unexpected extent, that an avalanche (in Porsche terms) of new model variations could be justified. In the same way, this development fuelled further sales which just helped the Stuttgart manufacturer to go from strength to strength. In so doing, Porsche became the envy of many other sports car manufacturers as they scrambled to grab a piece of this niche market which, in no small way, Porsche would help to keep alive during the ensuing fuel crises.

The Porsche stand at the Geneva Show, 1964, contained a mixture of models as the 356 was still a current model at that time. The 904 sports racer was really there as a halo vehicle as very few of these racers were converted for road use. Partly obscured by the yellow and red 356s, one can just make out a lone 901/911 in blue, marking a very passive entry for what was to become a world-beating sports car in the not too distant future

One of the first Typ 901 prototypes completed at the factory in 1963, pictured here with the engineering team responsible for its development. Ferry Porsche is standing in the foreground against the front left wing of the car

This photograph shows the Typ 901 (not yet identified as the 911) on the stand at the Geneva Motor Show in March 1964, but still wearing its introductory name plate from the previous year's Frankfurt launch

Translated, this advertisement reads – 'We attach more value to building exceptionally good cars rather than an exceptional number of cars' – basically, quality comes before quantity

The 1973 model year ended on a far from chilly note with strong sales. The 911 was still powered by the trusty 2.4-litre boxer engine, but the next year would see Porsche taking a bold step into the big league

Ten years on from its launch, the 911 had developed into an extremely handsome and respected sports car. Pictured here is the 1973 (US spec) 911 E 2.4-litre in both Coupé and Targa form

Porsche 911 production statistics

Model Year	Description	911 Production
1970	C-series	14,381
1971	D-Series	12,164
1972	E-Series	11,882
1973	F-series	15,438*

Source: Porsche

*This figure does include the Carrera RS 2.7 model as it was manufactured under the F-series designation, of which 1525 units were produced. However, this model is covered separately in the next chapter.

A LEGEND IS REBORN

Due to the importance of the Porsche 911 Carrera RS 2.7, it is necessary to devote a separate chapter to the development of this car which vaulted the company's name into the spotlight. The Carrera RS 2.7 was no ordinary 911 merely with a selection of 'go faster' parts fitted. This was a comprehensively re-engineered model of such significance that it would take a place in automotive history alongside the very finest super cars.

Through the 1960s, Porsche had been very successful on the track, thanks in no small part to a policy of producing road cars for the road, and purpose-built race cars for the track. This might sound a very obvious strategy to follow now, but other manufacturers had resorted to using superlight, modified versions of their road-going products with which to compete on the track. This had had two distinct benefits for the motor manufacturer, the first being that it reduced the cost of producing expensive one-off racers, and secondly there was an association factor where customers related the cars they bought through their local dealership with those they saw on the track.

As motor sport became more professional, and sponsorship money began to pour in, so manufacturers were able to allocate more and more funds towards developing full-blown race cars. However, with the forthcoming changes to the motor sport regulations in the early 1970s, Porsche were able to justify the development of a car that would bridge the gap between sports cars for the road and those for the track, just as the 356 Carrera had done almost two decades earlier. This prompted the Porsche engineers to once again consider producing a small run of road cars that would satisfy the homologation requirements of a Group 4 contender.

The Carrera concept was only given the green light by the Porsche Sales Department on condition that the majority of these race-ready sports cars were made available for road customers as well. In that way, the Sales Department could be more confident of selling any outstanding vehicles in the general market should the Race Department not be able to shift sufficient Carreras to their racing customers.

In the tumultuous days of the early 1970s, much of the automotive industry's design focus was concerned with colour, liberal thinking and radical ideas. As a result of this new wave of creative thinking, Porsche addressed the market's increasing requirement for a progressive approach to new model design. However, when the new Porsche broke cover, there were few cars on the market more radical than the 911 Carrera RS 2.7. It wowed the press and public alike during its introduction at the Paris Salon in October 1972.

With outrageous lettering splashed along its flanks and a 'duck's tail' spoiler attached to the rear engine cover, whatever were the Porsche engineers thinking about when they made this car? At launch, the potent new Carrera broke the mould and took the sports car world by storm.

Just three years had passed since the unforgettable Festival of Woodstock in 1969 had shaken the establishment, and the message being handed down by the

TIMELINE (1970-1972):

1967	1971	1972	1972	1973
Limited run 911 R introduced as lightweight racing car.	Dr. Fuhrmann gives go-ahead for 911 GT model to be developed.	911 2.7-litre prototype undergoes tests in the summer of '72.	RS Carrera 2.7 shown at Paris Salon October 1972.	Carrera RS 2.7 ceases production in July.
			First cars delivered weeks after Paris launch.	

upcoming generation was that 'grey' was dead. The market wanted to be shocked – ordinary was out and radical was in. Psychedelic colours and bold styling sold products and Porsche, needing to break into new markets, certainly pushed the boat out with the 911 Carrera.

Behind the scenes, a very nervous Porsche Sales Department waited with baited breath for the reaction of those at the Paris Salon. Their fears were allayed when a frantic scribbling of orders ensued and almost all the initial batch scheduled for production were swallowed up during, or immediately after, the Show.

The 911 Carrera RS 2.7 was a risky model for the Stuttgart company, especially as this car was intended to be the 911 flagship. The Porsche Sales Department was so sceptical about the sales prospects for such a high performance sports car that they restricted production to just 500 vehicles. They had held a similar view back

in 1967 when Baron Huschke von Hanstein, Porsche's publicity supremo, had proposed a run of 500 high performance 911 S models, based on the lightened and super quick 911 R, but that idea had been comprehensively squashed back then.

In 1973, the mainstay of the Porsche 911 range was its entry level 911 T, which was still powered by the 2341cc engine. However, the Carrera RS 2.7 opened the door for the company to develop the boxer 6-cylinder engine still further, as engine capacity continued to grow with larger engines powering future 911 models.

Porsche proudly displayed their new secret weapon, the 911 Carrera RS 2.7 sports car at the Paris Salon, in October 1972

Where Did The Name 'Carrera' Come From?

This Porsche publicity shot (November, 1972) shows the new Carrera in a typical German country setting near Esslingen, with the imposing fortress atop the Teck mountain in the background. This was a popular spot for gliders due to the favourable updraughts in the area. The early Carreras were all white with different coloured lettering and matching wheels. The red-on-white combination shown here was the most popular

An early photograph (November, 1972) of the company's 911 Carrera RS 2.7 Coupé press car. Registered S-AP 6492, this press car was well used by the media hacks and appears in many Carrera publicity shots

Photographed in front of the Ludwigsburg Palace, Germany's largest baroque palace (12km north of Stuttgart's city centre), this early Porsche 911 Carrera RS 2.7 Coupé looks ready to go. Built originally as a hunting lodge, Ludwigsburg Palace is a very appropriate site for this racer to be photographed as it, too, would gather many trophies

In order to appreciate the significance of the new and dynamic 911 Carrera RS 2.7, one must understand the origins and emotions associated with the name of 'Carrera'. In 1950, a race was organised in Mexico from the south of the country to the north, in celebration of the completion of that country's section of the Pan-American Highway, a transcontinental motorway covering a staggering 16,000 miles from Alaska to Chile.

In an effort to bring international recognition to this achievement and to attract tourists to their country, the Mexican government staged a road-race, *La Carrera Panamericana*, which turned out to be an all-out race across almost the entire length of the country. The Spanish word 'carrera' means competition or race, and the harsh uncompromising conditions of this diverse country served only to attract the best racing teams and competitors. Teams such as Ferrari, Mercedes, Lancia, Porsche and many more signed up, while top international drivers included Fangio, Maglioli, Kling and Phil Hill, as well as a Texas chicken farmer called Carroll Shelby.

Conditions for the drivers and teams were exceptionally tough as drivers battled not only the treacherous roads, but also crowds of over-eager spectators who had never seen such a spectacle before. By way of comparison, *La Carrera Panamericana* was twice the length of the Mille Miglia but, in contrast to the legendary road races of Europe, garage and pit facilities were non-existent, while heat and dust were the enemy of all. It was under these conditions that Porsche earned its stripes the hard way when, in 1954, the last year that the race was held due to high driver and spectator mortality, Porsche finished in third position overall behind two Ferraris. It must be remembered that Porsche had manufactured their first automobile only six years earlier, making this a truly monumental achievement.

As a result of the company's significant achievements in Mexico, the mechanics quite logically referred to the successful Porsche 550 racer's engine as the 'Carrera' engine, a name that stuck with the potent four-cam engine even after the team had returned to Stuttgart. However, it did not take long for the name 'Carrera' to take on further significance in Porsche's world when, at the Frankfurt Motor Show in September 1955, the Porsche 356 A 1500 GS Carrera was introduced to the world as a full production road car.

In recognition of the company's success in Mexico, the Carrera name was given to the highest performing model within the 356 range from that moment on. With the launch of the new 911 model at Frankfurt in 1963, however, there were more than a few raised eyebrows as questions were asked as to why there was not a high performance version of the new sports car being introduced at the same time. The questions, though, were premature, as seldom does a manufacturer introduce a full vehicle range of a new model at launch. However, the public and Porsche enthusiasts had grown to expect a true road racer from the Stuttgart stable. Although the 911 was introduced without a high performance version, the Carrera name was to be proudly carried on the flanks of a more potent racer for the time being, the 904, also known as the Carrera GTS.

Regular international Porsche campaigners in the South American scene, Fürst Metternich (right) and Constantin Graf Berckheim are seen after competing in the 1952 Carrera Panamericana in their Porsche 356 1500 Cabriolet

Jubilation as the Porsche team celebrate their third place finish in the 1954 Carrera Panamericana. The Porsche 550 Spyder was powered by the potent new four-cam engine which was later to take on the name 'Carrera'. From the left (sitting on the car), are Herbert Linge, Hans Herrmann and Huschke von Hanstein (wearing a white cap in the centre) with Czechoslovakian-born Jaroslav Juhan immediately to his left. The team's main sponsor, Fletcher Aviation, was the official distributor for Porsche aviation engines in America

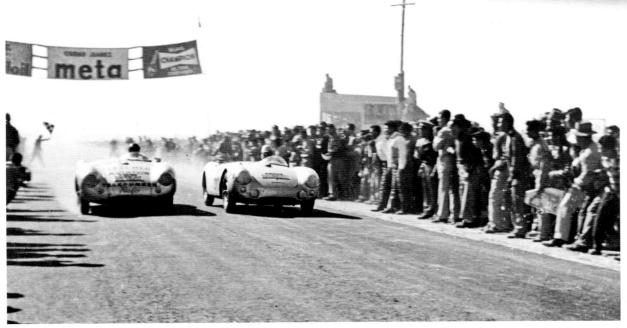

Crossing the finish line on the left in a Porsche 550 Spyder is Hans Herrmann. This was the fifth and last Carrera Panamericana (November 19-23, 1954) and Porsche achieved an outstanding third place overall and first in class for Sports Cars up to 1500cc, while the car on the right is driven by Jaroslav Juhan, who finished just behind Herrmann

What? No Carrera!

Why did the Carrera name not appear on the 911 model list at launch? Just as the Porsche 356 had had to first prove itself back in the early 1950s before a high performance Carrera road version was introduced, so too did the 911 have to undergo a period of introduction, development and refinement before Porsche would consider producing a specialised high performance road car in the 911 range.

The reasons were also more complex than that as the motor racing regulations at the time did not warrant the investment required to produce a hybrid road/race model within the range. More than that, Porsche already had two race cars which bore the name of Carrera, those being the Carrera GTS (or 904), and the Carrera 6 (or 906), and to introduce a road car with this name would certainly have been overkill.

The 911 S derivative had been introduced on July 25, 1966, just two years after the 911 first rolled off the production line. Under its engine lid, this new car had a more powerful version of the by-now trusty 1991cc boxer motor developing 160bhp, instead of the more conservative 130bhp in the standard engine. Although the 911 S proved to be an extremely successful car on the track, increased competition from other Group 2 racers forced the Stuttgart manufacturer to consider building a more powerful car to increase the performance gap between it and the opposition.

However, Porsche was prevented from developing the 911 S beyond that allowed by the rules in that class at the time, and so an altogether new and more powerful model was the answer.

The Porsche Carrera GTS (or Typ 904) was the first of Porsche's 'plastic' race cars, so called because they were fabricated from fibre glass and not the traditional aluminium. This photo shows Rolf Stommelen at speed in a 904 at the Nürburgring in 1965. Of interest is the car's registration plate, K-SR 904, where the 'K' stood for Cologne (Köln) and 'SR' for Stommelen Rolf, while the number '904' needs little explanation

Thus, work soon began on an even sportier and lighter version of the 911 powered by the Carrera 6 engine in the standard 911 body shell. Well, *standard* is a relative term at Porsche, because it was more like a stripped out, no-frills 911 body shell that was further lightened by replacing certain body panels with aluminium and fibreglass.

Manufactured in the spring of 1967, this 'missing link' in the Carrera history, the 911 R, was a very important vehicle in the overall development of a dedicated factory competition 911. Although intended only for competition purposes, 24 of these cars were built which showed the Porsche engineers that a lightweight 911 could certainly deliver the goods. Acting almost as an experimental model, 911 R developed an impressive 210bhp from its 2.0-litre engine, some 50bhp more than the standard 911 S, and proceeded to take several titles and set numerous speed and endurance records.

The final production 911 Carrera RS 2.7 was based on a lightened version of the 911 S featuring slightly wider rear fenders to accommodate the wider wheels. As explained in this chapter, the production Carrera RS 2.7 was available in two roadgoing versions, the M471 (Sport) and M472 (Touring), while the full-race version that the factory wanted in the first place was called the M491, or RSR 2.8.

The Porsche Carrera 6 (or Typ 906) was a full-blooded race car powered by a highly tuned version of the boxer six-cylinder engine found in the road car. Here, a Carrera 6 is seen participating in the 1000km race at the Nürburgring in 1966

This is a photo of the rare Porsche 911 R taken at a press launch at Hockenheim in December, 1967. Note the round rear lights, which were said to be much lighter than the standard lamp clusters

Carrera In The Making

A rarely mentioned but important prototype is the 911 S 2.7 that served as the test vehicle for the new 911 Carrera model. Taking a standard 911 S from production, the bigger experimental engine was installed and tests were carried out at Weissach to establish the correct engine specifications and suspension settings required to deal with the extra power and higher performance.

To avoid attracting too much attention to the project, the 2.4-litre badge was removed from the engine cover. In fact, there was little danger of anyone noticing this important prototype undergoing tests, as it looked just like any other 911 of the day – one advantage of an unchanging design. There were nine such 911 S 2.7 prototypes built which underwent extensive tests during the spring and summer of 1972.

The first 911 to carry the 'Carrera' lettering was the 911 Carrera RS 2.7 of 1973

Close inspection shows that the 2.4-litre badge has been removed from the engine cover of this 911 S 2.7 – which might have led an inquisitive motoring journalist wearing a detective's hat to correctly assume that the car was no longer a 2.4-litre 911. But frustratingly, the lack of information did not reveal what engine did indeed lurk beneath the engine cover

One of the nine 'Carrera' 911 S 2.7 prototypes undergoing high speed tests at the Weissach facility near Stuttgart

RS Stands For Rennsport (Racing Sport)

This image shows that at least one of the fleet of nine 911 RS 2.7s was given a new identity, as it proudly shows off its new 2.7 engine capacity. This car is clearly an F-series car as it still features the rubber bumper strip, but the wider fenders hint at greater performance

On Rolf Sprenger's arrival at the Porsche factory in 1967, the 911 was still a fairly young sports car, and not much had been done to develop the car to any serious competitive level. One reason for this had been that Porsche had their hands full with the introduction of the 911 through the 1960s, and they also wanted a fully developed fuel injection system to power their next high performance sports car.

"I remember when I arrived, we had the T and the S as carburettor cars and then we split them – the T, E and S and the output was relatively close together. There was no 'hammer', no very special strong engine, because we needed to develop the fuel injection," Sprenger recalls.

Originally the Carrera RS 2.7 was developed as a homologated sports car for customer competition. Working closely with the RS project from its inception, Rolf Sprenger explains, "Actually the project was more a kind of competition project for those customers who wanted to do smaller competitions, but we also knew there were some rich people who didn't want to drive so fast but they liked to have more comfort, and for that reason the M472 Touring was made".

The first batch of Carrera RS 2.7 cars were produced with a thinner gauge 0.7mm sheet steel in place of the 1.0mm normally used for the body shell. The windows were replaced with lightweight Glaverbel glass in an attempt to further reduce weight. The engine lid and rear spoiler was fashioned from fibreglass and, in order to accommodate bigger tyres, the fenders were widened to take the 6-inch front and 7-inch rear Fuchs alloy wheels.

The interior was a no-nonsense environment, as all comforts had been stripped out in the interests of weight reduction. All soundproofing and even the underbody corrosion proofing was omitted in the production process, although the lack of this latter item did cause these cars to rust quite badly later in life. The M471 option (Sport) was really a car for the track as it had a very spartan interior. With the removal of soundproofing, corrosion coating and electric windows, around 250lbs was saved in the Carrera RS 2.7 Sport.

Considering that a 911 S Coupé could be bought for DM 31,180, the basic Carrera RS was almost a gift at DM 34,000. The price was deliberately kept this low as the Zuffenhausen Sales Department was still nervous about the possibility of not being able to sell them all. The best thing of all for sports car enthusiasts was that the RS ran on regular grade fuel, making this one of the most versatile sports coupés on the market, and so poor sales were never an issue.

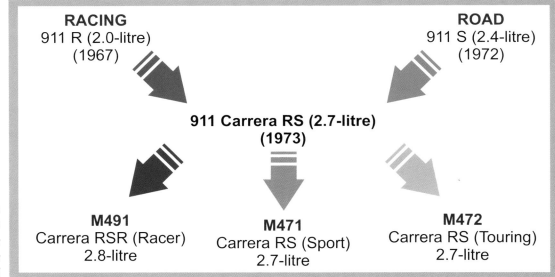

This family tree shows how the 911 Carrera RS 2.7 evolved from two distinct family lines, the lightweight racing version (911 R) combining with the bigger-engined, road-going 1972 model. The result, a year later, was three very potent sports cars that would have a massive impact on the motoring world

RACING
911 R (2.0-litre)
(1967)

ROAD
911 S (2.4-litre)
(1972)

911 Carrera RS (2.7-litre)
(1973)

M491
Carrera RSR (Racer)
2.8-litre

M471
Carrera RS (Sport)
2.7-litre

M472
Carrera RS (Touring)
2.7-litre

From the rear three-quarter angle, the Porsche 911 has perfect lines, almost like those of a dolphin with its bottle-nose front, tapering symmetrically down to a thin-edged tail

This is a very early Porsche Typ 911 Carrera RS 2.7 Coupé prototype from August, 1972, showing the 'positive' trial scripting along the sill (rocker) panel

The Carrera RS 2.7 Hits The Market

When the factory saw how quickly the first cars had been swallowed up by the market after their Paris launch, a further batch of 500 cars was immediately planned for production, but this time with the slightly thicker 1.0mm body, unlike the first lightweight batch. When they also flew off the shelf, a further batch of 500 was put into production – altogether, 1525 Carrera RS 2.7 cars were made which included test and homologation prototypes.

Production of the Carrera RS 2.7 continued up to July 1973. The vast majority of Carreras during this time were built in left-hand-drive form, with only a hundred or so right-hand-drive cars for the British market.

Ironically, the super fast 'Sport' version actually worked out cheaper than the 'Touring' model. Seems strange that a race car should be cheaper than its equivalent luxury road-going model! The Carrera RS 2.7 was only offered in Coupé form and, unfortunately for the Americans, it was not sold their side of the Atlantic.

Porsche 911 Carrera RS 2.7 – Sport and Touring versions:

MODEL DESIGNATION	DESCRIPTION	PRICE
M471	Carrera RS Sport. Fuel tank – 85 litres; Recaro sports seats; Rear seats removed; sound insulation removed; rubber mats replaced carpets; basic door trimmings; dashboard clock removed; passenger sun visor removed; 300 km/h speedo.	DM 34,700
M472	Carrera RS Touring. Interior furnishings and trimmings similar to the 911 S, adding 115kg to weight; 1,308 Carreras had Touring finish including interior clock, carpets, hood lining, sun visors, full door trim; steel rear bumper.	DM 36,500

Testblatt

FIA / CSI Homologation Nr. **637**

Gruppe A: **4**

FÉDÉRATION INTERNATIONALE DE L'AUTOMOBILE

Testblatt gemäß den Bestimmungen des Internationalen Automobil-Sportgesetz Anhang „J"

Hersteller   Dr.-Ing.h.c.F.Porsche KG, Stuttgart-Zuffenhausen

Baumuster/Typ   Carrera RS   Hubraum   2687   ccm

Baujahr/Modelljahr   1972/1973   Beginn der Serien-Fertigung Oktober 1972

Serien-Nummern Fahrgestell 911.360.0001 usf.   Motor   663.0001 usf.

Art des Karosserie-Aufbaues a)   Coupé

Art des Karosserie-Aufbaues b)

Art des Karosserie-Aufbaues c)

Grand-Tourisme   Herstellung des 500. Fahrzeuges erfolgte am   19

Serien-Grand Tourisme   Herstellung des 1000. Fahrzeuges erfolgte am   19

Tourenwagen   Herstellung des 1000. Fahrzeuges erfolgte am   19

Serien-Tourenwagen   Herstellung des 5000. Fahrzeuges erfolgte am   19

ONS/FIA Eintragungen

Datum der Antragstellung

November 1972

Antrag geprüft

Anzahl der Testblattseiten (Grundhomologation)   12

Anzahl der Nachtragseiten

FIA-Anerkennung

FIA-Stempel   Unterschrift

Einstufung gültig ab   1. MÄRZ 73

Liste Nr.

This is the first Carrera RS 2.7 to be photographed at the Weissach skid pad and is wearing the trial 'Carrera' identification along the sill panels. This was later changed to the 'negative' style which is now so familiar to all admirers of the 1973 Carrera RS 2.7

This is one of the most important pieces of paper in the history of the 911 Carrera RS 2.7. With this official FIA homologation document, the Carrera was declared eligible as a race car while still being road legal for the enthusiastic sporting motorist

A pair of Carreras go head-to-head in a mock contest for this publicity shot

An early Carrera RS 2.7 stands in the car park of Werk 2 at the Porsche plant in Stuttgart. This car, still covered in ice in the early morning winter sunshine, has the alternative 'Porsche' door lettering instead of the Carrera insignia. One Research Department engineer explained that this was informally referred to as 'Sports Option Number 1' amongst the factory workers. Some owners even chose to have the lettering removed altogether from the sill panels as they felt that the car looked too aggressive as an everyday car used for shopping or for evening trips to the theatre

VW-Porsche
Vertriebs-
gesellschaft mbH

Information

Pr 72/24(D,1Ex)

9/72

DEUTSCHLANDS SCHNELLSTE RARITÄT

PORSCHE CARRERA RS

In Fachkreisen - und nicht nur dort - gilt der Name Carrera als Qualitätsprädikat, seit zu Anfang der 60er Jahre ein 130 PS starker Porsche mit einem 4-Nockenwellenmotor als Flaggschiff der 356er Reihe diesen Namen trug. Das Fahrzeug war für die damalige Zeit eine technische Delikatesse und bewährte sich auf Rennpisten und Rallyestrecken. Zahlreiche Sport-erfolge sind mit dem Begriff Carrera verbunden.

In den vergangenen Jahren trat bei Porsche der GT-Sport etwas in den Hintergrund. Die Ursachen sind bekannt: einmal die technischen Anstrengungen, die erforderlich waren, um dreimal hintereinander die Markenweltmeister-schaft gewinnen zu können, zum anderen aber auch der Mangel an großen interessanten GT-Rennen. Jetzt hat die FIA eine GT-Trophäe ausgeschrieben, die voraussichtlich zum Championat werden wird. Da zugleich auch das Interesse der Öffentlichkeit an Rennen mit Serienfahrzeugen ständig wächst, hat man bei Porsche beschlossen, einen neuen Carrera auf den Markt zu bringen.

Ab November 1972 wird der Porsche Carrera RS mit einem 210 PS starken 2.7 l Motor und rennsportmäßiger Innen-ausstattung vom Band laufen. Der Wagen beschleunigt in 5,8 sec von 0 auf 100 km/h und hat eine Spitzengeschwindig-keit von 245 Kilometern in der Stunde. Durch die stark vereinfachte rennsportmäßige Innenausstattung und durch die Verwendung von Kunststoff und Aluminium konnte das

- 2 -

Announcing the arrival of the Porsche 911 Carrera RS 2.7, this press release dated September, 1972, explains why Porsche decided to introduce a Carrera model at this point. Due to the fact that the sport of GT racing had drifted into the background in the previous few years, the technical input required to produce a suitable road-going GT car could no longer be justified. With new rules introduced by the FIA, fresh possibilities presented themselves in the form of a GT championship category which made the construction of a 911 Carrera sports car feasible. This coincided with a revival in public interest for production-based GT and sports car racing. As a result, Porsche announced that the 911 Carrera RS 2.7 would be rolling off the production line in November of that year

Pictured inside the famous Solitude Castle overlooking Stuttgart, this Porsche 911 Carrera RS 2.7 Coupé is minus its rear spoiler. In fact, 30 such vehicles were manufactured in 1973 without the 'duck's tail' at the specific request of the respective buyers

The sales brochure produced for the Carrera was quite unusual, and followed a style not previously used by Porsche. Comprising a set of images in the form of photographs shot on a motor-drive camera, the Carrera RS approaches the lens in successive frames and then departs again down the same stretch of winding road. It was certainly quite novel for its day

gültig ab 3. 2. 1973

Preisliste
Modell 1973
Porsche 911
Carrera RS

That Famous Duck's Tail

Klaus Bischof, a 917 race mechanic at the time, remembers the early comments about the spoilers. "It was the very first production car which had been fitted with such aerodynamic aids. That was a trend setter for the whole world, but today we take it for granted."

Porsche engineering chief and creator of the Carrera RS 2.7, Norbert Singer, correctly determined that this potent new sports car would require some additional aerodynamic enhancements to help keep the back end firmly planted on the ground due to the car's high speed potential. The combination of extra power and reduced weight meant that the Carrera was a much more potent car than any other roadgoing 911 and keeping the back wheels squarely on the road ensured a more efficient delivery of the car's increased power.

Sporting a distinctive rear spoiler which significantly improved rear downforce, this revolutionary appendage (for road cars) was not well received, initially, by the top management at Zuffenhausen. Some felt that it did not do the styling of the original 911 any favours, but there were those who thought that the rear spoiler gave the car a menacing, more aggressive attitude. In addition to the now famous rear spoiler, further steps to improve airflow over and under the car, included the fitting of a deep front air dam to reduce front end lift at speed.

'Valid from February 3, 1973' says the official price list for the Carrera. Customers could still not believe their eyes that such a high performance car was so reasonably priced

The Carrera is regarded as one of the first sports cars to fit a rear 'duck tail' wing. It was not an easy concept to get approved by the Porsche management board

Spoiler—an aerodynamic device attached to a car (usually under the front bumper or on the decklid) to either reduce drag or induce downforce on the car. So called because it spoils the normal flow of air over or under the car.

Road & Track carried a useful feature in their January 1976 edition, giving brief explanations for certain mechanical components on vehicles in their 'Auto Dictionary'. This image clearly outlines where the spoiler sat in relation to the engine of the 911, while the magazine excerpt tells how the 'spoiler' modified the flow of air over or under a vehicle to aid the car's aerodynamic efficiency. The only problem with this image is that the spoiler shown here is that of the F-Series 911 Carrera RS 2.7 (1973) which was not exported to America, while the body of the car is clearly a G-Series (1974) as it has the concertina safety bumpers of the later model

More Downforce Was Needed

Getting the aerodynamics of the Carrera RS right was no easy task. Far from just bolting on a spoiler and going out on the road to test the results, Porsche spent many hours in the wind-tunnel comparing the airflow over the Carrera's body with, and without, the now-famous rear lip.

As the 911 body shape was already perfect in the eyes of the engineers, it was only the rear half of the body that required fine tuning which the wool tufts illustrate in the accompanying photographs.

This was the actual show car from the Paris Motor Show in October 1972. It is identifiable as a 'Sport' version of the Carrera RS 2.7 as the horizontal rubber strips are missing from the bumpers, their place being filled by a coloured paint strip corresponding with the colour of the door lettering and Fuchs alloy wheels. The profile of the upturned 'duck's tail' rear spoiler is quite different from the later flat profile of the 'tea tray' spoiler as fitted to the following year's model

Here a 911 Carrera RS 2.7 undergoes the same wind-tunnel test but fitted, as can be seen, with a rear wing

A 911 Carrera RS 2.7, at first without a rear wing, undergoes a wind-tunnel test at the Weissach test facility

Carrera Scripting

As a motor manufacturer, Porsche had not been known for putting any model identifying decoration on their cars that was not absolutely necessary. However, in 1973 all that changed quite dramatically.

Klaus Bischof, Porsche race mechanic from 1968-1981, and currently head of the Porsche Museum, recalls the introduction of the revolutionary Carrera lettering. "The time for marketing had come." This short statement accurately sums up the unprecedented surge in marketing effort in the 1970s by the automobile industry as a whole.

In an interview with the author, Porsche design chief from 1969-1989, Anatole (Tony) Lapine, described where the idea of lavish body embellishments originated from. "Whatever you see on racing cars participating in speed events, you would get a good deal of inspiration from that," he explained. The location of the lettering on the sill panels came from the race track, in particular the Ford GT40, and as the Carrera was to be raced, it was a good source, according to Lapine, of inspiration to follow.

Early experimentation with the 'Carrera' lettering included both positive and negative examples along the bottom of the doors, or sill (rocker) panels. The final decision on this, however, resulted in the negative form of the name being adopted. Another decorative feature that changed was the positioning of the name 'Carrera RS' which on some early cars is located in a high central position just beneath the top lip of the rear spoiler. On the final production vehicle, this wording was moved lower down and to the right side of the engine cover.

This early 15 x 8cm layout of an experimental Carrera hand-inscribed poster by Erich Strenger shows the car's potential top speed, power output and acceleration figures. The important thing about this poster is the bottom line of the wording just above the car, which, when translated, reads 'Only 500 men will have the opportunity of driving this car'. The implication here confirms that production was to be limited to just 500 cars, which places the poster at the very beginning of the car's development, as final production totalled around 1525 units. The wording was not, however, used on this poster, but employed on other promotional and marketing material

Porsche engineer and factory racing driver, Jürgen Barth, puts an early 911 Carrera RS 2.7 through its paces during a test session for Bilstein shock absorbers. This press photo was later used in the Christophorus magazine, and shows the Carrera's final production version of the rear spoiler

This press photograph again shows the 'positive' version of the 'Carrera' lettering along the bottom of the door. This form of the famous scripting was later dropped

Here the 'Carrera' lettering is shown in its final 'negative' style, a clever alternative to traditional automotive script embellishments of the day. However, this large style of scripting was not common to other Porsche models, the company preferring a more conservative or less ostentatious form of model identification on the rest of the range

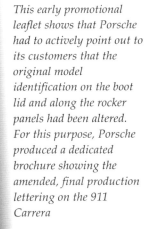

This early promotional leaflet shows that Porsche had to actively point out to its customers that the original model identification on the boot lid and along the rocker panels had been altered. For this purpose, Porsche produced a dedicated brochure showing the amended, final production lettering on the 911 Carrera

Zur Information:
Im Gegensatz zu dem im Prospekt gezeigten Schriftzug wird der Porsche Carrera RS mit dem abgebildeten neuen Schriftzug versehen.

Information:
Contrary to the lettering shown in our leaflet, the Porsche Carrera RS will carry the new lettering as picture shown above.

Information:
Au contraire des inscriptions montrées dans le prospectus, la Porsche Carrera RS est pourvue des nouvelles inscriptions montrées ci-dessus.

No longer conservative, this contemporary 911 Carrera RS 2.7 shows the bold, in-your-face 1970s style that some Porsche customers hankered after

Advertising The 911 Carrera RS 2.7

It is natural for any motor manufacturer to use their top of the range model when promoting or advertising the lesser models in their range. However, with a few exceptions, Porsche tended not to do that as they felt that each model had a specific market which was partially budget-driven by the customer, or just reflected personal preference as in the case of the mid-engined 914.

The 911 Carrera RS 2.7 on the other hand was in a league of its own. It was produced long before the time of customer track days with which we have now become quite familiar, as this sports car was aimed more at the driver who might want to try his hand at some amateur motor racing. As such, the Carrera RS 2.7 promotional material tended to be aimed at a more specific target market.

...oder doch lieber den Roten?

Meine Frau findet zwar den weißen schicker... Aber ganz gleich, welche Farbe ich wähle, ich werde in jedem Fall einen Wagen fahren, der mehr Spaß macht, mehr Technik hat, mehr Garantie bietet. Das Mehr an Porsche ist umfangreicher als Sie denken. Denn er ist nun mal sicherer, handlicher, wirtschaftlicher, umweltfreundlicher und jetzt auch langlebiger. Und mehr Spaß macht er auch. Deshalb informieren Sie sich bei uns. Damit Ihr einziges Problem die Wahl der Farbe bleibt.

PORSCHE
mit Langzeitgarantie.

Fordern Sie unsere Broschüre: »Porsche-Ingenieure plaudern aus der Schule« an.
Dr. Ing. h. c. F. Porsche Aktiengesellschaft. 7 Stuttgart 40. Postfach 400640

The irony of this advertisement is that it is not about the 911 Carrera RS 2.7 at all. In this scene, a successful businessman is sitting in his office telling his friend that his wife does not mind which colour 911 he buys, but that he is himself more interested in the technical attributes of the car. Interestingly, the 911 in the picture is the 1973 Carrera RS 2.7 which only came in white. The technical message that Porsche was putting across in this ad was that, from the 1976 model onwards, all 911 bodies would be galvanised, inside and out, a move that would all but eliminate the rust problems associated with earlier 911s. A further twist in this saga is that the 1973 Carrera RS 2.7 specifically had no rust preventative coating on the bare metal at all which was a weight-saving measure on that model. Obviously the legend of the Carrera name was very strong in the mid-1970s for it was very unusual to see a contemporary scale model available so soon after the production car. Unlike today, it usually took much longer back then for such scale models to come to market

Der Porsche Carrera RS: Nur 500 Männer werden ihn fahren.

The magazine advertisement states that only 500 lucky men would get to drive one, which shows that Porsche only expected that men would want to own one of these hairy-chested beasts. Such sexually discriminatory advertising would not be tolerated today, but one can question why Porsche decided to advertise the model at all, with such a limited production run. The answer though lies in the power of 'halo' advertising, where the top model drew customers to buy lower-priced 911s as well

The advertisement reads, "Germany's fastest rarity, only 500 cars". Although there is mention of the 911 T, E and S models in the accompanying wording, this ad is all about the Carrera and its superior performance capabilities

Deutschlands schnellste Rarität: Auflage 500

Er heißt Porsche Carrera RS, und ist der schnellste Seriensportwagen, den Porsche je gebaut hat. Sein Sechszylinder-Einspritzmotor mit 2,7 Liter Hubraum leistet 210 PS und bringt eine Spitze von 245 km/h. Sein Leistungsgewicht von nur 4,5 kg/PS ermöglicht eine Beschleunigung von 0 auf 100 in 5,8 sec. Sein rennerprobtes Fahrwerk sowie die beiden Front- und Heckspoiler sichern eine exzellente Straßenlage.

Durch die große Elastizität seines Motors fährt der Porsche Carrera RS selbst im dichten Stadtverkehr problemlos. Ein 85-Liter-Tank, den Sie jetzt auch in den Porsche 911 E und S-Modellen finden, sorgt für großen Aktionsradius. Zudem kann der Carrera — wie alle Porsche — mit Normalbenzin gefahren werden.

Über weitere Einzelheiten in Technik und Details sowie über die verbesserten und verfeinerten Modelle 911T, 911E und 911S berät Sie gern Ihr VW-Porsche-Händler.

Eine Auflage von 500 für einen Sportwagen von der Klasse des Carrera RS ist nicht groß.
Sie müssen also schon sehr schnell sein, wenn Sie Deutschlands schnellste Rarität fahren möchten.

PORSCHE

Marketing And Publishing Campaigns

Hiring models and setting up photo shoots for advertising and marketing campaigns can be an expensive game, especially when, like Porsche, there was not much money for such extravagant expenditure. This meant that whenever a marketing campaign was launched, Porsche made certain that the resultant photos had as wide an application as possible.

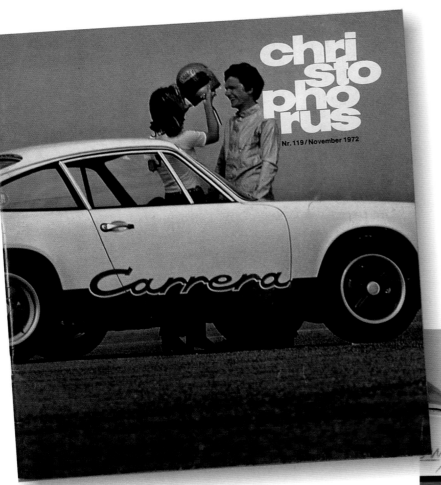

Shortly after the new Carrera's launch, the car was used on the front cover of Christophorus *magazine in November, 1972. At least they let the female model change her clothes a few times during this shoot to make them look like slightly different each time the photos were used, as the accompanying images show*

The Carrera quickly became the transport of choice for those who recognised the car for what it was. The photographer has picked out the red in the car and selected aircraft with similar colouring to match the Carrera

This is an early promotional page mock-up prepared by the Porsche advertising department for proofing before printing. One can see that the photograph on the left hand page is similar to the accompanying colour photo taken at the same airfield

Seine Besonderheit:
Der CARRERA RS ist ohne irgendeine Einschränkung voll alltagsverkehrs- und straßentauglich. Ein ganz gewöhnlicher PORSCHE, der ganz Ungewöhnliches kann.

Seine serienmäßigen Fahrleistungen: Von 0 auf 100 in 5,8 sec. Höchstgeschwindigkeit 245 km/h. Dennoch eine für einen Hochleistungsmotor überraschende Elastizität über den ganzen Drehzahlbereich, mit dem höchsten Wirkungsgrad zwischen 3000 und 5000 U/min. Bei einer Verdichtung von nur 8,5 : 1 gibt sich der CARRERA RS sogar mit Normalbenzin zufrieden.

Seine Ausstattung ist auf den Sporteinsatz zugeschnitten. Alles Überflüssige entfällt, nur das funktionell Notwendige ist vorhanden. Ergebnis: Ein Leistungsgewicht von 4,6 kp/PS.

Seine Repertoire: Per Achse zum Rennen und wieder nach Hause. Montag ins Büro. Dienstag nach Genf. Abends zurück. Mittwoch zum Shopping. City. Stauung. Kriechverkehr, aber keine Kerze verrußt, keine Kupplung streikt. Donnerstag Landstraße, Autobahn, Serpentinen, Feldwege, Baustellen. Freitag nur Kurzstrecken und immer wieder Kaltstarts. Samstag mit Urlaubsgepäck nach Finnland.

Ein neuer PORSCHE —
der CARRERA RS.

Sein Name erinnert an das längste und härteste Straßenrennen der Welt, bei dem einst Hans Herrmann, Fürst Metternich und José Herrarte auf PORSCHE Triumphe feierten:
Die CARRERA PANAMERICANA.

Seine Technik zeigt in jedem Detail die Summe aller Erfahrungen, die PORSCHE bisher im Sport und in der Serie sammeln konnte.
Sein Motor ist ein 6-Zylinder-Einspritz-Boxer. 2687 ccm. 210 DIN-PS bei 6300 U/min. Max. Drehmoment 26 kpm.

In the background is the Porsche 911 Carrera RS 2.7, but the red car in the foreground is its bigger, more potent brother, the RSR 2.8 race car. It is interesting to compare these two cars in this way, as there is little outward difference between the two. The most obvious variation, though, can be seen in the extended front and rear wings (fenders) of the RSR, allowing for wider competition tyres

Carrera RSR 2.8

Although the Carrera RS 2.7 was a more than competent sports car and occasional racer, Porsche's real weapon of choice for the track was the Carrera RSR 2.8, a 300bhp heavyweight capable of out-gunning most other cars in its class. Listed as the M491 on Porsche's option sheet, the RSR 2.8 was also built in 1972 as a thoroughbred racer and was not legal for road use at all.

M491	Carrera RS Racing – known as the RSR. Engine capacity increased to 2806cc, 300bhp; Available only with 5-speed gearbox.	DM 59,000

Carrera Oddity

Head of Porsche Advertising at the time of the 911 Carrera launch, Herr Georg Ledert, recently commented that, based on the dimensions of this illustration, the image was a possible magazine cover or page within the *Christophorus* magazine. The square layout ruled it out as a magazine advertisement or marketing poster. The contents of the image are in themselves very interesting, as this page layout was made up in recognition of the achievement by the Carrera RSR in winning the Daytona 24-Hours in January 1973. Ironically it shows a road-going Carrera RS 2.7, and not the RSR 2.8.

Even more confusing is the combination of Deutschmark coins and the wheel portrayed in the background. The four-stud alloy wheel fabricated by Fuchs was made specifically for the 4-cylinder 914 mid-engined sports car, and is not the 5-stud Fuchs wheel as used on a 911. As with many things in advertising, the manufacturer's message is carried through the association of the components in this image, rather than by direct implication.

In another comparative photo setting, the RSR on the right is easily distinguished by its extended wheel arches, front trunk securing straps and the radiator grille for the oil cooler in place of the number plate panel below the front bumper. Another important feature in this photo is that the RSR is missing the oil filler flap that the road-going RS has on the front left fender just ahead of the windscreen

The square dimensions of this rather curious image suggest that this was intended as a possible page for the Christophorus magazine

Once again the RS and RSR stand side-by-side in the grounds of the Stuttgart factory. Although the car in the foreground is the 2.8-litre RSR, it is still wearing a 2.7-litre badge and aerofoil on the engine lid. Obvious differences are the flared wings and, through the back window, one can see a racing roll cage

Carrera Market Positioning

Trying to get an uninterested motorist to appreciate the engineering merits and complexities of the 911 Carrera RS 2.7 is rather like trying to explain to your great grandmother some of the finer qualities of Deep Purple's *Smoke on the Water* from the album *Made In Japan*, at full volume. To many who remember that era, it's simple really, it just rocks you, but you have to be tuned in to those qualities to fully appreciate the five-star performance of both the artist and the engineer. You have to want to appreciate it, otherwise the meaning is lost on you. The awesome qualities and intensity of Ian Paice's six minute drum solo on the cut *The Mule*, is like taking the Raidillon Eau Rouge curve at the foot of the pit straight of the legendary Spa circuit at full chat. It is a life-changing experience.

In this way, a rock band, artist, sportsman or sports car manufacturer builds up a reputation or following over time and through sustained popularity becomes an acknowledged specialist in their field and might eventually take on legendary status. However, you cannot manufacture an icon. It is the public who decide whether something is worthy of such recognition, and they do this through digging into their wallets and buying your product or service regularly over a prolonged period of time. Porsche's engineers had no idea of the legendary status to which the RS 2.7 would rise.

However, not every RS 2.7 owner wanted his (or her) car to be a spartan, road-legal track car. Preferring some interior comforts to go with the awesome performance, around 550 owners sent their cars back down the Stuttgart-Zuffenhausen production line to be fitted with full 911 S trim and equipment. With just over 1000 vehicles, certainly the bulk of the total production, being finished as lightweight models, the Carrera RS 2.7 was actually homologated in Group 3, for standard Production GT cars.

Even within the relatively limited production run of the Carrera RS 2.7, there is a strong preference today for cars from the first batch of 500 produced – those fabricated with thinner gauge sheet metal. Enthusiasts today talk of their RS as being from the first batch, rather than the later production run. There is little doubt that the early cars do attract greater attention today, but all Carrera RS 2.7s are rare classics.

Ultimately, the Carrera RS 2.7 was for those who enjoyed the art of driving. However, the car could be easily driven around town or down to the corner shops on a normal day, such was the flexibility of the engine, and indeed the docility of the car as a whole. It was a car that literally anyone could drive, from the young female owner right up to the professional racing driver.

Back in the early 1970s, the Carrera RS 2.7 was to Porsche what The Rolling Stones were to music in the 1960s and 1970s. The Stones took rock 'n roll music, shook it violently, and created an in-your-face style that nobody else had dared to do, not to that level anyway. Parents of teenagers during that time were horrified at the brashness of this new confrontational genre of music, but this unique style appealed to a younger generation eager to break the bonds of parental control.

In the same way, the raucous and spartan world of the Carrera combined with its sensational performance, showed the two finger salute to the traditional automotive world. With the Carrera RS 2.7, Porsche stepped out from under the shadow of its early origins in the mountains of Austria and offered the driver the very essence of what all great sports cars should give – an adrenalin-filled, no holds barred drive of your life.

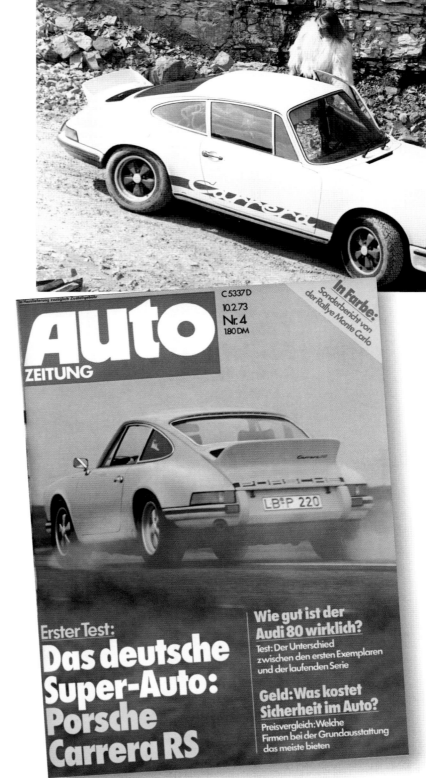

Judging by the muddy wheels and the rather rough setting in a quarry, this 911 Carrera RS 2.7 looks as though it has been put through its paces. But then the attractive young lady driver dressed in her fur coat appears quite unmoved by her challenging journey down the tricky road to this stone quarry!

Motor magazines around the world could not wait to get their hands on a 911 Carrera RS 2.7, and media coverage even in the early 1970s was extensive (this article featured in the German periodical, Auto Zeitung, February 10, 1973). Note the absence of any scripting on the rocker panel of this early press car. This is even more remarkable when one considers that Porsche initially only planned to make 500 of these sports cars – hardly a big production run

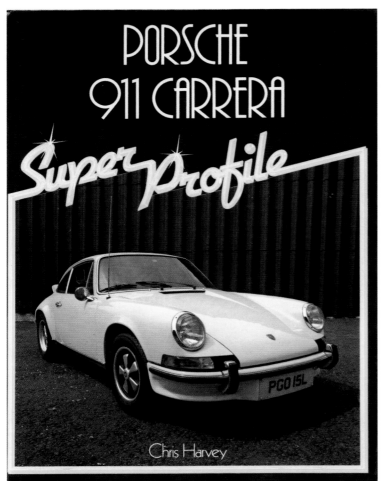

Published after the car went out of production (Haynes Publishing, 1982), this book is just one of many relating to the Porsche marque. Author, Chris Harvey, a Fleet Street journalist, wrote several books based on the 'Super Profile' theme with this one covering the Porsche Carrera specifically

This photograph taken at the 1973 Motor Show in Barcelona shows a rather packed Porsche stand with no less than ten 911s on display. A simple signboard behind the orange Carrera in the right foreground announces the Carrera RS specification: 2700cc, 230hp, 250km/h. However, for some reason this Carrera is without its familiar scripting along the sill panels. Although the Porsche display is far from glamorous, their unfortunate neighbours, Lamborghini, appear to have been stuck behind the pillars to the left of the Porsche stand

There is little doubt that this was the '70s. At the 1973 Geneva Motor Show, it appeared that Porsche went all out to win the most colourful stand of the Show award

It's a Small World

For those unable to afford the real thing, there is always the miniature version to consider. In fact, scale models and memorabilia are big business for most manufacturers these days, even if they are modern-day creations or replicas of earlier versions. For Porsche, this is especially big business, as the respect, enthusiasm and loyalty that the marque has built up around the 911 brand over the past 40+ years is enormous.

The degree of research that goes into making the models as accurate and authentic as possible is extraordinary and often the manufacturers of these models know almost as much about the real thing as they do about the scale models they manufacture.

This particularly attractive 911 Carrera RS 2.7 model is in 1/24 scale

When reproducing a model as significant as the Porsche 911 Carrera RS 2.7, there is added value in basing that model on a particularly important vehicle such as this original company press car (registration: S-AP 6492)

How low can you go? No matter which scale of model you collect, there is a 911 just for you: 1/87, 1/43 and 1/24 scale

If driving your 911 Carrera every day is not enough for you, then you can spend every waking hour with one tied around your neck

Porsche 911 production statistics

Model Year	Model Description	
1973 (Carrera RS 2.7 M471) 'Sport'	F-Series	Approx 1000 units
1973 (Carrera RS 2.7 M472) 'Touring'	F-Series	Approx 550 units

Source: Porsche

The success of the Carrera RS 2.7-litre engine was such that in a slightly detuned state, it would power successive generations of Porsche 911s, carrying the model forward through the next two-and-a-half decades and beyond. The boxer motor was the heart and soul of the 911, both on and off the track and was ultimately enlarged to a mighty 3746cc in the Carrera RS 3.8 of 1993.

The Carrera RS 2.7 would be described by some as raw and uncompromising, which by comparison with some of the other sports cars on the market at that time, may be justified. But one must remember that the car was first and foremost planned as a racer that was then adapted for road use in order to make up the production numbers.

Significantly, through both the marketing and competition successes of the 911 Carrera RS 2.7, this model has become one of the most recognisable sports cars of all time – ask any kid between 10 and 90 years of age!

THE VOLUME YEARS

Introduced in September 1973 (model year 1974), the G-Series was the first 911 to wear the new impact absorbing bumpers, introduced as a safety measure in the USA to ensure the protection of fuel lines, lighting and the opening of doors in the case of a minor accident. This vehicle protecting legislation sent shock waves through the design sector of the auto industry as manufacturers were forced to experiment with ways of incorporating these changes into their designs.

The G-Series is considered by many as the watershed model that separates the earlier 911s from the later models which carried more safety and emissions equipment and, as a result, lost some of the innocence of youth through becoming bulkier and heavier.

The casual observer may have been forgiven up to this point for thinking that each new model of 911 looked strikingly similar to its predecessor. Throughout the 1970s, the engineers in Stuttgart-Zuffenhausen worked hard to maintain the familiar looks of the 911. Under the skin, however, each new model was packed with more and more technology and this had to be carefully engineered into a relatively small motor car.

One of the most important engineering developments in 1974 was the standardisation of the 2.7-litre engine across the entire production car range. Although the engine capacity only grew by the relatively small margin of 346cc, for the engineers it was the culmination of what they had been itching to do all along – to give the 911 some really serious power. The G-Series was therefore the gateway for further engine development and, while the Carrera RS was given a 3.0-litre engine in 1974, the rest of the range would follow with the larger engine two years later.

Not a company to rest on its laurels for too long, Porsche introduced the production Turbo model in 1975. First shown as a concept at the Frankfurt Motor Show in 1973, Porsche developed the Turbo version for production following their vast experience with turbocharging in motor sport.

With the launch of the 911 J-Series (1976), Porsche AG was the first car maker to use steel panels hot-galvanised on both sides for its standard products. In this way it significantly increased the lifespan of the corrosion-proofed bodies and was able to offer an extended warranty of up to six years against rust penetration.

Almost three decades after the first sports car was introduced bearing the Porsche name, the company celebrated the production of its 250,000th vehicle on June 3, 1977. This milestone took place against a background of an exceptionally healthy financial situation, and the end of the 1976/1977 fiscal year concluded with sales revenue of DM 1-billion.

As with many family-controlled companies, there was friction at senior management level. As a result of personality differences, Dr. Fuhrmann exited the scene, his place being taken by German-American Peter Schutz. The cause of this split had been Fuhrmann's insistence that the 911 had run its course and the

TIMELINE (1974–1989):

1974	1976	1981	1983	1985	1989
Safety bumpers.	911 Turbo introduced.	Peter Schutz takes over as Chairman.	All 911 models called Carrera.	Porsche 959 introduced.	Speedster introduced.
All 911s with 2.7-litre power.	Fully galvanised body construction.		Prototype 959 shown at IAA.		

air-cooled boxer engine would soon be outlawed due to noise pollution legislation. He argued that the 924 and 928 front-engined, water-cooled sports cars were the way to go and that there would be no place for the 911 in the future model line-up. Ferry and the rest of the world, of course, disagreed and so Peter Schutz was ushered in to ensure the continuity of the much-loved 911.

Although Schutz is credited with the resurgence of the 911 through the 1980s, he was also responsible for calling all 911s by the name 'Carrera', a name previously reserved for the highest performing model in the Porsche range. Some felt that he had diluted the respect that this name carried by applying it to the whole range, but with hindsight this criticism is perhaps unjust. Borrowing some of the rich heritage of the Carrera name was in fact a clever marketing move by Schutz to give the 911 a much-needed sales boost in the early 1980s, without which there might not even have been a Porsche sports car on the market today. With sales in 1981 at their lowest for almost a decade, it is perhaps fitting that the strength of the 'Carrera' brand was used to save the company from possible obscurity.

The 1980s was a decade of development within the Porsche company, both on the technical and personnel fronts. Shown at the motor show in Frankfurt in 1985, the Porsche 959 was clear evidence that Porsche was pushing the envelope in terms of technical and design parameters. On the 25th anniversary of the 911 (1988), a special new model was introduced that used the knowledge gained in rallying. The 911 Carrera 4 was a landmark vehicle offering the ordinary customer the advantages of all-wheel-drive in a production car.

Peter Schutz left the company in 1988 and was replaced by his then deputy, Heinz Branitzki, while the following year marked the last full year that Professor Ferry Porsche would hold office as Chairman of the company's Supervisory Board, stepping aside in favour of his son.

The Porsche 911 Turbo 3.0 Coupé (1976 model year) was a fully equipped grand touring speed machine. Standard equipment included air conditioning, electric windows, rear wiper and leather upholstery

Porsche's 911 Carrera 2.7 Coupé (1974 model year) was a much improved model with more power, improved safety and all-round youth appeal

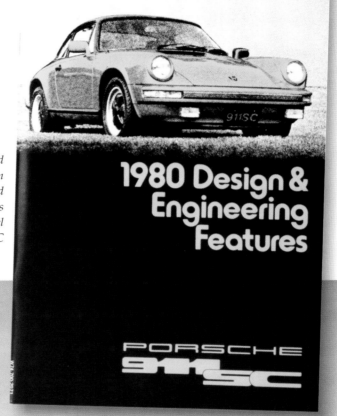

The factory produced this handy booklet on the Design and Engineering features for the USA model 1980 Porsche 911 SC

The bodywork and styling of the 959 show a marked difference from the rest of the 911 range as this front and rear shot of the 1986 car shows

Frankfurt Motor Show 1973

The 1973 Frankfurt Motor Show, or IAA (Internationale Automobile Ausstelung), was an important one for Porsche, not least because they were displaying their latest turbo-powered 911 prototype. The stand therefore required special attention to maximise the visibility and accessibility of their new prototype car for visitors.

Porsche had gained considerable experience in the use of turbochargers through their racing exploits, and it was only a matter of time before this technology found its way into their production cars. However, in typical Porsche fashion, the Turbo model would take a further two years to reach production.

During their planning for the 1973 Frankfurt Show, Porsche produced this scale model of their stand to ensure maximum impact

This 2.7-litre 911 Coupé on display at the 1973 Frankfurt Motor Show already features the impact safety bumpers planned for the 1974 model year

Porsche's Turbo prototype on display at the IAA 1973. In the scale model of the show stand in the accompanying photo, the Turbo's raised circular podium can be seen in the right hand corner

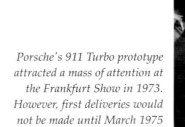

Porsche's 911 Turbo prototype attracted a mass of attention at the Frankfurt Show in 1973. However, first deliveries would not be made until March 1975

This scale model of a 2.7-litre fuel injected 911 engine was made to help the organisers of the 1973 IAA Frankfurt Motor Show plan the Porsche stand

The new G-Series 911 was praised by the media and its many safety features were welcomed by the industry. One of Germany's top selling auto journals, Auto Motor und Sport, was quick to get the new 1974 model on the cover of the August 1973 issue

Selling sports cars to the Italians was not without its challenges, as Porsche had to overcome the Ferrari-factor

**Le nuove Porsche 2,7 litri.
Sono sempre pochi quelli che si concedono ciò di cui gli altri sognano.**

The 911 Carrera 2.7 and RS 3.0

Three basic 911 models were included in the 1974 line-up, those being the 911, 911 S and 911 Carrera. Although the Carrera mentioned here featured the 2.7-litre engine, it was not the fire-breathing RS that had set the world alight the previous year, but a rather more rounded and comfortable cruiser. Known as the G-Series, this model had a smoother body shape, American safety bumpers and a distinctive reflective red strip that joined the two back light clusters and carried the name P-O-R-S-C-H-E.

In order to keep the Carrera's name in the spotlight on the racing scene, Porsche made a limited run of the new Carrera RS 3.0. Being a very different beast from the previous year's RS 2.7, the RS 3.0 was developed purely for racing and while some cars were converted for road use, the total quantity manufactured by the factory was only 110 cars.

The Carrera RS 3.0 also used the chassis from the G-series which was a totally new car from the earlier RS 2.7 and other pre-1974 cars. Delivery of the RS 3.0 began in late 1973, although even the factory is unsure of the exact delivery date of the road legal cars.

Although the RS 3.0 was designed as a customer racer, they could also be licensed for road use. Costing DM 64,980, around 50 cars were converted to RSR form which meant that they were destined for a life on the track

PORSCHE

PRESS RELEASE

EMBARGO DATE:

15th AUGUST, 1973

Introducing the Porsche range for 1974.

"THE

CARRERA

GENERATION"

The first major development of the very successful Porsche 911 model, based on the 2.7-litre Porsche Carrera RS which, when road tested by "Autocar", evoked the following comment as introduction to their report.

"SENSATIONAL,

EVEN BY

PORSCHE STANDARDS"

ISSUED BY PORSCHE CARS GREAT BRITAIN LIMITED

In this photo, a 1975 American spec Porsche 911 Carrera 2.7 Coupé is being demonstrated to a customer at a Porsche Sales Centre

In a press release dated August 15, 1973 in which the new 1974 model Carrera was introduced to the media, the Porsche press department quoted the words used in the Autocar test review – "Sensational, even by Porsche standards"

911 Safety Bumpers

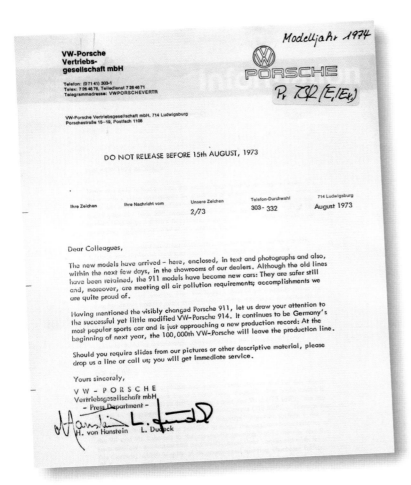

In another press release to the world's media on August 15, 1973, Porsche PR boss, Baron Huschke von Hanstein announced that the new 1974 model 911s would be arriving in the showrooms "within the next couple of days". He also took the opportunity to remind journalists that the popular and quick selling VW-Porsche 914 would reach the important milestone of 100,000 sales by early 1974. Von Hanstein never missed an opportunity to promote the company's achievements in the media

The design team at the Weissach-based Style Porsche set about turning this potentially problematic legal requirement into a styling success

US Federal regulations introduced in 1974 required vehicles to have bumpers fitted that were capable of absorbing an impact of up to 5mph (8km/h). Awareness groups like the self-styled American consumer lawyer Ralph Nader spent their days outlining the potential dangers of the automobile, and so emerged the age of safety consciousness which has continued to grow to this day.

While improved driver, passenger and pedestrian safety is always a good thing, this particular issue delivered what was thought to be a crippling blow to the typically sleek lines of sports cars around the world. While several prominent sports car manufacturers simply attached rubber blocks to their bumpers as overriders, Porsche took the challenge in its stride and actually made a feature out of the problem.

Design chief Tony Lapine and his team were determined to accommodate the latest Federal requirements without disturbing the styling of the timeless lines of the 911 created by Butzi Porsche. For Porsche, the design of their sports car had always been about style and function, never fashion.

Upon contact, the impact-absorbing dampers behind the bumper would travel backwards by up to two inches. Where the bumper bar met the bodywork at each end, neat rubber bellows allowed the bumper to move backwards into a recess in the fender without causing any damage, returning to their original position following this action.

Contrary to common belief, the 'safety bumpers' as they became known, were not intended to reduce shock and injury to vehicle occupants by absorbing energy in a collision. In fact, the stated purpose of these bumpers was concerned only with the maintenance of the integrity of exhaust, fuel, cooling and lighting systems and the ability to open the trunk, hood and doors following a collision.

Ahead of the rest of the country, the State of Florida required that all cars sold there after January 1, 1973 must be fitted with these bumpers. Although the new national safety bumper regulations were planned for 1974, their implementation was delayed for a year by the Federal authorities. However, as Porsche had already prepared their new model to comply with these requirements, they went ahead with this design for the '74 model range.

Ferry Porsche addresses guests on May 10, 1974, on the 25th anniversary of the start of Porsche production, at a company function held at Weissach

Ferry is seen enjoying a joke with family, staff and guests. It is amazing to see the simplicity of the event held in a marquee in celebration of the most significant milestone in the company's history at that time. Second from the left wearing glasses is Franz Xaver Reimspiess (developed the VW boxer engine), Hans Kern (Porsche finance director), Ferry Porsche, Herbert Linge (just behind), Dorothea Porsche (wife of Ferry), F.A. 'Butzi' Porsche and wife Brigitte, and on the right in the light suit is Louise Piëch, Ferry's sister

This may seem like a simple line-up of cars on display for the guests, but it is, in fact, motoring ballet. While the local band played music, the cars danced. One can see the cars are lined up in choreographed pattern of colours and in order of Coupé and Targa, each with a dancing ribbon attached to the fender making it a unique event for the time

This sheet was issued for the 1975 Vienna Stamp Exhibition, in recognition of the centenary of Professor Ferdinand Porsche's birth on September 3, 1875. It is a good example of the lack of quality control exercised by the Paraguayan authorities as the date of Professor Porsche's death is shown on the stamp as January 30, 1961. Professor Porsche, in fact, died 10 years earlier, in 1951. The stamp does, however, bring three important Porsche milestone cars together, the electric Lohner-Porsche (1900), the first 356 model (1948) and the 911 Turbo (1975)

Stamp Of Approval

Quite frequently, it is the underdeveloped and remote countries that issue some of the largest and most exotic stamps in the world. Some African and South American countries that are off the beaten track, as far as tourism is concerned, reproduce the natural beauty and wildlife of their nation on postage stamps that are sold on the international market.

However, this trend developed into a flood of stamps when those nations began to exploit the passion and drive of philatelists around the world as a means of earning foreign currency. The launch of such stamps became so frequent that the world's leading stamp catalogue excluded these issues as they were viewed as souvenir stamps. However, this volume of stamp production leads inevitably to a fall in quality which can be seen in the accompanying miniature sheet.

K-Jetronic Fuel Injection

'K-Jetronic – A new, ecologically favourable injection system in the Porsche.'

'An injection system, developed in collaboration with Bosch, which will be increasingly integrated into the Porsche range beginning with 1974 models constitutes a firm step forward in the battle to control exhaust emissions.'

So read the headline and opening sentence of the press release announcing the introduction of the new K-Jetronic fuel injection system across the 911 range. The K-Jetronic system provided better fuel economy, improved engine flexibility and lower exhaust emissions than before. The advanced fuel and air metering system offered by this Bosch petrol injection system placed Porsche in a strong position in the emission-conscious USA.

This Porsche press release is dated April 5, 1973, and explains the operation of the new K-Jetronic fuel injection system for the 1974 model 911

The age of driver aids had arrived. In this company announcement in 1975, Porsche revealed that an automatic speed control device could be ordered as an optional extra on all 911 models

Cruise Control

The 1970s was the age of invention and space travel. Men landed on the moon in 1969, and so to have an automatic device that controlled the speed of your car in 1975 seemed entirely within reason.

Called the 'Tempostat' by Porsche, this piece of equipment allowed the 911 driver to automatically set the desired speed of travel by means of a lever located on the steering column. The driver could then relax behind the wheel and not have to look down constantly at the speedometer to ensure that he or she was driving at the legally allowed speed.

This device could be set for any speed between 25-110mph (40-180km/h) and manual control could be resumed at any time by depressing the brake or clutch pedal, or indeed by switching the lever to the 'Off' position.

Getting Kitted Out

Porsche were quick to realise the value in supplying corporate products and apparel to its growing band of enthusiasts worldwide. Due to their many motor sport victories and international achievements, in no time at all the company built up a healthy business in calendars, posters, clothing and many other items.

With a growing international following, company apparel became an important part of the business. Located deep within the confines of their Stuttgart-Zuffenhausen headquarters, these two models display the latest 'his' and 'hers' fashion wear for 1974

On the occasion of Louise Piëch's (née Porsche) 70th birthday in August 1974, she was presented with the first 911 Turbo to be produced by the factory

The Turbo Era

The Porsche 911 Turbo prototype was first exhibited at the Frankfurt Motor Show in 1973, while the pre-production model was shown at the Paris Motor Show in October of the following year. The first 911 Turbos were finally ready for delivery in March 1975 marking the company's 25th anniversary of car production.

Known in-house as the Typ 930, the powerful 911 Turbo was the fastest production car in Germany at the time. Manufactured with the H-Series cars, this new model would be officially referred to as the 911 Turbo Coupé, although in some export markets it was called the Porsche 930 Turbo.

Being five inches (12cm) wider than the 911 Carrera, the Turbo was easily recognisable. Although Porsche undoubtedly carried over their vast turbocharging experience gained through motor sport, the 911 production Turbo model had its origins in a 2.0-litre prototype from 1969. The project did not progress any further at that stage, however, as the concept was considered premature.

This is an early example (1975) of Porsche's new 911 Turbo 3.0 Coupé, parked just outside the gates of the Ludwigsburg plant. This olive green car, still fitted with temporary factory plates, is complemented by an attractive, fur-clad model

Some customers requested special equipment to be fitted to their car by the factory. This 911 Turbo 3.0 Coupé (1975), equipped with additional driving lamps, awaits delivery in the factory grounds at Ludwigsburg

Starting with the 1976 model, the 911 was equipped with electrically-adjustable, heated, body-colour wing mirrors. Due to their rather large size and the fact that they stuck out in quite a pronounced fashion, these mirrors earned the nickname of 'elephant ears'. As a result, this H-Series model is frequently but affectionately known as the 'elephant ears' model, which is perhaps a little unkind as the 1976 Carrera 3.0 Targa is a very attractive sports car

The American sales brochure gave the new Turbo's engine capacity as 182.6 cubic inch – it sounds miniscule against the big block Chevy and Ford monsters, but the acceleration figures of 0-60mph (0-96km/h) in 5.7 secs offered blistering performance by any standards

No More Rust

Galvanised steel had already been in use on Porsche cars since 1971, but as from 1976, the whole body of the 911 was fabricated from hot galvanised rustproof sheet steel. The layer of zinc which coated the body panels varied according to the conditions to which it would be exposed on different parts of the body. Porsche was the first car manufacturer in the world to offer such comprehensive rust protection.

This Porsche prototype was pictured in the windtunnel at Weissach in 1976, but it is not known if this model went into production or not

Seen here in discussion at the 1977 Frankfurt Motor Show are (from left to right) Heinz Branitzki, Ernst Fuhrmann and Dorothea Porsche, wife of Ferry. On November 6, 1976, the Supervisory Board of Dr. Ing. h.c.F. Porsche AG appointed Dr. Ing. Ernst Fuhrmann as Chief Executive of the Board of Management with Heinz Branitzki as his deputy

America was the only country in which the 911 Turbo was known as the 911 Turbo Carrera. Perhaps this was done in order to leverage the value of the Carrera name with which most motor sport enthusiasts in the USA would have been familiar. With America being Porsche's biggest export area, it made sense to market their cars in the most advantageous manner. Road & Track (January 1976), carried a very glowing report on the new 911 models for the 1976 model year

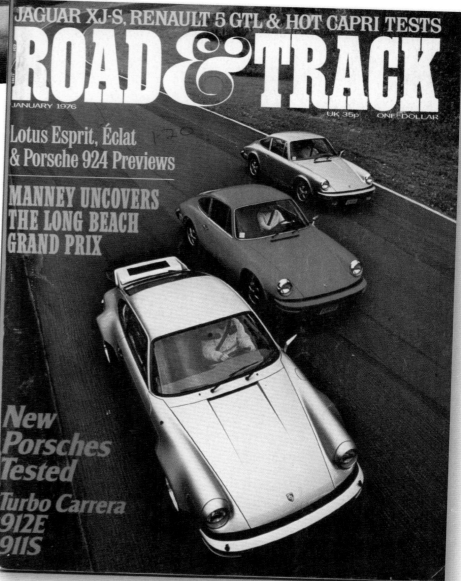

JAGUAR XJ-S, RENAULT 5 GTL & HOT CAPRI TESTS

ROAD & TRACK

JANUARY 1976
UK 35p ONE DOLLAR

Lotus Esprit, Éclat
& Porsche 924 Previews

MANNEY UNCOVERS
THE LONG BEACH
GRAND PRIX

New
Porsches
Tested

Turbo Carrera
912E
911S

Porsche Cars Great Britain

Michael Cotton, head of Press and PR for Porsche Cars Great Britain (PCGB), sent out a press release on March 21, 1977, announcing a £1 million expansion of the Porsche facilities in the UK. Both Ferry Porsche and Heinz Branitzki were present for the opening of the new British headquarters at Richfield Avenue, Reading, Berkshire. The new building housed Porsche sales and after-sales departments.

Taken in 1977, this photo shows a well stocked AFN showroom. Porsche Post editor, Bryan Walls, took this photo for a feature in the Porsche Club magazine

The AFN workshop was a busy place in the spring of 1977, as witnessed by Porsche Post editor, Bryan Walls

Pr 77/77 E

PORSCHE

PRESS RELEASE

EMBARGO DATE:

PORSCHE'S £1 MILLION HEADQUARTERS

Dr. Ferdinand (Ferry) Porsche, Chairman of Dr.Ing.h.c.F. Porsche AG and of Porsche Cars Great Britain Limited, today opened the brand-new British headquarters at Richfield Avenue, Reading. The total facility, including advanced technical equipment, represents a £1 million investment in the future.

Porsche Cars Great Britain Limited originated from A.F.N. Limited, formerly importers of German cars and now a wholly-owned London Porsche main dealer which retains its showrooms and workshops at Falcon Works, London Road, Isleworth. In 1973 PCGB moved to the old Isleworth film studios at Worton Hall on a temporary basis in order to expand.

The move to Reading coincides with the launch of the British 924 model, and with the announcement in Germany of the new 928. Since 1965 the 911 range of models has been the mainstay of the operation, recent sales averaging 450-500 cars per year. It's planned to sell an additional 600 Porsche 924s during 1977, so the expansion at Reading was vitally necessary.

The company secured a 3½ acre site overlooking the Thames, at Caversham, last June. Planning permission was granted in record time, and construction of the 44,000 square foot building started in August.

Today it is fully operational with a staff of 40 people (to be expanded soon to approximately 60), the majority recruited in Reading. John Aldington is the Managing Director, and with

/Cont...

ISSUED BY PORSCHE CARS GREAT BRITAIN LIMITED

The press release issued by PCGB on March 21, 1977, announcing the opening of their new headquarters in Reading

- 2 -

Peter Bulbeck, Director and Company Secretary, is delighted to welcome two Board colleagues from the German parent company - Dr. Porsche and Heinz Branitzki - who have come to England for today's ceremony.

Building work has been supervised throughout by Campbell Finley, who will take up a new appointment early in April as General Manager of A.F.N. Limited.

Unusually the company has only two main departments - sales and after-sales - managed respectively by Colin Richard and Iain Denham. The ground floor is occupied by four main [for new-car dewaxing and preparation; for major body repairs for mechanical repairs and the training of dealers' technica personnel; and for the £300,000 stock of replacement parts a components, which is computer controlled to ensure a compreh after-sales service to owners via the dealer network. The offices are air-conditioned, a staff restaurant is provided and a sauna is included in the plans.

The new Porsche 928 model will be on sale in Great Br from next Spring, giving PCGB and its 20 dealers a full yea train staff and prepare for this exciting car. The range then be the 924, the 911 models, the 928, and the Turbo whi will continue to be the prestige "flagship" model.

For the Porsche enthusiast who has everything, there is always the customised bathroom suite. The American magazine, Car & Driver, *carried this little humorous illustration of the 'World's Fastest Fixtures'. Offered by the manufacturer, Laufen Bath Fixtures, the 1.5-gallon tank and wash basin seen in this illustration would undoubtedly add panache to any bathroom!*

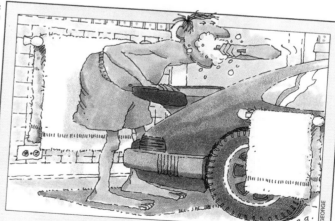

The World's Fastest Fixtures

Porschephiles can now give their bathrooms more panache with a new water closet and pedestal sink designed by Ferdinand Porsche. Laufen Bath Fixtures offers the stylish 1.5-gallon tank and washbasin in a variety of colors. No word yet on a rumored two-seater. Sadly, the trademark Porsche red is unavailable.

Porsche Production Reaches New Heights

High production volumes had never been a priority at Porsche, as the manufacture of quality, performance vehicles requires attention to detail rather than sticking to a mass production schedule. That said, reaching the milestone of 250,000 cars was for Porsche something of a small miracle in itself when considering their modest beginnings back in a wooden shed in the Austrian Alps.

Porsche's press department had this to say about their achievement, "The 250,000th Porsche sports car, a 911 Coupé, is about to leave the assembly line, less than three decades after production began in 1949". The press release went on to say, "Being a producer of exclusive cars with relatively low production figures, the Company of Porsche may yet be very proud of this figure".

Over their 28 years of production, 61.8% of Porsche output was attributable to a single model, the 911, a truly unusual situation in modern day motor vehicle manufacture.

German headlamps for a German car. Quality is an attribute that has long been synonymous with German manufacture, and the American car-buying public were well aware of this as this 1977 magazine ad suggests

AFN placed this advert in the spring 1977 issue of Porsche Post, *the Porsche Club Great Britain's official magazine*

In June 1977, Porsche achieved the landmark production figure of 250,000 vehicles

Ferry Porsche is pictured here in 1979 with his family in the garden of the Villa Porsche in the north of Stuttgart, Feuerbacher Weg 48, on his 70th birthday. From the left, standing, are his sons Gerhard (born 1938), Hans-Peter (born 1940), Ferdinand Alexander (born 1935) and Wolfgang (born 1943). Seated at the front are Dorothea Porsche (1911 - 1985) and Ferry Porsche (1909 - 1998)

Customised 911

From the very outset, Porsche sports cars had been a favourite amongst the many vehicle modifiers that had sprung up to cater for this demand. It was popular in this market for several reasons. Offering good performance and having a well-proven history of motor sport victories, it was fairly easy to extract yet more power from a willing power-plant.

Another good reason was that this type of high performance was not readily available at this price from other sports car manufacturers. Modifications were not restricted to the engine bay, as customers wanted their 911s to be personalised both inside and out. One such company that pandered to the customer's every wish was B+B in Frankfurt/Main, West Germany (in 1978, one still had to differentiate between East and West Germany).

It was around this time that Porsche introduced its own *Sonderwunsch-Programm* or 'Special Wishes' department at the Stuttgart plant, for customers wanting that little bit extra. Located in Werk 1 at the Porsche factory, this department catered for all modifications from personalised upholstery to almost 'works' type competition engine mods, special paint colours and even audio systems. Modifying 911s had become big business.

The American magazine, Road & Track, *ran a special feature on the B&B outfit which specialised in modifying Porsches*

The 'Telephon' wheel was first used on the Porsche 928 as from 1978. However, the first 911 to be fitted with this wheel as standard was the Carrera 3.2 in 1986. Customers could, however, opt for the more expensive Fuchs wheel. Later, in 1989, the Fuchs alloy wheel was standard on the Carrera 3.2 and the Telephon wheel became an option

End Of The Line

Increasing engine emission constraints had led Ernst Fuhrmann to the conclusion that the future for the company lay with front-engined vehicles. His reasoning for such a view was based on the reduction of engine noise, a problem that could have potentially signalled the end of the air-cooled, rear-engined 911. Water-cooling would be required to solve this problem, a solution deemed too difficult and too expensive on the 911 due to the need to reposition the radiators at the front of the car. So, the end of the 911 seemed unavoidable – according to Fuhrmann.

This view did not sit well with 911 enthusiasts around the world, but more importantly, it did not please Ferry Porsche. Continuing tensions between these two leaders resulted in a parting of the ways and Fuhrmann left the company for a second time. It was announced to the press late in 1980, that the new Chairman would be Peter Schutz. German-born but raised in America, Schutz quickly reassured customers that the 911 was here to stay.

Professor Ernst Fuhrmann was the father of Porsche's famous four-cam Carrera engine which did so much to raise the Stuttgart manufacturer's fortunes in the 1950/60s. Here he stands between the two cars at the centre of the storm, the front-engined Porsche 928 and a 911 (1978)

American brothers, Bill and Don Whittington together with German driver, Klaus Ludwig, brought the Kremer 935 K3 home in first place at the 1979 Le Mans 24-Hour race. The number 41 car had led the race since midnight on Saturday night and crossed the line a full seven laps ahead of the second-placed car, yet another Porsche 935 driven by actor Paul Newman, Rolf Stommelen and Dick Barbour. A second Kremer Racing Porsche 935 was placed third

Victory At Last!

Few would have given the number 41 'Numero Reserve' Kremer Racing Porsche 935 K3 any chance of crossing the finishing line first at the 1979 Le Mans 24-Hour race, but those few would have won a lot of money had they bet on it. After 10 years of trying at Le Mans, the privateer outfit from Cologne finally made it.

Porsche had only recently decided against developing the 935 any further as a factory racer, leaving the task instead to a small number of highly professional privateer teams around the world. Kremer Racing created their own bespoke aerodynamic body kits, while experienced race mechanic Walter Heuser weaved his magic on the engine, pushing the maximum power output to an astonishing 740bhp. The 935, which was originally developed by Porsche engineer Helmuth Bott, would go down in motor sport history as Porsche's most successful race car ever, winning over 150 races between 1976-1986.

In 1982, the FIA discontinued Group 5 in favour of a new Group C class, but the 935 lived on in competition in privateer teams in the IMSA GTP category right up until 1986. Kremer's three most memorable victories must undoubtedly include the 1979 Le Mans 24-Hours and, in 1980, winning both the Daytona 24-Hours and the Sebring 12-Hours, where, in fact, 935 K3s took the first five places.

911 SC · Targa · SCS

PORSCHE

Porsche 911 SC

The 911 range was trimmed to just two models in 1978, those being the 911 SC and the Turbo. The 'SC', which stood for Super Carrera, was powered by a 3.0-litre engine that year and was available in either Coupé or Targa form.

After 18 years without a convertible in the line-up, the 911 SC family was finally joined by a Cabriolet in 1983 and it was soon billed as one of the fastest convertible sports cars in the world. Some 50% of the Cabriolet's folding hood comprised structural steel sheets which allowed the car to drive at high speeds without the roof material 'ballooning'.

This 1979 sales brochure was prepared for the Japanese market and covers the 911 SC, Targa and SCS models. The SCS was the Japanese name for the equivalent of the UK's 911 SC Sport, with uprated chassis and upgraded interior components, plus a rear spoiler and other body detailing

The 911 SC was powered by a 2994cc engine from 1978-1983, after which the SC designation was discontinued. This photo shows a pair of US spec SCs in 1980

This sticker announces the launch of the 911 SC Cabriolet at the 1982 Geneva Motor Show

On The Bookshelf

Over the years, there have been many books written on every Porsche subject imaginable. One of the main reasons for this is that the Porsche marque is one that is packed with emotion, technical innovation, motor sport victories against all odds, iconic design and much more. Because of the role that the 911 has played in the company's success and growth over the years, it is perhaps not unexpected that so much attention has been given to this remarkable car.

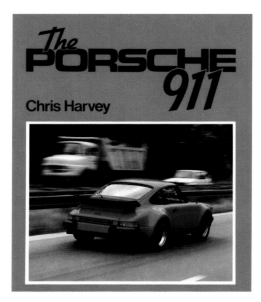

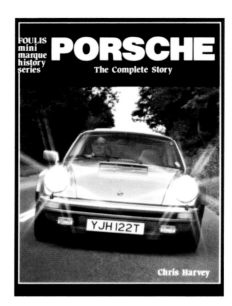

Chris Harvey's book, The Porsche 911 *(Haynes Publishing, 1980 & 1986), covers all aspects of owning a 911. From the idiosyncrasies of owning one to motor sport and restoration, Harvey's marque experience is impressive*

In Porsche: The Complete Story, *Harvey (Haynes Publishing, 1983) charts not only the different Porsche models, but also the people and the engineering behind each model*

Porsche sports cars have always been produced with the discerning person in mind, and this is reflected in their sponsorship of such events as professional tennis since 1978

For many business executives, air travel became an increasing part of their lives from the '70s onwards. Not surprisingly, quite a few also drove Porsches and so the company added branded luggage to the range

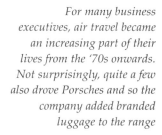

For those all-important weekend getaways in your 911, a set of tailored Porsche suitcases and personal bags, specially designed to fit in the front trunk, was essential

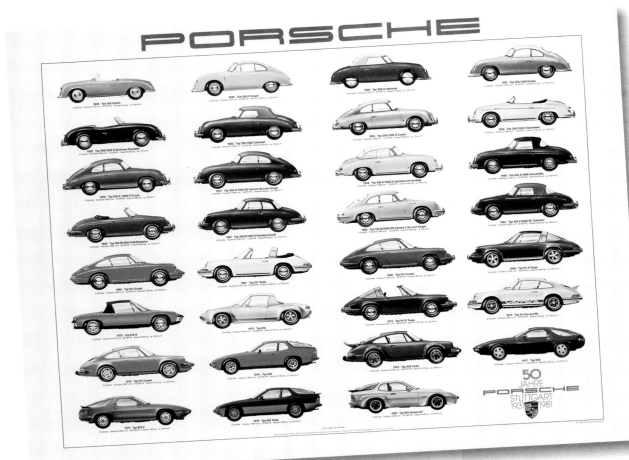

PORSCHE

ODD 911 Turbo

The South African motoring publication, *CAR*, has been a highly respected magazine in its field for many years. When Technical and Features Editor of *CAR* magazine, Dave Trebett, had an opportunity to get behind the wheel of an ODD modified 930 (911 Turbo), he jumped at the prospect. However, his determination to drive this car was not based on his love for Porsches, but rather on his dislike of them.

Original Design and Development (or ODD) of Johannesburg, South Africa, performed their magic on this 3.0-litre Carrera which combined the best of the Carrera mechanicals with the 'slant-nose' styling of Porsche's racing 911.

Trebett's impressions were at first a little subdued but later his mood was lifted as the engine's flexibility and the car's general behaviour had even this seasoned journalist searching for superlatives.

'50 Years Porsche Stuttgart 1931-1981' – this poster celebrates the 50th anniversary since the inception of Dr. Ing. h.c. F. Porsche GmbH, the design office founded by Ferdinand Porsche in Stuttgart in 1931

South African CAR magazine ran this feature on a locally modified Porsche Carrera in their May 1981 issue

PORSCHE 'CARRERA

Photographs by Steve Tronson.

David Trebett tries a Porsche 911 that has undergone an ODD 'body development course' and emerged as a 'Carrera'. A sheep in wolf's clothing? Hardly...

The Value Of Advertising

The value of 'halo' advertising is probably best illustrated by this 1981 Porsche magazine ad. The halo model here is the 911 Turbo which at the time was quite simply the bees knees in sports cars. Young boys at the time, including the author, would stumble and drop their school bags on the pavement when one of these drove by, such was the presence and respect that the Turbo demanded.

The marketing impact of Porsche's turbo-powered race car victories was very effectively converted into sales; magazine ads like this one just served to rub salt into the wounds of many of Porsche's competitors. Placing all four Porsche models in one double-page magazine spread like this had a mesmeric effect on most full-blooded sports car enthusiasts and it is still an extremely effective ad.

Many people did not warm to Schutz's swift American style of management, as this approach paid scant regard for the time-honoured, traditional Swabian way of life which also filtered into the workplace

THE 924 OPTION.
An introduction to unequalled engineering and craftsmanship, the Porsche 924 was voted best 2 litre sportscar in the world, four times running. The 924 Turbo is possibly the fastest.

THE 911 OPTION.
The Porsche Classic, yet still ahead of its time. First created in 1965 it is the blueprint for all Porsche racing and rallying cars today. The 911 Targa is the convertible option of this motoring classic.

Porschefolio.

THE 928 OPTION.
The most comfortable Porsche ever built. A powerful 8-cylinder engine combined with unequalled luxury creates a perfect balance of form and function. The 928S, as one would expect, has an even more powerful engine with increased performance to match.

THE 930 OPTION.
The ultimate in high performance motoring, the Porsche 930, otherwise known as the 911 Turbo, has an astonishing performance of 221 kW from the 3.3 litre engine. This makes it one of the fastest production sportscars in the world.

NO OPTION.
Lindsay Saker are the sole importers and distributors of Porsche and Porsche parts in this country.
Authorised dealers:
Johannesburg Lindsay Saker, 30 Eloff Street, Johannesburg. 21-2511.
Cape Town Motors W.P., 26 Paarden Eiland Road, Paarden Eiland. 21-1030.
Durban South Coast Motors, 359 South Coast Road, Rossburgh. 45-1981.
Port Elizabeth Embassy Motors, 287 Cape Road, Port Elizabeth. 54-4311.

Lindsay Saker PORSCHE

RIGHTFORD SEARLE-TRIPP MAKIN J1840

Motor Buyers' Guide: Supplement to Finance Week. September 24-30, 1981

Motor Buyers' Guide: Supplement to Finance Week. September 24-30, 1981

Lindsay Saker were the official Porsche importers in South Africa from the very first Porsche that landed on the sunny shores of that country in 1957. They remained the sole agents there up until Porsche reclaimed that right in the 1990s

Peter Schutz And The Carrera

When Peter Schutz arrived as CEO of Porsche in early 1981, he set about changing things, but not all of his changes were to everybody's liking. One of the first things he did, though, was to re-establish the future of the 911 by applying the Carrera name to the whole model range, with the exception of the 911 Turbo.

Following the uncertainty surrounding the long-term survival of the 911 at the end of the 1970s, many saw this naming as a strong signal that the 911 was still going to be around for many years. This move undoubtedly ruffled a few feathers as others felt that the distinctive Carrera name had been diluted, but his insistence in this matter was instrumental in restoring confidence in the marque and, as a result, sales flourished.

This potential new lease of life for the 911 served to strengthen not only the 911's place in the market, but also cement the new Chairman's position within the world of Porsche.

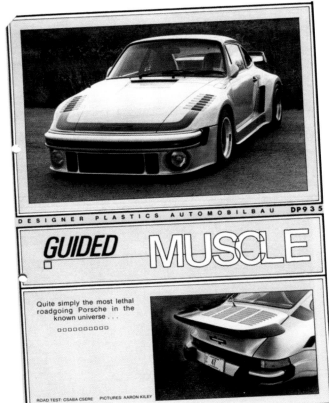

SCOPE magazine in censorship-ridden and conservative South Africa was the 1980s' equivalent of today's lads' magazines. Featuring plenty of bikini-clad models, there was also always a healthy selection of motoring material in each issue which is, of course, why the author bought this copy as a teenage lad at the time. This article is from the August 1983 issue

911 Slant Nose

Never before had Porsche rushed a new model into production and it was not about to happen now just because a Porsche 935 had won the 1979 Le Mans 24-Hours. Where most other manufacturers may have been tempted to hurry a road-going version of a successful race car to market, Porsche would rather deliberate and conduct exhaustive tests before making any such announcement.

When the Kremer Racing Porsche 935 swept to victory that year, it was only a matter of time before the aftermarket customisers began to offer 935 look-alikes. When Porsche saw what a lucrative market existed for the 935 body modification and engine performance kits, they decided to have their slice of the action too. Very much the brainchild of Rolf Sprenger, the 911 Flachbau or Slant Nose, became the sports car of choice for the discerning Porschephile.

When a normal 911 Coupé cost DM 60,620 in 1983, the Slant Nose would set you back a whopping DM 183,272. Only 948 of these extremely powerful sports cars were produced between 1983-1989.

The 911 Turbo 3.3 Coupé Flachbau developed 330bhp and, combined with the lightweight construction, a top speed of 164mph (264km/h) was possible

Porsche 911 Carrera Replaces 'SC'

In the late summer of 1983, as the 911 celebrated its 20th birthday, the 911 SC models were superseded by the 911 Carrera models. These cars were fitted with a revised 3.2-litre flat-six engine and the new models were immediately available in Coupé, Targa and Cabriolet body styles, while the 1984 models were also available in the 'Turbo Look' wide body style which had proved so popular in America.

The 911 Carrera is widely regarded as the model which saw the 911 blossom into a full product range. With the exception of the Turbo which used a 3299cc engine, the 911 Carrera was powered by the same 3164cc flat-6 engine from 1984 right up until the end of the 1989 model year. Even the very distinct Speedster (1989) used the same power plant.

The company produced this wall poster to celebrate 35 years of successful sports car manufacture (1948-1983)

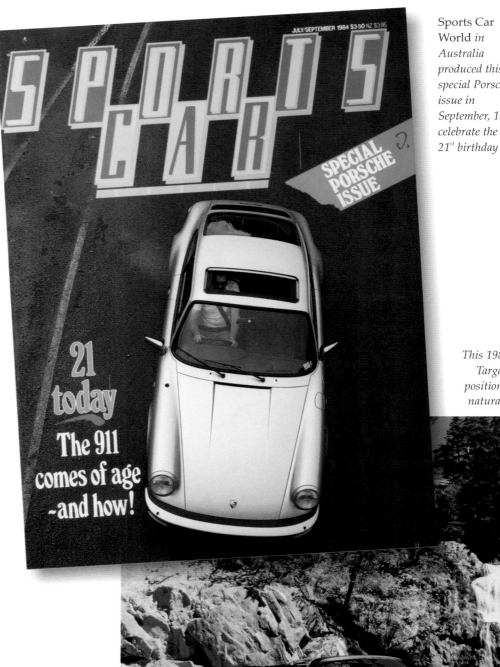

Sports Car World in Australia produced this special Porsche issue in September, 1984 to celebrate the 911's 21st birthday

This 1984 US spec 911 Targa is attractively positioned in beautiful natural surroundings

Turbo Look 911

The popularity of the 'Turbo Look' body in the States (mainly) had come about because some customers liked the look of the wider body. There was of course the slight advantage that the non-Turbo 911, which cost DM 64,500 (US$25,277) in 1983, was not as thirsty as the full-blown model, but then in America the price of fuel was not really a big issue. The 911 Carrera Cabriolet 'Turbo Look' in 1985 would set you back DM 100,150 or $34,306 in American money.

A burgeoning aftermarket trend developed in which many coachbuilders and specialist firms fabricated wide body panels for 911 customers who wanted the look of the Turbo car. This developed into a very lucrative market and Porsche promptly reacted by offering their own factory version of this modification.

Far from just being a standard 911 Carrera with wider body panels, the 'Turbo Look' was in fact a Turbo car with the standard 3.2-litre engine. However, the 'Turbo Look' Cabriolet body was substantially reinforced as the Turbo suspension generated higher forces than the standard set-up. Despite the additional weight and body width, these cars boasted the same performance figures as the 911 Carrera models.

So successful was this 'Turbo Look' style - most were Cabriolets and Targas - that it became a listed model in the Porsche catalogue from August 1984 and, even to this day, it has a strong following.

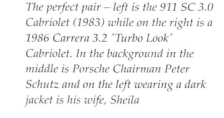

The perfect pair – left is the 911 SC 3.0 Cabriolet (1983) while on the right is a 1986 Carrera 3.2 'Turbo Look' Cabriolet. In the background in the middle is Porsche Chairman Peter Schutz and on the left wearing a dark jacket is his wife, Sheila

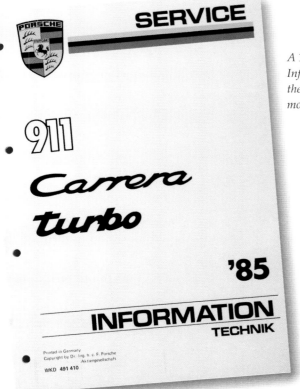

A 1985 factory 'Technical Information' service book for the 911 Carrera and Turbo models

The Flat Nose Carrera 'Turbo Look' is an extremely rare model and is seen here being driven by Norbert Haug. With his background in motoring and motor sport journalism, Haug later became the head of Mercedes-Benz motor sport

Kremer Racing, Cologne

A name synonymous with Porsche motor sport is the racing stable of the Cologne-based Kremer Brothers. Respected the world over, Kremer Racing, a privateer racing team, frequently improved on the Stuttgart factory-produced race cars and was a regular podium finisher from the 1960s through to the 1990s.

Cologne-born brothers, Erwin and Manfred Kremer, established a specialist motor repair and servicing workshop in 1962, dealing with customer's Porsche sports cars. From humble beginnings, the Kremer name was soon thrust into the motor sport spotlight as Erwin beat even the factory team in his well-prepared 911 race cars.

With many titles behind them and years of experience at the trackside, the Kremer brothers decided to hand over the reins to professional drivers in 1975 so they could concentrate their efforts on their newly-created retail dealership. Though Erwin stepped back from active racing as a driver, he continued to manage the race team while Manfred continued to build race engines.

Together with the racing operation and their large retail dealership, Kremer Racing employed 50 staff at its peak, but this was cut right back when Porsche decided to cancel all dealer licences in 1988. At a stroke, all existing dealers were required to reapply to Porsche for their licences no matter how well-established or long-standing the agreements were.

At this point, Kremer decided not to renew their dealer agreement as they wanted to focus their activities around their core racing business.

The Kremer Racing headquarters in Cologne in 1985 featured a large dealer showroom and a very busy racing division

Aero Engines

Ever wanted to take your 911 for a quick flight? Well it is not as crazy as it sounds, as the PFM 3200 aero engine (Porsche Flugmotor) is derived straight from the 3.2-litre boxer engine that powered the 911 Carrera Coupé.

A Mooney M20 aircraft painted in Rothmans racing colours and powered by the PFM 3200 engine drew an obvious link with the Rothman's sponsorship of the hugely successful Porsche 962 racing car at the time.

In 1986, Porsche Aviation Products was founded in Washington IL, as a sales company for the Porsche PFM 3200 aero engine which had demonstrated its reliability the previous year in the course of a record round-the-world flight.

"Lights, camera, action!" Prior to the 1985 round-the-world flight, the Mooney M20 aircraft was the subject of a good deal of media attention

The Mooney M20, painted in Rothmans racing colours, shows off its PFM 3200 engine

Porsche 959
– A Wolf In Sheep's Clothing

Although the 959 is to all intents and purposes a road car, it has its origins in the world of motor sport. Changes in the racing regulations in the mid-1980s permitted greater flexibility in the development of standard-looking vehicles for racing in the Group B class. The Porsche engineers set about building a new race car based on the 911 but utilising a 4-wheel drive layout with the possibility of this also being adapted for normal road use.

The brainchild of Porsche engineer Helmuth Bott, the concept was first introduced to the public at the Frankfurt Motor Show in 1983 where it was exhibited as an undeveloped prototype called the 'Group B Studie'. Conceived with racing in mind, the prototype's body had smoothly contoured outlines and rounded surfaces that were to be echoed in later generations of the 911.

Porsche created another big stir in 1985 when it launched the road-going production version of this Group B racer. Technically, the 959 was quite unlike anything anybody had ever seen before. Fitted with twin compound turbochargers, the 2.85-litre boxer engine in the road-going 959 developed a whopping 450bhp and could reach a mind-blowing 196mph (315km/h). For those wishing to acquire one of the 292 cars made, there was the small matter of parting with DM 420,000 (or US$144,000).

Based on the 911, the floorpan of the 959 was re-engineered to take the 4-wheel drive layout and revised suspension, while many of the body panels were fabricated from aluminium and fibreglass-reinforced epoxy resin. The rear body section and engine lid were integrated with the large rear spoiler and could be raised as one unit while the aerodynamic body was designed as a no-lift body shape. The front headlamps and fenders were reminiscent of the 1983 high performance 911 Turbo Coupe 'Slant Nose' which was itself a variation of the awesome 935 racer from the late-1970s. What a pedigree!

The 959's first competition victory was in the 1984 Rallye Paris-Dakar in the hands of Frenchman René Metge. The following year, the 959 won the Pharaohs Rallye in Egypt and in 1986 the Porsche 959 took first, second and sixth places in the Paris-Dakar event.

The media were let loose in a 959 at a press weekend event at Gstaad in southern Switzerland, January 1987. Testing the car to its limits on a large icy surface minimised any chance of serious damage while at the same time it demonstrated the car's awesome capabilities

This stunning front cover on the February 1984 issue of CAR AND DRIVER captures the silhouette of the 959 beautifully

Helmuth Bott regards the 959 as one of his favourites as it was his dream car which he took from concept to fruition. Here Bott is pictured at the wheel of an early 959 in September 1984

Money Matters

The financial year 1985/86 saw Porsche increasing activities on all fronts. With turnover up by 12% and vehicle production reaching 100 cars per day, the company reported that they had sold their entire production for that year. In the mid-1980s, there were not too many motor manufacturers that could boast of being in such a strong situation.

Export sales to the United States had increased 15% over the previous year, which, being Porsche's biggest export market, was very good news indeed. This increase in fact pushed the US market to a whopping 54% of total sales. This growth in production and global sales obviously required more staff and at the end of the 1986 fiscal year, Porsche employed 8458 personnel, an increase of 543 (7%) over the previous year.

Every year the Porsche calendar was issued together with a bronze medallion. Long-serving Porsche employees were given a set of these medallions in silver covering the last 12 years and they were displayed in an attractive case

Porsche distributed these favourable company and financial results to the press at the end of their 1985/86 fiscal year

PORSCHE
Presse-Information

Pr 86/33 (E,1.Ex.)

Porsche AG: more employees, higher production numbers and increased turnover

The Stuttgart sports car manufacturer Porsche has achieved the targets set for the business year 1985/86 (August 1, 1985 - July 31, 1986): a sales volume amounting to over 53.000 cars and a turnover of exceeding 3.5 billion Marks.

Turnover

With 3.568 million Marks (without value added tax) the total turnover exceeded last year's turnover by 12 per cent, the car business having a share of 3.195 million Marks (2.812 million Marks last year). The other turnover rates achieved by sales of spare parts, development work and other services, increased by 3 per cent to 373 million Marks compared to last year.

in mio. DM	1984/85	1985/86	change
turnover	3.176	3.568	+ 12 %
home market	804	780	- 3 %
export	2.372	2.788	+ 18 %
export share	75 %	78 %	+ 3 %

Production

The daily production at Zuffenhausen reached by the end of the last business year, amounting to 100 cars, remained the same throughout the whole year under report. At AUDI AG an average of 144 units of the models 924 S, 944 and 944 Turbo were produced daily during business year 1985/86. Thus production capacities were fully exhausted during the whole business year.

Units	1984/85	1985/86	change
production	50.514	53.625	+ 6 %
911/928	18.980	21.500	+ 13 %
924/944	31.534	32.125	+ 2 %

Sales

The sales situation was again favoured by the high demand on the export markets. Compared to last year, car sales to the United States increased by 15 per cent and those to other export countries by 8 per cent. The USA-share in total sales was thus raised from 50 per cent to 54 per cent. The decrease in sales on the domestic market faces highly increased customer deliveries, reducing the stock of dealer organizations.

Units	1984/85	1985/86	change
sales	49.365	53.254	+ 8 %
home market	12.224	11.340	- 7 %
export	37.141	41.914	+ 13 %
export share	75 %	79 %	+ 4 %

Dr. Ing. h. c. F. Porsche Aktiengesellschaft · Porschestraße 42, Stuttgart-Zuffenhausen
Postanschrift: Postf. 40 06 40, 7000 Stuttgart 40 · Tel. (07 11) 827-0, Fernschreiber 721 817 · Fax (07 11) 827-58 88

Employees

By the end of business year 1985/86 Porsche AG employed 8.458 persons, i.e. 543 more than last year. The additional jobs were mainly provided due to expanded production and development capacities.

	1984/85	1985/86	change
employees	7.915	8.458	+ 7 %
blue-collar workers	5.098	5.419	+ 6 %
white-collar workers	2.817	3.039	+ 8 %

Investments

The medium-term investment program was carried on and 272 million Marks were invested. Last year's investment volume could not be achieved due to unexpected delays in planning and realization of construction works. The lion's share of investments was again allotted to extending and improving the model range as well as expanding and modernizing production facilities. This concerns especially the new paintshop, which was put into operation as planned during the first six months of 1986. Other important investments were made in research and development. The increase in financial assets concerns the raise in capital of two existing participations. The financing of the investments was again effected by funds achieved through the enterprise.

	1984/85	1985/86	change
investments	291	272	- 7 %
fixed assets	286	265	- 7 %
financial assets	5	7	+ 40 %

Profits

Profits achieved during the year under report were satisfactory, resulting from the favourable development of sales and turnover as well as fully exhausted capacities - despite the negativ exchange rate for US exports and exports to other important countries. On March 27, 1987 the following suggestion will be submitted to the General Stockholders' Meeting: namely to decide on a DM 15,-- dividend for common stocks and a DM 16,-- dividend for preference shares.

Prospects

The unsteady situation of the exchange rate, especially the continuous devaluation of the US dollar and the other exchange rates of important markets, are expected to impede business conditions during the year under report - a situation which will, however, affect the main competitors in the same way. Yet, the present excellent automobile business, an attractive model range, the Porsche employees' qualification and readiness to work, a solid financial base and internal rationalization following the rapid growth period of the past are good preconditions for coping with the challenges of business year 1986/87 successfully. To guarantee long-term competitiveness high investments are planned.

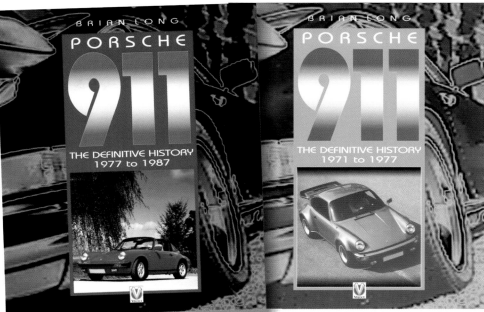

These are just two of the five books in the Brian Long series covering the 911 from 1963 to 2004

Once again, Harvey outlines the achievements of the 911 on the track as well as its phenomenal performance in the dealers' showrooms. Porsche 911 In All Its Forms offers a wealth of technical detail as well as anecdotes and model history

A devoted Porsche enthusiast, Tony Corlett has an engineering and design background and lives on the Isle of Man. This book is the first definitive book on the 911 3.2 Carrera, the product of many years of work and outlines this model during the period 1984 to 1989

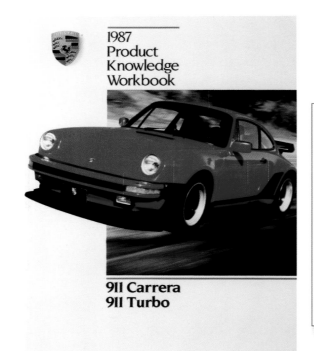

1987
Product
Knowledge
Workbook

911 Carrera
911 Turbo

Auto Motor und Sport produced this dedicated supplement in July 1988 to commemorate the 25th anniversary of the Porsche 911

Champagne Time

A 25th anniversary is important in anyone's life, and none more so than for Porsche who had grappled with the larger manufacturers both on and off the track. This silver anniversary milestone was pounced on by the world's media, much to the delight of the management back in Stuttgart-Zuffenhausen.

Auto Motor und Sport, was, and still is, a very highly respected motoring publication in Germany and they published a dedicated supplement to commemorate this milestone in the 911's history.

A company marketing poster shows the open-top appeal of the Speedster

911 Speedster

The Speedster was an instant classic. Designed as a no-frills modern version of the 356 Speedster of 1955, this rather surprising model was snapped up as quickly as it came off the production line.

The Speedster's body consisted of a 'Turbo Look' wide body with a cut-down windscreen where the upper corners of the windscreen were rounded, rather than squared off like the Cabriolet. The philosophy behind this model was to provide a fun, go-in-the-sun model with little in the way of comfort features. At DM 110,000 the Speedster cost significantly more than the Cabriolet but around the same price as the 'Turbo Look' Cabriolet.

Electric windows were replaced with wind up ones while an electrically-operated hood mechanism was not deemed clever enough to deal with the complex folding requirements of the Speedster's hood. Besides, it would have added unnecessary weight and would definitely not have been in keeping with the spirit of the original spartan model.

A batch of 171 narrow-bodied Speedsters were made for export only with an additional 2103 units being manufactured for Europe and the UK. The hump-back styling was not everybody's cup of tea, but these early cars hit the mark and are today extremely collectable.

911 Speedster

PORSCHE

The extremely low silhouette of the Porsche 911 Carrera 3.2 Speedster was certainly quite different in 1986

The Speedster's Driver's Manual explained the reason for the car's flimsy, lightweight top in the following manner: "The 911 Speedster was essentially designed as a 'fine weather vehicle', specially for those who love 'open-air driving'. In contrast to the 911 Cabriolet, which naturally has a fully adequate folding top, your 911 Speedster is fitted with a light emergency folding top. Depending on the conditions in which it is used and on the weather, certain drawbacks such as draughts, wind noise, leakages at the joins between the folding top and body, or door windows, cannot be avoided.
"The Speedster cannot be washed in car washes and therefore must only be washed by hand.
"We wish you many sunny days, many miles of pleasurable driving in the open air and a great deal of enjoyment in your new Porsche."

This unusual hinged top belongs to the Porsche 911 Carrera 3.2 Speedster Clubsport, a one-off concept car built for the 1987 Frankfurt Motor Show. Although it featured the same mechanicals as the standard Speedster, at 100kg lighter it was quicker and intended as a more sport-oriented vehicle

Porsche 911 production statistics

Model Year	Model description	Units
1974	G - Series	11,642
1975	H - Series	8,189
1976	J - Series	10,677
1977	K - Series	13,793
1978	L - Series	10,684
1979	M - Series	11,543
1980	A - Programm	9,874
1981	B - Programm	8,698
1982	C - Programm	10,735
1983	D - Programm	13,229
1984	E - Programm	13,669
1985	F - Programm	12,348
1986	G - Programm	17,074
1987	H - Programm	16,441
1988	J - Programm	14,380
1989	K - Programm	16,488

Source: Porsche

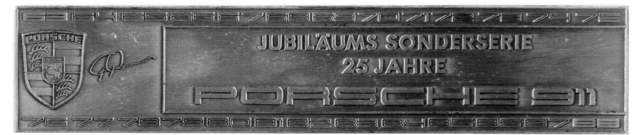

This 1988 plaque commemorates the 25th anniversary of the introduction of the Porsche 911 at the Frankfurt Motor Show back in 1963

THE 1990s - SERIES 964

Although to the casual observer the new model, the Typ 964, looked like little more than a face-lifted version of the outgoing 911, nothing could have been further from the truth. Beneath the skin, the first model in this new 964 series boasted a permanent 4-wheel drive system which required a substantial redesign and re-engineering of the chassis and suspension.

Essentially, the 911 was a car of the sixties, and, when it was introduced, nobody could have imagined what automotive technical advances might be made in the next quarter of a century. As a result of the new 4-wheel drive system, a massive 85% of the Typ 964 consisted of completely new parts, and yet the Porsche engineers were able to maintain the familiar look of the 911, no small feat in itself.

This development was inspired by the considerable experience and knowledge gained through the success of the 959. Following the sizeable investment that had gone into the development of the 959's high performance 4-wheel drive system, the Porsche engineers were given the challenge of putting this technology to good use in a production 911, while maintaining the familiar 911 body shape.

Furthermore, the company planned both a 4-wheel and a 2-wheel drive version of the 964. Although these two versions were developed simultaneously, the Carrera 4 was launched ahead of the Carrera 2. This was done to prevent the slightly cheaper Carrera 2 from stealing sales from the ground-breaking Carrera 4. Launching the two models together was also not an option for the same reason.

Just as the Porsche engineers were busy with technical and engine developments, so too were the designers hard at work exploring the boundaries of the 911 shape. This resulted in a 1989 design study called the Panamericana, which you either loved or hated!

The period between 1988-1993 saw Porsche celebrating two important milestones. The first of these was the introduction of the 964-series itself in August 1988, which coincided with the 25th anniversary of the 911 model (1963-1988). The second milestone was the launch of the 30th anniversary version of the 911 in 1993.

The 964-series also witnessed the return of the Carrera RS badge as well as the introduction of the biggest Porsche boxer engine to date, the RS 3.8. As with so many previous Porsche models, the RS 3.8 was produced to enable the homologation of the awesome RSR 3.8 racer introduced in 1993.

TIMELINE (1989-1993):

1989	1990	1992	1993
Introduction of Typ 964 4-wheel drive.	Carrera 2 launched.	Carrera RS badge returns.	'30 Jahre' anniversary model introduced.
Panamericana concept.			

The Porsche 911 Carrera 2 3.6-litre Cabriolet was introduced one year after the Carrera 4. This is a USA spec model from 1992

A 1991 Porsche 911 Carrera 4 3.6-litre Coupé is put through its paces at Weissach

Carrera 4 (1989)

A 911 family gathering with, from left to right, a red 911 Carrera 2 3.6 Speedster, 911 Carrera 4 3.6 30 Year Jubilee model, 911 Carrera 2 3.6 Cabrio, while at the rear is a yellow 911 Turbo 3.6

Introduced in the 911's 25th anniversary year, Project 964 was the first attempt by the company to market an all-wheel drive production car for the everyday Porsche driver. Although the company had had some considerable experience by now with four-wheel-drive systems, substantial changes were needed in order to prepare this model for normal assembly line production.

A totally new floorpan had to be developed. This was to allow the driveline that transmitted drive to the front wheels to be installed in the assembly process from below, rather than from inside the vehicle, thereby also easing any future maintenance requirements. Considering that the wheelbase and track dimensions are virtually unchanged, the Stuttgart company had worked wonders in introducing an almost entirely new vehicle while sharing as few as 15% of its components with its predecessor.

Even in a top-of-the-range sports car such as the Carrera 4, the 959 4-wheel drive system would have been too expensive for a 911 production model, and so a somewhat cheaper mechanical differential was developed for the 964. It was also the first model to feature power steering and ABS brakes as standard features on a 911. To carry this extra weight around, more power was needed and so at the time of its launch, the Carrera 4 was fitted with a bigger 3.6-litre engine and became the most powerful naturally-aspirated model in the 911 range. Developing 250bhp and giving a top speed of 160mph (260km/h), it covered the 0-62mph (0-100km/h) sprint in just 5.9 seconds.

While the interior came in for some mild upgrading, it was the underside of the car which received a radical makeover. Just like the 959, the new 964 road car was fitted with a full-length belly pan. This provided several benefits, one of the main being a reduction in engine noise in compliance with European regulations, as well as lowering the level of noise for the cabin occupants. While noise reduction was regulated by the authorities, this did not necessarily please the Porsche enthusiasts who craved the sound of that sweet six cylinder boxer engine in full flight.

A revolutionary new rear spoiler automatically extended from the engine lid at speeds above 50mph (80km/h), and retracted again when the speed dropped below 6mph (10km/h). This extending rear spoiler was no gimmick as the company explained in a press release in 1988:

"Porsche [has] led the way with the introduction of today's common additional spoilers for nose and tail. The extendable spoiler of the Carrera 4 now underlines the functional character of an aerodynamic lift-reduction aid, something Porsche would never see as a styling attribute".

Adoption of this extendable 'lift reduction aid' was driven by the fact that the company did not want a fixed rear spoiler as used by the Carrera RS 2.7 or the later Turbo 930, because they wanted to retain the original, unspoiled 911 silhouette.

As a production car, the potential advantages of the all-wheel drive system envisaged by the engineers was expected to far outweigh any negative perceptions arising from an almost 20% increase in the car's price.

However, reworking a 4-wheel drive system into a production vehicle involved more than simply adapting the existing bodyshell to receive the new drivetrain. The current wheels and steering set-up could not accommodate the requirements of ABS braking, while the luggage compartment and bulkhead would have to be modified to take the front differential. Furthermore, the air conditioning unit which had by now become a modern day necessity, could no longer be contained within the old bodyshell.

The full advantages of all-wheel drive would become obvious when accelerating in a curve, especially on a more slippery surface, while wheelspin when pulling away from a standing start would also be eliminated. Additionally, it improved straight-line stability in cross winds.

At the August 1988 introductory price of DM 114,500 (1989 year model), the Carrera 4 Coupé represented good value for money with its all-wheel drive system, comfort, performance potential and Porsche's renowned build quality. Even at launch, the entire first year's production of the Carrera 4 had already been sold. With hindsight, the 4 served as a crucially important platform on which future generations of 911s would be built.

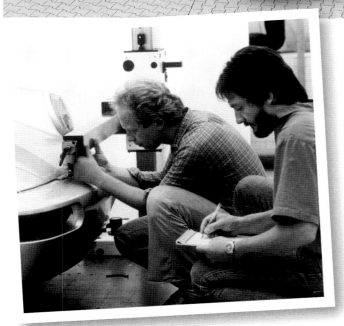

Two design engineers put the final touches to the 911 Carrera 4 in 1988 in Porsche's design studio. The model was launched the following year

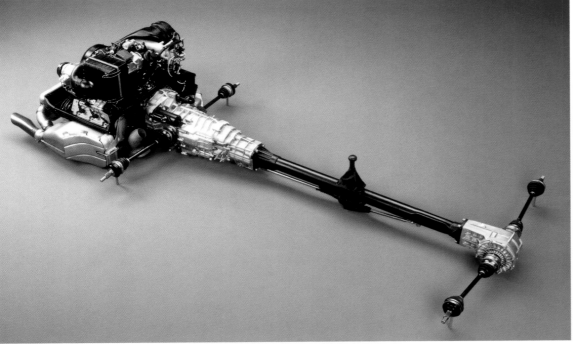

A 1991 Carrera 4 3.6-litre Coupé is captured outside the Intercontinental Hotel in Stuttgart

The complete drivetrain of the 1989 Porsche 911 Carrera 4 3.6-litre is revealed in this shot

There is something dramatic about contrasting the advanced technology of a sports car with the apparent starkness of an industrial plant, as this location in the Emsland region of Germany near the Dutch border, illustrates so well. The model in question is another 1991 Carrera 4 3.6 Coupé

New Design Team

On April 1, 1989, Dutch-born automobile designer, Harm Lagaay, took over the management of Porsche's styling department from Anatole Lapine, who had held this post since 1969. Lagaay worked for Porsche in 1971 on the 911 and 924 before moving to Ford in 1977 and then on to BMW Technik before returning to Stuttgart as head of Style Porsche in 1989. He also oversaw the design of the Typ 993 before retiring from Porsche in July 2004.

Lagaay's colleague, Dr. Ulrich Bez was born at Bad Cannstatt in Germany in November 1943. Bez graduated from the University of Stuttgart with a Doctorate in Engineering and proceeded to build a formidable reputation for himself as an engineer, designer and racing driver.

This more than qualified him for the post of design and development engineer at Porsche, where he led the Vehicle Research and Development programmes. He directed design and development of the 911 Turbo (930), the Carrera RS 2.7, the 968 and the 993.

Ulrich Bez, pictured here in 1988, holds a doctorate in engineering from Berlin University. Bez later became CEO and Chairman of Aston Martin Lagonda Ltd

A youthful-looking Harm Lagaay, Porsche designer, photographed in 1992

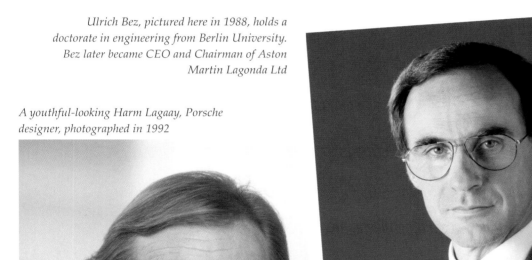

Panamericana Concept

The Panamericana was introduced to a rather bemused press and public at the Frankfurt Motor Show in 1989. In a press release issued at the time, the company announced: "Porsche presents a study of unusual shape and technology based on the Carrera 4." They weren't joking either!

Based on the 964 Carrera 4, the Panamericana was intended to demonstrate a forward-thinking attitude by Style Porsche, the company's design studio, and was presented to Dr. Ferry Porsche as a gift on the occasion of his 80th birthday. 'Future-orientated thinking, long-term conceptual certainty, creativity and competence in technology' – this rather typically abstract marketing terminology was used to explain the Panamericana concept in the corporate press release.

Whether or not the Panamericana tugged at your heartstrings, it represented an important step in the company's thinking at a time when Ulrich Bez and Harm Lagaay had just arrived at Porsche. Hired to breathe new life into the 911, the Bez/Lagaay team probably developed the Panamericana concept as a test of public reaction more than anything else.

Stylistically, the Panamericana was a mixture of several schools of thought. The sweeping roof line which tapered down to the rear wings offered several configurations – hard-top, Targa, Convertible or Coupé.

While the overall shape was rounded and very smooth, the front-end treatment utilised some 928 design cues with its sunken headlamps. The rear end was distinctly un-Porsche-like and certainly the least attractive aspect of the car was the rather aggressive open wheel styling, which made the vehicle appear more like a beach buggy on steroids.

Here the Porsche Typ 911 Panamericana concept vehicle is being put through its paces at the Weissach proving ground in 1989

Given to Ferry Porsche on his 80th birthday, the Panamericana represented fresh thinking within the design department at Porsche

An example of this Panamericana 1:43 scale model was given to all Porsche staff on Ferry Porsche's 80th birthday on September 19, 1989. It was Ferry's belief that his staff should also share in his birthday celebrations

"Oh - go get yourself a Porsche."

Apparently, Porsche sports cars are even appreciated in the Pavo cristatus world, where peacocks are members of the pheasant family

Carrera 2 (1990)

If the sales success of the Carrera 4 was a benchmark, then its 2-wheel drive sibling introduced in August 1989 proved to be an even bigger winner. For many, the Carrera 2 represented a purer form of Porsche motoring, with its traditional rear-engined, rear-wheel drive layout.

It only became apparent later, but the Carrera 2 was the model that most thoroughbred Porschephiles really hankered after. It had the added bonus of weighing 100kg less than its all-wheel drive brother and, at an introductory price of DM 103,500, it was DM 13,100 cheaper than the Carrera 4 which had increased in price since its launch a year earlier.

Introduced on the Carrera 2 was Porsche's brand new Tiptronic gearbox. A company press release at the time of the car's launch explained the move. "The new Porsche Tiptronic that was designed especially for the 911 Carrera 2 opens up new dimensions in 911 motoring."

The Carrera 2 made use of the same double ignition 3.6-litre engine as the Carrera 4, a system that was inspired by Porsche's aircraft engine technology. Externally, it is indistinguishable from its all-wheel drive brother except for the '2' or '4' alongside the Carrera lettering on the engine lid.

Some diehard supporters in the Porsche 2-wheel-drive camp saw the Carrera 2 as the spiritual successor to the Carrera 3.2 of 1984. While you could argue the benefits or otherwise of 2-wheel versus 4-wheel drive *ad infinitum*, the truth is that the Carrera 4 represented a major technological step forward for the company which elevated the Porsche marque into the highest echelons of the sports car world. If you did not support the 4-wheel drive concept, then you could buy a Carrera 2 and save yourself some money in the process!

The stark backdrop to this 1992 Carrera 2 3.6-litre Coupé serves to highlight its smooth, compact lines

Porsche created a range of 964 model accessories for those enthusiasts wishing to extend their passion from the garage to their office desk

This 1992 model year Porsche Typ 911 Carrera 2 3.6-litre Cabriolet 'Turbo Look' is finished in metallic Amethyst and features Tiptronic transmission

Tiptronic – A Simple Selection

With effect from November 1989, Porsche offered a new 4-speed Tiptronic gearbox which offered the driver either fully-automatic gear shifts or a means of selecting gears manually. This Tiptronic transmission was the result of a joint development between the manufacturers of the gearbox, ZF Friedrichshafen AG, Robert Bosch GmbH (who were responsible for the electronics) and Porsche.

Far removed from the relatively disappointing Sportomatic 'box of 1967, this new piece of technology relied on the experience gained with the Porsche dual-clutch (PDK) used in the successful 962 Group C competition model.

Tiptronic, first offered on the Carrera 2 model, enabled the car to be driven in a conventional automatic manner with the added benefit of 'intelligent' gear-change programmes which fine-tuned the automatic change process. Alternatively, by moving the gear lever from the D-position into a second gate to the right of the main gate, the driver could manually change gears at will. In this position, the lever could be 'tipped' forward or backward for manual up-changes and down-changes.

In all the markets that Porsche sports cars have penetrated, you will find no end of specialist workshops offering to make your car go faster, look better, or just give it a plain old service

The speedometer of this 1992 Carrera 2 3.6-litre shows the selected drive position in the vertical left central column beneath the speedo needle. By knocking the selector over to the right to effect manual gear changes, the relevant gear was shown in the right hand vertical column

Close inspection will reveal the simple operation of the Porsche Tiptronic gear shift in this 1990 Carrera 2 3.6-litre

This is not quite what you would want to happen to your beloved 911, but it was just as well to know where to go if the unthinkable did occur

Any Porsche racing series involving the 911 was always going to be a success, such was the popularity and flexibility of the car. With all the participating cars being prepared by the factory, a level playing field was ensured which led to very close racing and excellent entertainment for the spectators. No major developments were made to the cars during the first two years of the series, but in 1992 the Cup cars were based on the Carrera RS instead of the Carrera 2 model

Carrera Cup And Supercup Racing

The world première of the Porsche Carrera Cup took place at Zolder in Belgium on April 1, 1990, with 40 identical Porsche 911 Carrera 2 Cup cars on the starting grid.

Following the success of the Turbo Cup, which had used front-engined Porsche 944 Turbo cars, the management wanted to initiate a series that utilised the 928 model, also a front-engined model. In order to get the new series off the ground, Porsche brought stalwart Herbert Linge out of retirement and put him in charge of the overall programme.

Herbert Linge recalls, "The idea after the 944 Turbo Cup was to do a series with the 928, and I told them immediately, if you want to do it with the 928 I am not going to do it."

When asked why not with the 928, he replied, "Because the car was not built to be a race car. The car was a very good GT road car, but it was not a racing car; it was too heavy and too big. I told them that if I was to run the series, then I do it with the 911. 'Oh.' they said, 'the 911, it is too expensive. It is going to cost a lot of money,' but I said, 'No, it will cost less than the 928'. So they finally agreed that I can do it with the 911."

MEISTERSCHAFTS-ENDSTAND 1991

1. Roland Asch (D)
2. Wolfgang Land (D)
3. Jürgen von Gartzen (D)
4. Olaf Manthey (D)
5. Oscar Larrauri (ARG)
6. Philipp Müller (CH)
7. Peter Aslund (S)
8. Andy Bovensiepen (D)
9. Harald Grohs (D)
10. Bruno Eichmann (CH)

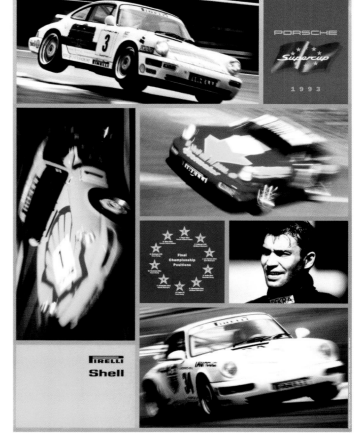

The Supercup series began in 1992 as a curtain-raiser to Formula 1 races around the world. Now in its 17th year, the Supercup has undoubtedly brought Porsche unprecedented exposure at the highest levels of the sport by sharing the stage with Formula 1

It's In The Bag

Porsche was the first manufacturer in the world to offer driver and passenger airbags as a standard safety feature on all production models, as from February 1, 1991. Although airbags for both front occupants had been available as an option since 1986, these were now included across the entire production car range as standard.

Model prices increased by DM 3,500 but this was no ordinary airbag system, as Porsche sought to maximise both their active and passive safety systems in the car. The combination of Porsche's 3-point safety belt and airbag system optimised the hold back effect for both driver and passenger, decreasing the risk of injury in a frontal collision.

If you were really enthusiastic about your 911 Turbo, then you could purchase a matching pair of lapel badge and tie pin, leaving the world in no doubt as to what car you drove

Wendelin Wiedeking first worked at Porsche as Director's Assistant in the Production and Materials Management area from 1983-1988 before leaving the company for alternative pastures. However, he returned to Porsche in 1991 where he has remained, and now serves as President and Chief Executive Officer of Porsche Automobil Holding SE (formerly Porsche AG), while also filling the post of Chairman of the Executive Board

A New Start

Chief Executive Officer Arno Bohn left the company on October 1, 1992, making way for Dr. Ing. Wendelin Wiedeking to assume leadership of the Board of Management. Following a difficult economic period which had seen a significant fall in sales (911 sales fell by over 60% between 1991-1993), new organisational and production procedures were introduced under an initiative called 'Lean Management'.

Based on the Japanese system of 'Kaizen', the 'Porsche Improvement Process' (PVP) was drawn up and involved the entire workforce. Literally translated, 'Kaizen' means continuous improvement which created a continuous process flow to bring production problems to the surface. The initialisation of this PVP process had the effect of boosting the company's performance potential and productivity.

This dramatic streamlining of working methods and procedures was accompanied by shorter working hours and a reduction of personnel by some 1850.

911 Carrera RS Coupé (1992)

In Porsche terms, 'less' normally means 'more', because if the car contains less by way of comfort and luxury, then it usually translates into less weight, higher performance and higher specification for sporting purposes.

First shown at the 1991 Birmingham Motor Show, the Carrera RS boasted an even more powerful version of the same 3.6-litre boxer engine that powered the Carrera 2 and 4 models. Classified by the media as a 'lightweight super sports version of the Carrera 2', this extreme sports machine could trace its roots back to the legendary Carrera RS 2.7 of 1972. This rear-wheel drive Carrera RS, however, amounted to little more than what could be called a street legal 'Cup' model, which in marketing terms was the base model for their homologated GT race car.

Carrying a price premium of DM 26,330 over the Carrera 2 Coupé, the Carrera RS came in at a weighty DM 145,450 (US$ 93,375) and was only available in the 1992 production year. For your money, you got the same blueprinted engine as in the Cup model producing a hefty 260bhp (10bhp up on the Carrera 2).

Weighing in at about 10% less than the Carrera 2, the RS's increase in engine output seemed marginal, but combined with the remapping of the engine management and a lightened flywheel, performance was significantly enhanced. Top speed was given as 162mph (260km/h) and the 0-62mph (0-100km/h) sprint was achieved in just 5.3 seconds - nearly half a second faster than the Carrera 2.

The road-going Carrera RS obviously did not carry a roll cage and power steering, while a more comfortable 'Touring' version of this model did offer power-assisted steering. The Porsche Carrera RS made its world début at the Birmingham Motor Show in September 1991 and, although the company planned to build 1800 cars in total, over 2000 of these cars were produced through the summer of 1991 and into 1992.

This is a rare shot of Ferry Porsche and Wendelin Wiedeking together in public. They are engaged in conversation at a Porsche Club meeting in 1993

Dieter Röscheisen, a Porsche engineer and their official test driver for northern Europe, did most of his testing in Scandinavia. Here he is seen in 1991 putting the 911 Carrera RS 3.6 through its paces at the Weissach test track. Röscheisen, a keen amateur photographer, supplied the Porsche PR department with many useful photos taken 'up north'

'Die Porsche AG gratuliert Ihnen zu Ihrem 911 Carrera RS' (Porsche AG congratulates you on the acquisition of your 911 Carrera RS) – Porsche rewarded Carrera RS buyers with this attractive desk model

The 1992 Carrera RS 3.6 Coupé was a handsome-looking car, but beneath that pleasing exterior lurked a 260bhp 3.6-litre engine capable of pushing this beauty to over 160mph (260km/h)

It must be every schoolboy's dream to be driven around a race track in a Porsche, as this young man's smile certainly suggests. After a few laps around South Africa's premier race circuit, Kyalami, the author's son reported quite casually that the driver had spun the car several times. "But it was really cool, Dad." The car in question, a replica 911 Carrera RS Coupé N/GT, was just one of several racing Porsches belonging to members of the Porsche Club of South Africa who generously offered the public a few laps around the Kyalami circuit in order to raise funds for a local children's charity

911 Carrera RS
3.8 Coupé (1993)

Just when everyone thought the flat-six boxer engine had reached its limit at 3600cc, the Porsche engineers did a little bit more stretching, which for an engine that started life as a 2.0-litre with planned development up to 2.7-litres, was some achievement. With motor sport never very far from the minds of the Porsche engineers, it was inevitable when they produced the Carrera RS 3.8 that it would end up on the race track, and it was therefore fitting that this model was developed and built by hand at the Porsche Race Sport Department. Using the 1993 Carrera 2 as the starting point, Porsche had to make at least 50 road-going cars in order to qualify this new model for the German ADAC GT Cup, which served as the basis for a motor racing variant to come, the Carrera RSR 3.8.

While retaining the same stroke of 76.4mm, the bore was increased to 102mm to produce an engine capacity of 3746cc, or 3.8-litre in marketing terms. Power output was up 15% on the 3.6-litre RS, coming in at a storming 300bhp. Gone was the extendable rear spoiler of the C2 and C4 models, and mounted in its place was a fixed spoiler rising almost to roof height, ensuring that the back end stayed firmly planted on the road. The model designation 'RS 3.8' was inscribed on its side supports. The Carrera RS 3.8 could do the 0-62mph (0-100km/h) dash in 4.9 seconds, topping out at 167mph (270km/h).

The standard Carrera RS 3.8 Coupé was offered at a monstrous DM 225,000 (US$136,130).

Snapped in the parking lot of Werk 1 in Stuttgart, you can see the RS 3.8 badging on the flank of the aerofoil uprights

The 1993 Carrera RS 3.8 Coupé left one with little doubt that this was a very potent driving machine. Its 6-cylinder 3746cc engine developed 300bhp (221kW) and had a top speed of 167mph (270 km/h)

RS America

Because the 911 Carrera RS was not certified for sale in the United States, the 911 RS America was built especially for that market. Based on the Carrera 2, it was fitted with 17" 'Cup' wheels, a fixed rear wing and tuned suspension.

The interior of the RS America featured a pair of sports seats, electric windows, central locking and an alarm. The RS America was sold for US$53,900.

The Porsche 911 RS America was a model available only in America, as the name suggests. Built between 1993-1994, only 701 of these 3.6-litre, 247bhp beauties were produced. The USA publication, European Car, *carried a detailed feature on this model in their January 1993 issue*

Companies recognised the marketing strength of the Porsche 911 and used it to good effect to promote their own products, as did this car polish company

This 1992 studio shot of the Porsche 911 RS America shows the car's strong and handsome lines exceptionally well

RUF

Tucked away in the quaint town of Pfaffenhausen, which is set in the tranquil and idyllic mountains of southern Germany's Allgäu region, is one of the foremost Porsche specialist workshops in the world. Pfaffenhausen, a small rural village at the foot of the Alps, is about the last place you would expect to find a high tech Porsche specialist.

RUF Automobile GmbH was started by Alois Ruf Senior back in 1939, and is today run by Alois Ruf Junior in the same family style. AUTO RUF would undergo several changes between then and the super-efficient, high tech workshops of today.

Ruf is insistent that they do not modify Porsche cars, but that they manufacture bespoke Porsche models. A visit to their operating-theatre style workshops will reveal the extent of this re-manufacture, with customers from all over the world paying for their Porsche cars to be upgraded here. Such upgrading can range from a personalised hi-fi system and upholstery improvements to a full-race spec 911 including all engine, suspension and braking components.

The Pfaffenhausen company offer a full range of engineering services from the restoration of classics to modern Porsche upgrades, manufacturing and spray painting.

The RUF RCT, which stands for RUF Carrera Turbo, was built between 1992-1994. Based on the production 964 Turbo 3.6-litre model, this car was certainly no chicken. Power was boosted from 360bhp to 370bhp thanks to the increased compression ratio and, together with RUF's own 6-speed gearbox, lifted the top speed from 174mph (280km/h) to a whopping 190mph (305km/h)

By 1993, even the spartan 911 Carrera 2 Speedster featured some comforts previously not available on this model. The improved hood offered better protection and the interior now boasted leather-upholstered Carrera RS bucket seats. Only a handful of the 930 vehicles made were fitted with dual airbags as it was thought that the low-cut windscreen would not withstand the pressure of an inflating airbag. For the DM 131,500 (US$79,500) asking price, you got electric windows while Tiptronic transmission was available as from 1993. It was all rather a far cry from the stripped out 356 Speedster of 1955

Carrera 4 '30 Jahre 911'

To commemorate the 30th anniversary of the 911, Porsche launched the '30 Jahre 911' model in 1993, based on the Carrera 4 with Turbo attributes. This combined the technical advantages of electronic and dynamically controlled 4-wheel drive together with the widened body of the Turbo model and 17-inch Cup wheels, to underline the sporting elegance of the model.

The fixed rear spoiler of the Turbo body was replaced with the extendable spoiler of the Carrera 2/4, retaining the classic 911 silhouette. Output and performance figures of the 3.6-litre boxer engine remained the same at 250bhp and a top speed of 158mph (255km/h) with the 0-62mph (0-100km/h) sprint being covered in a sporting 5.7 seconds.

The exterior was given a new anniversary body colour, Viola Metallic, specially created in the Porsche Design Studio for the occasion. Below the silver '911' engine cover badge was the wording '30 Jahre', unmistakably setting this limited edition model apart from the normal range.

Full leather fittings were trimmed in a new anniversary interior colour, Rubicon Grey. Embossed into the folding rear seat backs was the '911' script in celebration of this special model. A metal plaque set on the rear parcel shelf carried the number of each car produced in this special series – a total of only 911 cars in anniversary trim were built. Other cars with combinations of these individual attributes would make up the series total of 1500 vehicles.

Around 15 Speedsters were converted to wide body 'Turbo Look' specs, which makes this model extremely rare indeed. They cost DM 147,910 (US$89,500)

One can clearly see the wide-body attributes of this 1993 911 Carrera 4 3.6 Coupé 'Turbo Look' 'Jubiläumsmodell', featuring a 250bhp 3600cc boxer engine

"So baut man Sportwagen" says this Porsche marketing poster in the top right hand corner, announcing to the world that the 30th anniversary of the Porsche 911 was a milestone in automotive history

The Porsche 911 – a milestone in 100 years of motoring history.

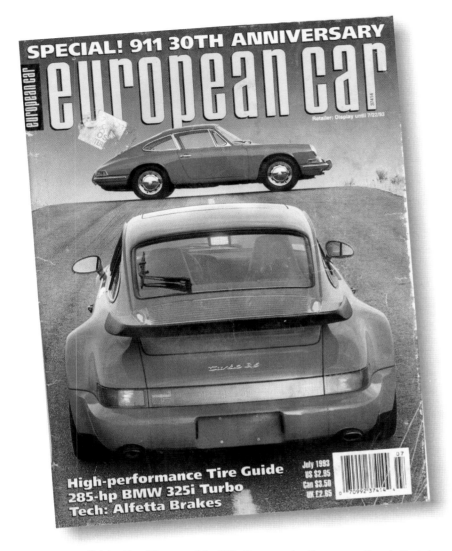

Some 911 enthusiasts prefer the profile of the Targa. This 1990 911 Carrera 4 3.6 Targa is certainly very pleasing

Celebrating 30 years of the 911, the magazine European Car *dedicated a significant slice of their July 1993 issue to the three decades of 911 development. Here the original 911 that started it all is pictured together with the latest anniversary model*

Carrera 964-Series –
The Pinnacle Of 911 Development?

Porsche have always strived to maintain a very strong family resemblance throughout the 911 range over the years, and this approach has set them apart from most other manufacturers. That the 911 appeared to remain largely unchanged for a quarter of a century without any major redesign shows just how advanced it was when it was first introduced. Once again, with the introduction of the 964 model, this enduring styling theme was retained, despite 85% of the car's components being totally new when compared with its predecessor.

Altogether, 33 prototypes were built and tested during the development phase of the 964. While developing the concept, however, feedback received from dealers and selected customers, who were aware of the impending new model, was quite clear – don't mess with the original 911 shape. These research groups were emphatic that the factory maintain the strictest adherence to the traditional 911 silhouette.

Building an entirely new car that housed a load of different technology and a revised engine, whilst retaining its traditional brand and image qualities, is, at best, quite a challenge. To do this utilising a 25-year-old shape is even more difficult. Building in the capability to support the next few generations of the same model is nigh on impossible for most design teams. In fact, not only did the 964 meet these stringent parameters, it clearly surpassed them in many respects as the Carrera 4 was a great success, receiving the accolade of the 'best 911 ever' up to that time.

Many Porsche customers, enthusiasts and company insiders felt that with the 964 the end of the line had come for that much-loved, and most recognisable of sports car shapes, the 911. Bristling with innovative features, all-wheel drive technology and aerodynamic efficiency, there were those who felt the immortal 911 had lost some of its original charm in its quest for high-tech advancement.

When Ulrich Bez arrived as head of Research & Development, he was immediately faced with the challenge of convincing Porsche's management that the 911 had not reached its development ceiling. In fact, the 964's successor, the 993, would usher in a whole new generation of development for the Porsche 911.

This medallion, featuring the 911 Turbo 3.6, was illustrated on the 1993 Porsche calendar, the year of the car's manufacture

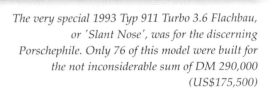

The very special 1993 Typ 911 Turbo 3.6 Flachbau, or 'Slant Nose', was for the discerning Porschephile. Only 76 of this model were built for the not inconsiderable sum of DM 290,000 (US$175,500)

A total of 1437 examples of this potent 911 Turbo 3.6 Coupé were manufactured in 1993. Boasting 360bhp, this powerhouse model had a top speed of 174mph (280km/h) and would set you back DM 204,000 (US$123,427). Porsche's Exclusive department offered a limited run of slant-nose conversions featuring pop-up headlamps and unique front spoiler with air ducts for the oil cooler. This Exclusive package offered a higher output engine, 385bhp, with larger turbocharger, altered cam profiles, modified cylinder head and inlet manifolds, auxiliary oil cooler and a four tailpipe exhaust system

Like father, like son. Ferry Porsche is pictured here in 1993 with his oldest son, Ferdinand Alexander Porsche, on the 30th anniversary of the launch of the Porsche 911. First manufactured in 1964, the 2.0-litre, 130bhp model on the left stands proudly alongside the 1993 Carrera 4 Coupé, which by this time, had increased to 3.6-litres and 250bhp. Ferdinand Alexander, or 'Butzi' as he was known, took over the management of the design studio of Porsche KG in 1961. In 1972, he, together with all other members of the Porsche family, resigned from the company when it was restructured. In 1975 he started his own design studio, Porsche Design GmbH, in new premises in Zell am See, Austria

Porsche 911 production statistics

Model Year	Model description	Units
1989	K - Series	16,488
1990	L - Series	17,768
1991	M - Series	20,072
1992	N - Series	12,415
1993	P - Series	7,265

Source: Porsche

LAST OF THE AIR-COOLED 911s

The successor to the outgoing 964-Series was a visually and mechanically much-modified 911, and first revealed at the Frankfurt Motor Show in October 1993. The internal design designation for this model was the Typ 993 (R-Programme) while publicly it would be marketed as the 911 Carrera Coupé. The world première of the new Typ 993 Cabriolet took place later, at the Detroit Motor Show in January 1994, while the European début took place at the Geneva Motor Show in March of that year.

The Typ 993 is regarded by many enthusiasts and admirers as the best of the breed, being the last 911 model ever to use the air-cooled boxer engine, Porsche's hallmark since the very first 356 model back in 1948. This was the first time in the history of the 911 that the model's basic shape was changed, with wider and flatter front wings allowing more streamlined and integrated headlamps.

TIMELINE (1994-1998):

1994	1995	1996	1997	1998
Typ 993 introduced.	911 Carrera 4, Carrera RS & GT2 launched.	1-millionth Porsche produced.	911 Carrera S launched.	Ferry Porsche dies March 27.
		GT1 launched.		Porsche 50th Anniversary.
				End of air-cooled engines for 911.

The engine underwent a thorough redesign and although the overall capacity of 3.6-litres was retained, the unit now produced 272bhp as opposed to 250bhp in the 964-Series. The manual gearbox was now a 6-speed unit as standard with a revised 4-speed Tiptronic transmission as an optional extra, while the Tiptronic S model featured steering wheel paddles for quicker gear changes.

For the 1995 model year, Porsche introduced the Carrera 4 which was immediately available in both Coupé and Cabriolet forms. The Geneva Motor Show that year witnessed the launch of the new 911 Turbo, while additional new models included a Carrera RS and, for the even more sporty drivers, the 911 GT2 was available. All in all, the first two years of the 993's existence were a busy time for the factory with so many new models and product innovations appearing. In 1996, Porsche enjoyed their highest production year yet with over 21,000 cars manufactured.

During the years 1995-1996, it seemed as though Porsche wanted to introduce as many different models as they could. This period saw the launch of the Carrera Speedster, Cabriolet Turbo, Carrera RS Coupé and Clubsport, 911 Turbo Coupé and the 911 GT2 Coupé.

The 993 T-Programme (1996 model year) also witnessed the launch of the ingenious Targa sliding roof concept, the first Targa model since the 964 Targa was phased out in 1993. The year 1997 saw the introduction of the Carrera S Coupé which married the Tiptronic S model with the wide Turbo body styling. The 1996-1997 model years also saw the launch of the 911 Carrera 4 (with improved performance) and the 911 4S Coupé.

There was no let-up in the level of activity in the 993's last full production year as Porsche introduced 21 road legal examples of the awesome GT1 in 1997, a direct off-shoot of the victorious Le Mans racer. Visually the GT1 possessed a passing resemblance to the 911 silhouette, but under the sheet steel and carbon-composite body lurked the suspension and mechanicals of a thoroughbred racer.

The Porsche Exclusive Department, the set-up responsible for building limited run or bespoke Porsche derivatives, constructed 345 examples of the Turbo S model in 1998 and, in April of that same year, 21 street-legal examples of the GT2 were built.

In 1998, the 993's final year of production, Porsche kept certain models of the air-cooled car in production overlapping with the production of the new 996 model, Porsche's first water-cooled 911. It was said at the time that this overlap in production existed in order to allow Porsche customers to become accustomed to the new generation 911 but, if truth be told, it was more likely to have been an insurance policy in case the market rejected the new water-cooled derivative.

From this angle, you can see how the front wings of the Typ 993 have been lowered, thereby improving the aerodynamics of this new 1994 911 Carrera 3.6 Coupé.

Based on the 911 Turbo body, the 1995 Porsche 911 GT2 was the fastest model introduced that year. One can see the plastic bolt-on wheel flares which replaced the normal body metal. The plastic ones were lighter as well as quicker and cheaper to replace

Launched at the 1995 Frankfurt Motor Show, the innovative 911 Targa 3.6 certainly made a big impact in the media. The new Targa was shown together with the 911 Carrera 4S for the first time at this show

This 1997 911 Turbo 3.6 Coupé belongs to Horst Marchart, an engineer with Porsche from 1960-2001. He retired while head of Research and Development after an extraordinary career spanning 41 years with the company

911% Faszination

The Last Of A Breed

The 1994 Porsche 911 Carrera 3.6 Cabriolet really did live up to its name as one of the fastest soft tops in the world, with a top speed of 167mph (270km/h)

The first public sighting of the new Typ 993 was at the Frankfurt Motor Show in September 1993. As the last of the air-cooled 911s, the Typ 993 is an important model in the company's history and, for many Porschephiles, it marked the passing of the true 911. However, the 993 Carrera ushered in the age of motoring sophistication, an era in which some sports cars matured into more luxurious grand tourers as they strove to attract the car-buyers' attention.

Electronic driver aids were deemed necessary as more people, who perhaps lacked the ability to handle a high powered sports car adequately, were now buying the 911. As a result, Porsche now offered an improved ABS anti-lock braking system, which consisted of a dynamic limited-slip system with an ABD (Active Brake Differential - effectively a traction control aid) and a limited slip differential. Launched with the Carrera 4 was the optional Tiptronic S transmission with steering wheel-mounted shift buttons to eliminate the risk of drivers dropping their eyes to the gear stick while changing up or down.

Launched as a 1994 year model, the bodywork of the 911 Carrera was smoother than its predecessor with a noticeably more aerodynamic front end, showing some styling cues from the 959. Styling of the 993 was by Englishman Tony Hatter under the supervision of design chief Harm Lagaay. The redesign, or major face-lift as Porsche writer Paul Frère put it, was widely seen as highly successful and compared favourably with the models of the early 1970s before the impact-absorbing bumpers disturbed the 911's design. The 911 models belonging to the G-Series (mid to late-1970s) and even the 964-Series, tended to look rather chunky below the waistline, but the 993 saw a return to the more elegant styling.

Mechanically and structurally, the Typ 993 was more of an evolution of the previous model, sharing the same roof and bonnet panels, while some mechanical parts were also carried over. The 993 was notable for its aluminium components used in the new multi-link rear suspension, which was mounted on a subframe. This unit was dubbed the LSA axle, which stood for Light-Stable-Agile.

The sense of speed in this picture has been enhanced by the photographer's use of a slow shutter speed. This vehicle is a 911 Carrera 3.6 Coupé

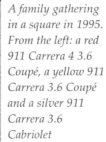

A family gathering in a square in 1995. From the left: a red 911 Carrera 4 3.6 Coupé, a yellow 911 Carrera 3.6 Coupé and a silver 911 Carrera 3.6 Cabriolet

One of Britain's top performance motoring publications, Performance Car, wanted to do a comparative photo shoot with similarly-coloured Coupé and Cabriolet versions of the new Typ 993. While the Cabriolet was no problem, as this was the official 1994 Porsche UK press car, the team had to search for a yellow Coupé, eventually finding a privately-owned one in Scotland

A group of journalists is pictured while taking a rest during the Performance Car 'Car of the Year' shoot out around the Cadwell Park race circuit. The Porsche 993 is seen leading the pack in this comparative test during a stop-over in the area around the Yorkshire Moors

911 Carrera RS 3.8

The 911 Carrera RS was a model for all sporting-oriented drivers. Available as a standard (if one can use that term) factory RS, this car came fitted with front and rear spoilers and at 1270kg, was a full 100kg lighter than the 911 Carrera model. The 3746cc RS was only available in rear-wheel drive form.

For those wishing for yet more performance, there was the 'Club Sport' package which offered a choice of two gearboxes (for track work), a full roll cage, battery-kill switch, fire extinguisher and a six-point harness. This gave the Sport option Carrera RS a 0-62mph (0-100km/h) sprint time of 5.0 seconds with a top speed of 172mph (277km/h).

The red Carrera RS in the background is equipped with the optional Sports Package, while the yellow model is the standard street car. The 911 Carrera RS 3.8 produced a whopping 300bhp

In preparation for the car's launch, a prototype 911 Carrera RS 3.8 Coupé was put through a series of chassis tests in 1994 at the Contidrom, the dedicated test facility belonging to Continental Tyre, near Hannover

"What are the chances we'd both have brand new black Porsches?"

World Rally Champion, Carlos Sainz, was drafted in to test the Porsche 911 Carrera 4 3.6 Coupé in 1994

Der neue Carrera: 911% Faszination.

If you want to go shopping for Porsche memorabilia, you need to have the right bag for your goodies. The image on this shopping bag is of the 911 Carrera Coupé with the special Weissach performance package

Launched in the autumn of 1994 (1995 model year), the Porsche 911 Carrera 4 3.6 was immediately available in both Coupé and Cabriolet forms. It employed the proven 3.6-litre engine, but customers could opt to have their car modified by Porsche Exclusive Department, with a 3.8-litre engine developing 285bhp

Racing The 993

Amateur and professional drivers alike were quick to recognise the performance potential of the Typ 993. During the lifespan of this model, the Porsche Carrera Cup and Supercup race series continued to grow in popularity around the world with both drivers and spectators.

The year 1994 was the first in which the 993 was used in the Supercup series. Here Frenchman, Emmanuel Collard, is seen in action at Hockenheim in August of that year. In its maiden season, the 993 was still raced with the car's standard, extendable rear spoiler

For the Supercup series the following year, the 993 was fitted with a fixed high level rear spoiler. This is a presentation model of the 1995 season car

The 'Spring/Summer' edition of the Performance Products *mail-order catalogue cost US$5.00, and offered an attractive 15% discount off certain items until the end of April 1995. This company, which had been going since 1964, the same year in which the 911 was introduced, specialised in components and restoration parts for all manner of 911s*

Typ 993 Turbo

This 911 Turbo was introduced in the spring of 1995 at the Geneva Motor Show and now featured twin turbochargers. It was the first standard production Porsche so equipped and the first 911 Turbo with all-wheel drive. The similarity in specification and performance levels inspired several comparative road tests with none other than the Porsche 959, which shared the same technology in their twin compound turbochargers.

Porsche Exclusive Department offered the long-awaited sports suspension upgrade for the Turbo in the model's last year of production, 1998. In the model cull at the end of the 1997 production year, the Turbo escaped the axe and lived on until the introduction of the Typ 993's successor.

At the 1997 Geneva Motor Show, the 911 Turbo shared the stand with the awesome Porsche GT1

First produced in 1975, the Turbo had matured into a powerful and luxurious grand touring sports car. This is the 1997 model 911 Turbo 3.6 Coupé

Built only between November 1997 and April 1998, the 911 Turbo S 3.6 was yet another development by the Porsche Exclusive Department. Only 345 of these cars were made and cost DM 304,650 (US$175,000)

Build quantity – one vehicle! This is the only 911 Carrera Speedster made in 1995 and it was a special one-off for F.A. 'Butzi' Porsche, created by the Exclusive Department (the licence plate 'S FP 222' stands for 'Stuttgart Ferdinand Porsche'). The car was based on a 911 Carrera and fitted with a Tiptronic gearbox. Price – not for sale!

No 252, January 1995

Christophorus
Porsche Magazine 1/95

Lifestyle:
fascinating trip
to Piemonte with the
Carrera 4 Cabriolet

Motor sport:
Porsche's new
race car for the
1995 GT season

Perspectives:
Porsche concept
for a Chinese
family car

Adventure:
through the
Mongolian High Altai
on horseback

911 GT 2

Christophorus magazine ran the GT2 model on the front cover of their January 1995 issue

This well-known 911 GT2 racer was also made in 1:43 scale by the toy maker, Minichamps

Porsche showed off the race version of their 911 GT2 car at the Essen Motor Show in February 1995

This badge was presented to journalists attending the launch of the 911 Turbo in the French resort of Domaine de Châteauneuf, a splendid 18th century country house in the foothills of the Sainte-Baume mountains in Provence

911 Turbo

Domaine de Châteauneuf

Featured on the cover of the July 1995 issue of Porsche Report *is the potent 911 GT2 Coupé*

May 1995

July 1995

The new (1995) 911 Turbo Coupé was shown on the May 1995 cover of Porsche Report, *the Porsche Club of South Africa monthly magazine*

THIS MONTH — ON THE ROAD with 'OFF ROAD' — ELECTION RESULTS — OCTOBER DRIVING SCHOOL — EVOLUTION OF THE AUTO

PORSCHE CLUB OF AMERICA SAN DIEGO REGION — Windblown Witness — DECEMBER 1995

The land of bright sun and long beaches, southern California, is Porsche-territory. The San Diego chapter of the Porsche Club of America produces its monthly magazine called the Windblown Witness. *Covers for December 1995 and June 1996 are shown here*

THIS MONTH — PROGRESSIVE DINNER AD — HEART ASSN GOLF TOURNY — HYDROPLANING GLASS CLEANING — AUTO MUSEUM RECIPE

PORSCHE CLUB OF AMERICA SAN DIEGO REGION — Windblown Witness — JUNE 1996

911 Targa

In spite of the technically advanced roof system, form still followed function and the 911 Targa 3.6 was capable of a top speed of 170mph (275km/h)

Launched in the autumn of 1995 (1996 model year), this new Targa featured an altogether different roof system from any previous Targa. The 1996 version was based on a modified Cabriolet body, to which was attached a complete pre-assembled roof unit. This consisted of three glass components: a wind deflector, a moving roof section and the rear window.

Opening the glass roof, either partly or fully, raised the small front shield to act as a wind deflector. With the main roof in the open position and with the wind deflector raised, the electrically-operated 'inner' shade could be partially or fully closed for additional protection against draughts or the hot sun, if needed. The advantage of this new Targa system was that the driver did not need to stop to remove the roof panel as with the earlier version. At the touch of a button, the glass roof would slide back underneath the rear windscreen without impairing rearward vision, allowing the occupants to enjoy the feeling of open-air motoring.

This photo shows the sliding roof open with the large glass roof panel fully retracted and now positioned 'underneath' the rear windscreen

Here the sliding glass roof is half open with the wind deflector deployed

Porsche's model line-up for 1996: front row, from left to right – 911 Turbo 3.6, 911 Carrera 4S 3.6, 911 Targa 3.6. Back row, from left to right: 911 Carrera 3.6 Cabriolet, 911 Carrera 3.6 Coupé and 911 Carrera RS 3.8

The 911 4S, launched together with the Targa model in the autumn of 1995, featured wide Turbo bodywork, but had an extendable rear spoiler instead of the Turbo's fixed wing. The 4S was only available with a 6-speed gearbox and all-wheel drive. This centre page spread was taken from the 911 model range brochure for the 1996 model year

The new 911 Carrera 4S

First: four-wheel drive.
Second: Turbo brakes and visual enhancements.
Third: Turbo interior.
Fourth: 911 Carrera 4S.

The result is a feast for the eye: the car has lowered suspension, and features the nose and braking system of the 911 Turbo. It has flared sills and a flared rear body, 18-inch wheels, and a dynamic differential locking system. Not to forget air conditioning, trip computer, all-leather interior, electric seat adjustment, rear windscreen wiper, radio and stereo sound system as standard equipment.

The 911 Carrera 4S offers you not only visual enhancements, but impressive engineering benefits too.

This smart gift set consists of two lapel badges, featuring the 911 Carrera 4S and Targa models, and was to be given to journalists at the Frankfurt Motor Show in 1995. In fact, so many were made that they were also given to general visitors to the Porsche stand that year, and even the following year

July 15, 1996 signalled an important milestone in Porsche's history, with the production of the one-millionth Porsche sports car, a Typ 993 Coupé. In a long-standing tradition upheld by Porsche and the state of Baden-Württemberg, Ferry Porsche and Dr. Wendelin Wiedeking handed over the police patrol car to Erwin Teufel, Prime Minister of the German state for use by their 'Autobahn' Police. The picture, taken at the Porsche Werk 2 in Stuttgart-Zuffenhausen, shows Ferry Porsche with the millionth Porsche sports car

RUF 911

As mentioned elsewhere in this book, RUF Autos in Pfaffenhausen, southern Germany, manufactured some of the highest-performing Porsche sports cars in the world. Effectively, each time that Porsche produced a new model themselves, RUF would get an influx of orders for their own version.

RUF manufactured these models to the highest standards, making many components themselves or having them manufactured especially. This makes most RUF Porsches unique.

'Porsche Polizei Typ 993' – Porsche number 1,000,000 became a symbolic state patrol vehicle, being used mostly for parades and public relations rather than apprehending criminals

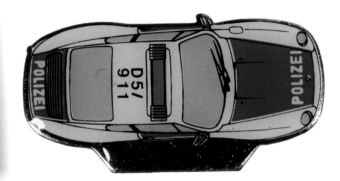

The RUF Turbo R, built between 1994-1997, lifted the standard power output from 408bhp to 490bhp. The 0-62mph (0-100km/h) sprint dropped from a rapid 4.5 seconds to a blistering 3.6 seconds, while the top speed increased by 13% to a whopping 204mph (328km/h). This exclusivity did not come cheap at DM 298,000 (US$184,000)

An 1:18 scale model was produced of the one millionth Porsche sports car

With the introduction of the 993 Carrera, RUF produced their own version of this Coupé in 1994

Aloise Ruf stands next to the very powerful RUF CTR II, a 520bhp supercar with a top speed of 211mph (340km/h). Built between 1996-2000, this model was extensively upgraded and included a reshaped nose providing more downforce and the roof gutters were removed for improved aerodynamics. The reshaped engine lid, with integral rear wing, extended across the full width of the car with ducts channelling air to the intercoolers. DM 425,000 (US$282,500) would buy you the basic car, while the 4-wheel drive option cost an extra DM 21,000 and the lightweight Kevlar body panels added a further DM 27,600

PORSCHE

Modellspiegel
1970 – 1996

All the specifications of Porsche's production cars between the years 1970-1996 are contained within the pages of this handy reference manual

Pikes Peak International Hill Climb, that famous and most dangerous of motor sport events in Colorado, USA, has produced some epic battles over the years. Drivers in a wide range of vehicles battle it out over the twisting 12.4 mile course to the top of this 14,110 foot peak. Jeff Zwart won the 1998 event in a Porsche 911 Turbo S 3.6

A private entry in the 1997 Le Mans 24-Hour race saw the 911 GT2 (number 74) of Bruno Eichmann, Andy Pilgrim and André Ahrlé finish strongly in 10th place overall

PORSCHE
993
The Essential Companion™

KING OF PORSCHE

A...

Adrian Streather produced this weighty tome on the Typ 993, charting every little detail and modification during the manufacturing life cycle of this model. This publication has 688 pages and 1300 photographs making it extremely comprehensive

The fourth in a five-book series by Brian Long covers the Porsche 911 between the years 1987-1997

BRIAN LONG

PORSCHE
911
THE DEFINITIVE HISTORY
1987 to 1997

This important little badge given out at the Geneva Motor Show commemorates two very significant Porsche milestones. Here, the lower car, the last of the air-cooled Porsche 911 sports cars, shares the same platform as the first of the new water-cooled cars, the Boxster of 1997. The 911 Carrera S was the last air-cooled 911 model to be made

The Porsche Club of Great Britain used to produce a monthly publication, Trading Post, *giving details of vehicles and parts that members had for sale. Having started in the early 1990s,* Trading Post *ran as a separate publication until it was incorporated into their monthly magazine,* Porsche Post, *in 2000. This is a copy of the April '97 issue of* Trading Post

TRADING
Post

PORSCHE CLUB GB

April 1997   Newsletter & Advertiser   No. 4/97

On time or not?

Turbo Day 97
6 April 1997

16th Grand National Porsche Autojumble

GT1 Racer

Initially two of these rather special road-going cars were built in 1996 to satisfy GT1 racing rules. The cost was a mere DM 1,550,000 (US$1,030,200). However, only a single external buyer would ultimately be successful in acquiring one of the pair as the other car was retained by the factory. With 544bhp on tap and a top speed of 193mph (310km/h), this was not a car for the faint-hearted.

The rest of the eager band of buyers would have to wait until the following year when a further 20 road-legal cars were built. This later batch more closely resembled the next generation 911, the Typ 996, and so this model will not be covered here.

This roadgoing example of the 911 GT1 was pictured driving through the streets of Stuttgart in 1996 still wearing its trade plates

The 50th anniversary (1948-1998) issue of the Porsche in-house magazine, Christophorus, appropriately shows the image of the first 356 model made in 1948, reflected in the wing mirror of the 1998 Typ 993 model

Porsche Magazine

Christophorus

Anniversary Edition · June 1998

50 years of Porsche
1948 – 1998

In celebration of Porsche's 50th anniversary in 1998, a procession of Porsche sports cars wound its way through the streets of Stuttgart. Here a 911 GT1 passes an observation point in the city

Pictured at a classic car fair in Stuttgart, this selection contained Porsche models manufactured by various toy companies around the world

The last air-cooled Porsche 911 left the Stuttgart-Zuffenhausen assembly line on March 31, 1998. Sadly, Ferry Porsche died just a few days prior to this date, ironically on the same day as the engine for this final car was manufactured. This last air-cooled 911 was ordered by American comedian, Jerry Seinfeld

Corgi, the model maker, produced this striking Porsche presentation set. Although it contains models other than the 911, it is perhaps significant that five out of the 10 models in the set are 911s

Porsche 911 production statistics

Model Year	Model description	Units
1994	R - Series	12,128
1995	S - Series	14,647
1996	T - Series	21,602
1997	V - Series	15,972
1998	W - Series	13,783

Source: Porsche

THE ICONIC 911

Back in 1964 when the first 911s were being delivered to lucky customers, electronic driver aids, airbags and ABS brakes were the things of science fiction. Such advanced technology and the implications they held for automotive engineering had not yet even been considered. In most production cars, seats belts, if fitted, consisted of a basic lap strap - inertia reel belts were still a good 15 years away.

TIMELINE:

1959	1963	1964	1974	1989	1993	1998
First '911' concepts take shape.	901/911 is shown to the public at IAA Frankfurt.	First 901s delivered to customers.	G-Series 911 introduced.	Typ 964 introduced.	Typ 993 introduced.	Ferry Porsche dies March 27, 1998.
						Porsche 50th anniversary.

Air conditioning was mostly for wealthy folk who could afford cars large enough to accommodate the huge compressor with the ancillary plumbing necessary in those days. The author can remember sitting in the front seat of a top-of-the-range Mercedes Benz S-Class in 1973 and having blue knees from the powerful blower of the air conditioning unit. This had been factory-fitted as an optional extra and, as the air outlets sat beneath the dashboard, they delivered a blast at knee level; air conditioning was still an uncommon extra and not properly coordinated into the production process.

The Porsche 911 had to grow in stature to accommodate the demands of the car buyer who increasingly came to expect more than just performance from his or her sports car. By the late 1980s and early 1990s, such cars had become an extension of the person and thus needed to portray a certain image. That image was success, wealth, achievement or recognition. Performance was not always paramount and comfort began to play an increasingly important role. A greater percentage of customers were women and, as women are generally shorter than men, seat positioning and steering wheel adjustment became important.

Accommodating these extra features resulted in the car becoming heavier, which necessitated a bigger engine and greater performance for those who did expect their Porsche to be a high performance car.

Taking these developments into account, the Porsche engineers did an outstanding job, constantly adapting the 911 to accommodate the myriad safety regulations increasingly demanded of manufacturers. Additionally, they worked wonders in preserving the basic shape of the 911 and enabling it to swallow the large quantity of electronic sensors and motors necessary to move seats at the touch of a button, operate the sun roof and windows, operate ABS brakes... The list goes on.

In the spring of 1995, Porsche launched its Tequipment programme of accessories and add-on items for customising owner's existing cars, while the Exclusive Department catered for modifications to new cars at the production stage.

The art of progress – produced in the same year, a 1964 Porsche 911 2.0 Coupé on the right sits alongside its predecessor, the 356 C Coupé, in the grounds of Porsche Werk 2

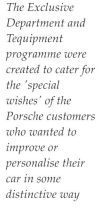

The Exclusive Department and Tequipment programme were created to cater for the 'special wishes' of the Porsche customers who wanted to improve or personalise their car in some distinctive way

Exclusive & Tequipment

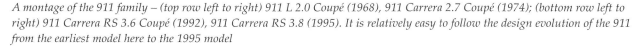

A montage of the 911 family – (top row left to right) 911 L 2.0 Coupé (1968), 911 Carrera 2.7 Coupé (1974); (bottom row left to right) 911 Carrera RS 3.6 Coupé (1992), 911 Carrera RS 3.8 (1995). It is relatively easy to follow the design evolution of the 911 from the earliest model here to the 1995 model

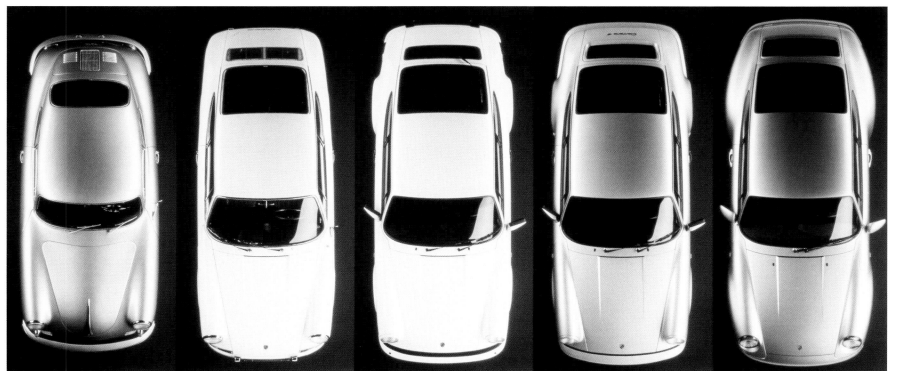

This collection of studio images (from left to right) shows the Porsche 356 B Carrera 1600 GT (1960), 911 2.0 Coupé (1963), 911 Carrera 3.2 Coupé (1987), 911 Carrera 2 3.6 Coupé (1989) and 911 Carrera 3.6 Coupé (1993). It is interesting to note how much larger the 993 is when compared with the first 911. The 993 had dimensions (length x width x height): 4245 x 1735 x 1300mm, while the first 911 measured: 4163 x 1610 x 1320mm

911 Silhouette Design Icon

Early Porsche publicity referred to the 'timeless shape' of the car. What makes the 911's lines ageless is that the original car's design philosophy was dictated by function and not fashion. In 1948, when the first 356 was penned by Erwin Komenda, it followed the basic shape of the Volkswagen Beetle, which was itself a very 'flow oriented' design. There was nothing on the market quite like the streamlined 356 back then, as the little car from the mountains of Austria dared to challenge the standards of accepted mechanical/engineering convention with its rear-mounted engine.

Placement of the engine in the tail of the car had several advantages, both from a design and engineering perspective. With no engine up front, it meant that the nose could be lower which resulted in the whole car having a lower silhouette. With the air-cooled engine hanging over the rear axle, no front-mounted radiators were required which saved weight, allowed improved rear wheel traction and handling, and also provided greater interior space.

For the new 911, Ferry Porsche again wanted a shape that would not be influenced by short-term thinking or industry trends. In essence, the 911 was to be a modernisation of that natural and timeless 356 design, a form that was based on a tear-drop shape. With such a strong foundation on which to build, the 911 could most certainly follow on where the 356 left off.

Of course this runs the risk of becoming predictable or repetitive in your design, but when you can continually refresh your brand, as Porsche have done, the marketing payback can be far beyond that of the competition. To continue to design a car that looks so similar in shape and style, whilst still incorporating new and innovative technology and engineering advances, is more difficult than to design that same car to look totally new and different every time.

Ferry Porsche was adamant in 1963 that the 356 successor should also have a fastback shape with the capacity for two occasional seats in the rear, and not be a full four-seater. One of the requirements for the design of the 911 back in the early 1960s was to modernise the basic flowing shape of the 356 to the extent that the new car could be as recognisable as its predecessor, but also provide a platform for future design development. Not in their wildest dreams could the company have foreseen the success that the 911 would eventually become.

Designing successive new 911 models according to the original style created by Butzi Porsche was risky for the company, should they get it wrong, but it was demanded by the devoted army of followers and enthusiasts around the world. If today's 911 looked significantly different from the first '901' shown at the Frankfurt Show back in September 1963, then it would no longer be a 911, so entrenched has this model become in automotive folklore.

From top to bottom we have the Porsche 356 B Carrera 1600 GT (1960), 911 2.0 Coupé (1963), 911 Carrera 3.2 Coupé (1987), 911 Carrera 2 3.6 Coupé (1989) and 911 Carrera 3.6 Coupé (1993). This photographic comparison shows how similar the silhouette of the Porsche 356 and the Typ 993 are, despite the 33 year age gap

The 911 In Society

In human terms, the 911 might have been likened to pioneers such as Amelia Earhart or Donald Campbell, dedicated adventurers in their respective fields. In the movie world, it may have been compared to endearing classics like *Dr. Zhivago*, *Lawrence of Arabia* or *The Italian Job*. In the world of music, the 911 might have resembled the evergreen Tom Jones or perhaps the vivacious Celine Dion or maybe even the raucous Rolling Stones. The common thread running through all of these timeless classics is the high personal achievement or exceptional quality of the production which has survived the ravages of time.

When any of these actors or artists performed, you would know exactly what to expect, or when one of those classic movies appeared on the screen, you knew that you would be in for a good evening's entertainment. Their reputation preceded them because their performance was predictable in so far as quality is concerned. In the same way, the Porsche 911 has evolved from its pioneering and uncertain beginnings, into a very desirable and respected automobile, and today you know exactly what you will experience behind the wheel - good quality, high performance, intoxicating sound and a highly recognisable symbol of sports car motoring.

The most iconic thing about the 911 is its instantly recognisable shape, which stands as a testament to its creator. Walk into the parking lot at the local superstore, and a Porsche 911 will stand out even if it is parked in the furthest corner. It is in this area the Porsche designers have succeeded where others have failed, as through the familiar shape of the 911, the company has created and maintained the value of its greatest asset. Instant recognition of your brand by the market is the ultimate measure of success that any company can achieve for its product, and Porsche has done so successfully by not changing the basic design of the 911 since its launch.

Taken in September 1996, this aerial view of Porsche Werk 8 (Weissach) shows how the test facility had developed into its own little community, when compared with the photos of the site earlier in this book. By 1995, around 1800 employees were based at this site

Touring with a 911 is 'driving in its purest form', the Porsche marketing slogan tells us. This is a 1994 Carrera 3.6 Coupé

The caption reads – '2400 guests, including 120 top sporting figures, celebrated the German Ball des Sports in Wiesbaden. Star of the evening was a red 911 Coupé which was raffled off as a first prize in a draw for German Sports Aid'. Porsche CEO, Dr. Wendelin Wiedeking was there to present the prize to the winner

A Porsche GT2 is surrounded by some high-powered personalities, including two space shuttle astronauts, who were special guests at Weissach in 1995. Standing inside the door on the left is Klaus Bischof, head of the Porsche museum. Also in attendance are several Porsche test drivers as well as Jens Torner, from the Porsche Historisches Archiv in Stuttgart

Pictured here is a very handsome 1992 model 911 Carrera 2 3.6 Cabriolet. The Cabriolet body style was reintroduced into the model line-up in 1983, this time as a 911 derivative, after the last 356 C Carrera 2 Cabriolet had gone out of production in 1964. Today, the Cabriolet is a permanent member of the 911 line-up

On the left is a 1965 911 2.0 Coupé (belonging to the Porsche Museum) while on the right is a 911 Turbo 3.6 from the 1993 model year. Despite the obvious differences in size and detailing, this photo highlights just how advanced the 1965 model was in its day. Having said that, the 993 model certainly represented a significant and very noticeable maturing of the original 911 design, with smoother and more rounded curves and corners

Heavy metal band, Judas Priest, wrote a song which captured the power and urge of the Porsche turbo. Called *Turbo Lover*, the song appeared on their *Turbo* album released by CBS Records in 1986. In writing this song, band members Glenn Tipton, Rob Halford and KK Downing were celebrating the 911's Turbo engine.

Then we race together. We can ride forever
Wrapped in horsepower, driving into fury
Changing gear I pull you tighter to me

We hold each other closer, as we shift to overdrive
And everything goes rushing by, with every nerve alive
We move so fast it seems as though we've taken to the sky
Love machines in harmony, we hear the engines cry.

I'm your turbo lover
Tell me there's no other
I'm your turbo lover
Better run for cover

Verses two and three of the song, which appear above with the chorus, leave the reader (or listener) with little doubt as to what the subject matter is all about. The album cover shows a hand gripping the gear shift of a car with the title Turbo written above the driver's wrist (Turbo' by Judas Priest, reproduced by kind permission of Sony BMG Music Entertainment (UK) Ltd.)

One Good Porsche Leads To Another!

The 911's history is peppered with short production model runs and concept racers that have in some way contributed to a significant or even legendary model later on down the line. As has been explained elsewhere in this book, Porsche have never been hasty in bringing a new car to market or preparing one for the track at short notice, as all steps in this process first need to be thoroughly tested and proven.

An example of this would be the 911 R of 1967, which ultimately led to the production of the 911 Carrera RS 2.7 of 1973, which provided the sporting enthusiast and amateur competitor with a ready-to-race dream car. The M471 (Sport) and M472 (Touring) set the sports car industry on its head, with the affordability and flexibility that the whole 911 sporting package offered.

The heritage created by the 1973 Carrera RS 2.7 was later carried through to the Carrera Club Sport of 1987 and on into the 964 RS (1992) as seen in the accompanying photograph.

Pictured (left) is a 1987 911 Carrera Clubsport. This car, one of only 53 right hand drive cars made, was owned by well-known British motoring photographer, John Colley; the 964 RS in the middle is the official 1992 press car from Porsche Cars Great Britain, while the car on the right is a 1973 Carrera RS 2.7

Personalised 911

After many years of modifying cars within the customer repair department run by Rolf Sprenger, Porsche decided to create two distinct channels through which the special wishes of the customer could be handled. Firstly, the Exclusive Department dealt with changes to a new vehicle still in the production phase, while the Tequipment programme catered for improvements to a customer's vehicle after it had left the showroom.

Although in theory the same products could be fitted to a car by either of these two departments, the Exclusive Department dealt only with parts fitted to the vehicle itself, while Tequipment also marketed accessories that enhanced or protected the vehicle, such as a special car cover or ski rack.

This development arose out of the increase in customer requests for the personalisation of their cars, and it was thought that the creation of individual formal marketing and technical programmes for these services should be created.

Such special wishes for the Tequipment service included the installation of a preferred sound system, a mobile telephone, a certain upholstery colour or a respray of the whole car. Other requests even extended as far as an upgrade of the engine to race spec or the full restoration of a customer's cherished classic Porsche sports car.

One Arabian Sheik had his 959 reupholstered throughout in his own personal shade of orange leather, including the steering wheel, which carried his family coat of arms in solid gold. This work would all have been carried out by the Exclusive Department. This particular customer had seven 959s in his collection

This 993 has been comprehensively upgraded by the Exclusive Department to include a full-width carbon-fibre finish dashboard with a similar appearance for the steering wheel. The seats, dashboard and carpeting were all in a matching colour while the mobile telephone aerial can be seen prominently fixed to the windscreen frame

The Exclusive Department issued this marketing booklet in 1995 promoting the special range of options available to customers

Through the Exclusive Department, one could also order this handy Porsche tyre pressure gauge with a new 911

Porsche issued this dedicated Tequipment poster showing a 1995 Carrera with upgraded front and rear spoilers which were available through this options programme

Mirror, Mirror ....

A photographic study reveals how the changes in shape and style of 911 exterior rear view mirrors has evolved over the years. From the small round chrome ones, through larger rectangular ones, to the 'elephant ears' of the mid-1970s. Thereafter followed a trend towards more streamlined mirrors in the 1990s.

The 1960s saw a very contemporary round, conical shape to the exterior mirror

1970 saw the earlier shape slightly flatter in profile but still rounded

With the launch of the Carrera RS 2.7 in 1973 came a swing to the larger rectangular shape

Under the skin, the 1988 Porsche 959 was all about power, speed and technology. On the outside, the supercar's streamlined body contours meant the wing mirror had to be a body hugging shape

The 1976 year model could be recognised by their electrically adjustable, heated, body-coloured wing mirrors. Because these mirrors stood out in such a pronounced fashion, they were dubbed 'elephant ears'

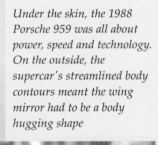

The Typ 993 was merely an evolution of both the 959 and the Typ 964, and was actually quite an attractive style, as mirrors go

Making The Right Impression

In the autumn of 1994, Porsche began to sell 'Selection' lifestyle products. This extensive programme included textiles, leather accessories and a specially developed set of suitcases for the 911 series.

In an effort to encourage a wider group of drivers to use their cars, the company launched the 'Porsche Travel Club' at the 1995 Frankfurt Motor Show with a large selection of international adventure and experience tours. With the 'Travel Club', the 'Selection' lifestyle products, and their 'Tequipment' and Exclusive programmes, the company now catered for the driver who wanted to enjoy touring to the full.

Ludwigsburg is the main centre for Porsche's marketing operations in Germany and the range of products offered through the Selection programme can be seen in this factory showroom in February 1997. Products included scale models, briefcase, bicycle rack, tie pins, cuff links, clothing, leatherwear, watches, handbags and much more

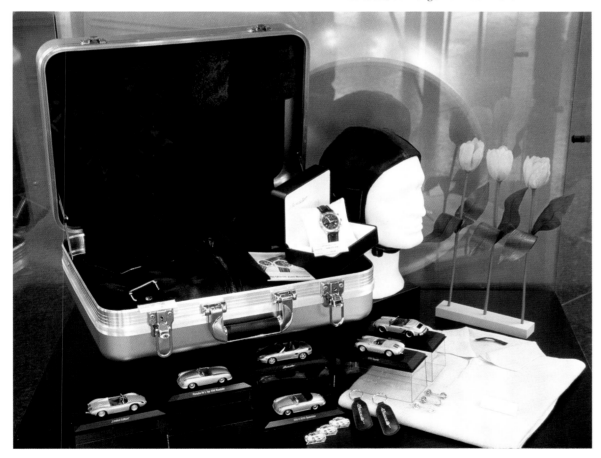

PORSCHE

Travel Club
Destination Excitement

Porsche issued this booklet when it launched the Travel Club in 1995

Money Matters

After three difficult trading years, and with a cumulative deficit of DM 450m (US$314m), CEO Dr. Wendelin Wiedeking was able to confirm at the end of the 1994/95 fiscal year that the economic turnaround had been successful. Thanks to improved sales and, above all, to the measures taken to boost productivity, the company was able to publish greatly improved figures.

The following year brought independent confirmation of the productivity improvements when the company was awarded the title 'Industrial Plant of the Year' jointly by the weekly publication, *Produktion*, and the business consultancy, A.T. Kearney. This confirmed Porsche as having the most efficient production facility in Germany.

In 1998, Dr. Wendelin Wiedeking announced at the stockholders' general meeting that the profit before tax for the 1997/98 financial year had risen dramatically to DM 324.4m (US$184.5m). This resulted in after-tax earnings of DM 276.9m (US$157.4m), the highest in the company's history.

INTERN *Carrera*

Engine assembly at Porsche's main plant in Zuffenhausen. Boards above the various workstations highlight the range of cost cutting and productivity improvement goals that helped the company to achieve its overall objective to reverse the downward financial spiral

Informationen aus dem Unternehmen

Auszeichnung *Die Porsche AG wurde zur „Fabrik des Jahres 1996" gekürt*

„Alle Produktionsmitarbeiter haben diesen Preis verdient"

Stellvertretend für die ganze Mannschaft nahmen etwa 20 Mitarbeiter aus der Produktion gemeinsam mit ihrem Vorstand Dr. Uwe Loos die Siegertrophäe im Wettbewerb „Fabrik des Jahres 1996" in Empfang.

Produktionsmitarbeiter mit Siegertrophäe: „Mit ihrem Engagement dazu beigetragen, daß Porsche den Titel errungen hat"

Zwei Tage lang haben die Mitarbeiter der Produktion ein ganz besonderes Interesse auf sich gezogen: Etwa 150 Vertreter aus über 70 Unternehmen waren nach Stuttgart gereist, um sich über Konzeption und Arbeitsweise der „Fabrik des Jahres 1996" zu informieren.
Den ersten Preis im von der Unternehmensberatung A. T. Kearney und der Wochenzeitung „Produktion" branchenübergreifend ausgeschriebenen Wettbewerb nahmen Produktionsvorstand Dr. Uwe Loos und gut 20 Produktionsmitarbeiter gemeinsam und stellvertretend für die gesamte Mannschaft entgegen.
„Schließlich haben alle Produktionsmitarbeiterinnen und -mitarbeiter mit ihrem einzigartigen Engagement dazu beigetragen, daß Porsche diesen Titel errungen hat – also haben alle diesen Preis verdient", unterstrich Dr. Loos in seiner Dankesrede.

Dr. Roland Hornstein, Hauptbereichsleiter Produktion der Canon Giessen GmbH, die im vergangenen Jahr als Sieger aus dem Unternehmensvergleich hervorgegangen war, überreichte dem Porsche-Team die Siegertrophäe.
Insgesamt hatten sich 64 Firmen um den begehrten Titel beworben und alle relevanten Daten über 61 Themenkomplexe hinweg für die branchenneutrale Fragebogenauswertung zur Verfügung gestellt und einem Ranking unterzogen – die Porsche-Produktion ging dabei als Sieger hervor. Die Hauptkriterien, die die Jury in diesem „Benchmarking" als ausschlaggebend für die unternehmerischen Erfolge ermittelte, betrafen insgesamt herausragende Leistungen in den Disziplinen Kostenreduzierung, Kundenorientierung und Organisation, speziell auf den Produktionsbereich des Unternehmens bezogen.

Im Rahmen des zweitägigen Seminars im Dorint-Hotel „Fontana" in Stuttgart-Vaihingen (Generalthema: „So arbeiten die besten Fabriken") berichteten die Porsche-„Produktioner" über die erfolgreichen Strategien, für die der Sportwagenhersteller ausgezeichnet worden ist. Die neue Fabrik wurde im Film vorgestellt, die Mitarbeiter erläuterten die Arbeitsweise in den Bereichen Roh-bau, Lackiererei und Montage. Porsche wurde darüber hinaus für die beispielhafte Mitarbeitermotivation im Rahmen des Porsche-Verbesserungs-Prozesses gewürdigt.
Über die Inhalte und Ziele der PVP-Schulungen und über das gut funktionierende Betriebliche Vorschlagswesen informierten die Porsche-Mitarbeiter die Seminarteilnehmer ebenfalls „aus erster Hand". Die Vertreter der übrigen neun Unternehmen aus den Top Ten des Wettbewerbs – mit nur einer Ausnahme gehören alle weiteren Gewinner der Automobil-Zulieferindu-strie an – stellten dem Fachpubli-kum ebenfalls ihre von der Jury prämierten Produktionskonzepte vor.

Porsche's in-house newspaper, Carrera, *carried an article in the December 1996 issue announcing the Industrial Plant of the Year award had been conferred on the company. The lady in the centre is holding the trophy*

Systemverantwortliche *Der direkte Draht von Zuffenhausen nach Weissach*

Werker und Entwickler im Dialog

Die Prozeßfähigkeit eines neuen Systems soll bereits im Entwicklungsprozeß berücksichtigt werden

ster". „Oftmals liefern sie Vorschläge zur Verbesserung gleich mit. Diese Zusammenarbeit haben wir in unserem Team sehr zu schätzen gelernt. Wir haben uns klar entschieden, den engen Bezug zur Produkti-on in Zukunft noch intensi-

Ferry Porsche Dies

On March 27, 1998, Professor Ferry Porsche died in Zell am See, Austria, aged 88. Three days later he was laid to rest in the memorial chapel on the family's Schüttgut estate. An official memorial service was held at Porsche's Zuffenhausen plant on April 3.

Dr. Wolfgang Porsche addresses guests and attendees at the memorial service held for Ferry Porsche at the Zuffenhausen plant. Behind the speaker is a large image of Ferry Porsche

The Exclusive Department gave this customer's 993 the wooden finish. This would have been arranged with the factory prior to starting to build the car

PORSCHE tiptronic

In December 1989, Tiptronic transmission was offered on the Carrera 2. This was the first automatic gearbox to be fitted to a 911 since the demise of the Sportomatic in 1979. An automatic transmission was regarded as something of a luxury item on a Porsche, but was really aimed at the American market

The ex-TWR Porsche WSC95 entered by the Joest team and driven by stalwarts Davy Jones/Alexander Wurz/Manuel Reuter was the overall winner of the 1996 Le Mans 24-Hour event

Prior to the 1996 Le Mans 24-Hour race, the Reinhold Joest run ex-Tom Walkinshaw Racing Porsche WSC95 was very much an unknown quantity, as this car had been dragged out from under the covers to do duty in the French race. Dusting off the cobwebs, the car was promptly put on pole. The next two slots were filled by a pair of factory Porsche GT1 cars which had also never raced. At the end of 24 hours, these three cars filled the top three places.

1. Manuel Reuter (D), Alexander Wurz (A), Davy Jones (USA)
   Joest-Racing, Joest-Porsche, 354 Runden **(Gesamtsieger)**
2. Hans-Joachim Stuck (A), Thierry Boutsen (B), Bob Wollek (F)
   Porsche AG, Porsche 911 GT1, 353 Runden - **(Sieger der Klasse GT1)**
3. Yannick Dalmas (F), Karl Wendlinger (A), Scott Goodyear (CAN)
   Porsche AG, Porsche 911 GT1, 341 Runden
4. Lindsay Owen-Jones (GB), Pierre-Henri Raphanel (F), David Brabham (AUS)
   West Competition, McLaren-BMW GTR F1 LM, 337 Runden
5. John Nielsen (DK), Thomas Bscher (D), Peter Kox (NL)
   Gulf Racing, McLaren-BMW GTR F1 LM, 335 Runden
6. Andy Wallace (GB), Olivier Grouillard (F), Derek Bell (GB)
   Harrods Mach One Racing, McLaren-BMW GTR F1 LM, 328 Runden
7. Henri Pescarolo (F), Franck Lagorce (F), Emmanuel Collard (F)
   La Filière, Courage-Porsche, 327 Runden
8. Nelson Piquet (BR), Johnny Cecotto (YV), Danny Sullivan (USA)
   Team Bigazzi SRL, McLaren-BMW GTR F1 LM, 324 Runden
9. Ray Bellm (GB), James Weaver (GB), J.J. Lehto (FIN)
   Gulf Racing, McLaren-BMW GTR F1 LM, 323 Runden
10. Price Cobb (USA), Mark Dismore (USA), Shawn Hendricks (USA)
    Canaska Southwind Motor, Chrysler Viper GTS-R, 320 Runden
11. Jacques Laffite (F), Steve Soper (GB), Marc Duez (B)
    Team Bigazzi SRL, McLaren-BMW GTR F1 LM, 318 Runden
12. Guy Martinolle (F), Ralf Kelleners (D), Bruno Eichmann (CH)
    Roock-Racing-Team, Porsche 911 GT2, 317 Runden - **(Sieger der Klasse GT2)**

LE MANS '96

Porsche triumphiert zum 14. Mal

1st.

2nd.

3rd.

Porsche's results at Le Mans 1996.

Result for you: winning technology.

PORSCHE

Porsche 911 GT1 sports racing cars made their début at Le Mans in June 1996, scoring a one-two victory in the GT1 class and taking second and third places overall. The second placed car (number 25) was driven by the hugely experienced trio of Bob Wollek/Thierry Boutsen/Hans-Joachim Stuck, while just behind them came Yannick Dalmas/Scott Goodyear/Karl Wendlinger in the number 26 car

PORSCHE

On October 18, 1996, Hans-Joachim Stuck collected his 911 Carrera 4S 3.6-litre from outside Werk 1 in Stuttgart-Zuffenhausen

Niki Lauda poses with his Carrera 4S outside his Lauda-Air headquarters in Vienna in 1997, 18 years after he started the operation

High Profile 911 Drivers

One of the benefits of being a modern-day racing driver is that you can generally choose the car you would like to drive. In the case of Hans-Joachim Stuck, he had been one of the most successful Porsche racing drivers the company had ever had, with his victories spanning several decades.

Two other 911 drivers were Niki Lauda, who was Formula 1 World Champion in 1975, 1977 and 1984, and Ralf Schumacher, whose 10-year F1 career ended in 2007.

Ralf Schumacher receives the keys to his 911 Turbo 3.6-litre in 1996

Last New 911 Model

It is appropriate to end this 35-year exploration of the fascinating Porsche 911 model, by examining the exclusive, and very powerful, 911 Turbo S. The Turbo S was the last new production model manufactured by Porsche that still carried the air-cooled boxer engine.

The significance of this car extends beyond the fact that it was the last 911 model, as it is an embodiment of what the Porsche 911 had come to stand for – quality, innovation and progress. In 1998, the Turbo S was also the most powerful road-going production 911 ever, producing a whopping 450bhp from its 3.6-litre compound turbocharged engine. Such power gave the Turbo S a top speed of 186mph (300km/h) and it could do the 0-62mph (0-100km/h) sprint in 4.1 seconds, giving true supercar performance. The Exclusive Department built only 345 examples and they reduced the purchaser's bank balance by DM 304,650 (US$173,235).

Interestingly, its power output matched that of the mighty Porsche 959 of 1987, while visually, the Turbo S also borrowed the well-styled rear wing air intakes from the earlier car.

There could hardly have been a more appropriate model with which to celebrate the legend that the air-cooled 911s had created over 35 years.

Änderungen von Konstruktion,
Ausstattung und Lieferumfang
sowie Abweichungen im Farbton
bleiben vorbehalten.

Dr. Ing. h.c. F. Porsche AG
Exclusive Programm
Porschestraße 42
D-70435 Stuttgart
Tel. ++49-711-911-5330
Fax ++49-711-911-6227

911 Turbo S

The Turbo S was a very special model in the 911 model range, and Porsche produced this dedicated sales booklet for it in 1998. Porsche have had their promotional literature distributed by the same company for many years, and in the bottom right hand corner on the back cover is printed an internal Porsche 'WVK' reference number for distribution purposes. However, some copies of the Turbo S booklet were printed without any reference numbers (as in this example), a first for the company, making those copies extremely collectable today

Changing Of The Guard

Porsche had spent 30 years (1963-1993) honing and perfecting the shape of the 911 by the time the 993, the last of the traditional air-cooled Porsche sports cars, was launched.

From the 1960s, the 911's transition into an icon in the 1970s was almost seamless. The '80s saw the 911 take on an altogether more sophisticated guise while the '90s witnessed a maturity of power and athleticism that could only be the result of endless development and refinement. The 911's evolution through the decades can be measured in steady increments, with the occasional radical development such as the 959. No other sports car manufacturer has sustained such a strong and identifiable personality in a single model, over such a prolonged period, other than perhaps Morgan.

What was the feeling then amongst the 911 enthusiasts when the air-cooled engine was discontinued in favour of the water-cooled unit? How did the average club member feel about this? After all, this was the backbone of the Porsche ethos, it is what made Porsche different and unique. I put these questions to Stephen Mummery, motoring journalist and member of the Porsche Club Great Britain:

"Funnily enough, what was good for the Boxster was seen, by a significant number, as heresy for the 911. Did we really want a 928 replacement sullying the unique model name? The 996 was somehow different, less charismatic in the eyes of many, and hence the attention that was placed on the outgoing 993 iteration of the air-cooled classic. And Porsche probably recognised that too. It wasn't long before the 996-and-a-half emerged – and it began to sound like a 911 again. References to the heritage were obvious at the appearance of the 997 and the launch traded heavily on the 911 history."

The Porsche 911 is considered by many motoring enthusiasts to be one of the greatest sports cars of the 20th century. Its timeless design has continued to captivate consecutive generations of driving enthusiasts since its introduction in the early 1960s. For the basic tear-drop shape of the 356 (built in 1948 but first shown at the Geneva Motor Show in spring 1949) to have survived for 60 years is remarkable in the truest sense of the word.

The first Porsche 911 2.0 Coupés are regarded by many enthusiasts as having the purest lines. The early models certainly have an uncluttered, almost innocent look to them

When the last of the air-cooled 911s left the production line at Porsche's Stuttgart-Zuffenhausen plant in 1998, it marked the end of an era. This blue Typ 993, the last air-cooled 911 to be produced, was ordered by the American comedian, Jerry Seinfeld

In closing, it is perhaps appropriate to display the Porsche badge. With its origins dating back to 1948, the car from Württemberg has had a few critics, but at the same time it has surprised and delighted many others. Above all, it has become a symbol of admiration throughout the world and examples have been treasured by those lucky enough to own one

PRODUCTION FIGURES

The introduction of the Porsche 914 in 1970 boosted the company's production enormously, actually trebling the output of the year before. Production during the 1970s peaked with over 43,000 units in 1973, dropping back briefly before reaching similar levels once again in 1977 with the introduction of the Porsche 924.

Ten years after the demise of the 914 model, Porsche reached record production in 1986 of over 53,000 units, the bulk of which was made up of 944 sales. That year also saw the highest annual 911 production of 17,074 units. Production for the five year period from 1985-1989 (213,433 units) was up 13% on the previous five year figure (188,748) which certainly kept the factory running at a healthy level.

The next real high point for 911 production came in 1996 with 21,602 units produced, but this was after production of the 928 and 968 models had ceased. 911 production would have to increase to fill the gap, although plans for the introduction of the all-new water-cooled, mid-engined Boxster were well advanced by then. The Boxster went into production in the autumn of 1996 and was marketed as a 1997 model.

Although Porsche produced its one millionth vehicle in 1996, the figures in these graphs fall just short of this because they exclude those 356s made before 1965. Total 356 production was just short of 78,000 units, which gives us the magical million referred to in the book.

Although the 911 has undoubtedly been the mainstay in the Porsche range, it is questionable if the company would have survived with just this one model during some difficult years. It cannot be denied that the other Porsche sports cars, the 914, 924, 928, 944, 959, 968 and Boxster all played their part in bolstering the company finances admirably, as each model has satisfied a different segment of the market. This has allowed Porsche to continuously develop the 911 to where it is today.

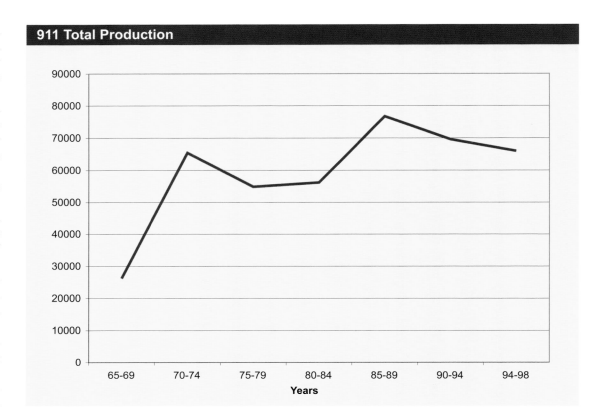

911 Total Production

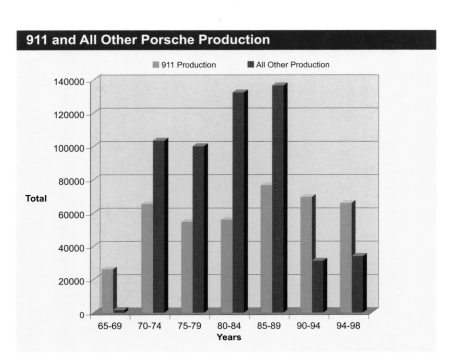

911 and All Other Porsche Production

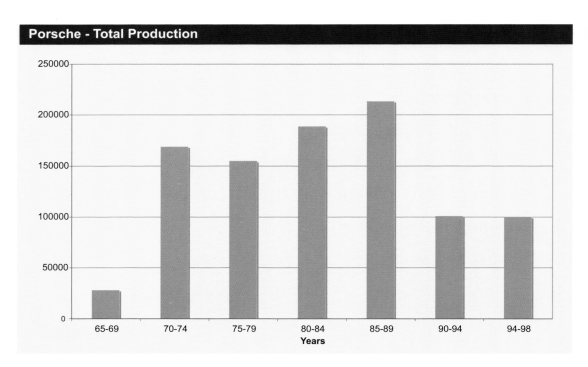

Porsche - Total Production

The accompanying images show the competitors' rule book and a race poster from the fifth and last La Carrera Panamericana in 1954, an event in which Porsche 550s performed with distinction.

While the first race in 1950 was run in a southerly direction, the four subsequent events started at Tuxtla Gutiérrez in the south near the Guatemalan border, and ran northwards to Ciudad Juarez near El Paso on the American border. Drivers had to cope with extreme conditions over the 2,000-mile course, and race engines that performed satisfactorily at sea level sounded really sick at 10,000 feet, requiring teams to tune and retune their engines on a regular basis

WINS PORSCHE TRANS-AM AND IMSA GT 1974

Brumos Porsche
59
KENDALL GT-1

FINAL STANDINGS TRANS-AM

1. PETER GREGG • PORSCHE CARRERA RSR
2. LUDWIG HEIMRATH • PORSCHE CARRERA RSR
3. HURLEY HAYWOOD • PORSCHE CARRERA RSR
4. AL HOLBERT • PORSCHE CARRERA RSR
5. JIM COOK • PORSCHE CARRERA RSR
6. TONY DE LORENZO • CHEVROLET CAMARO

FINAL STANDINGS IMSA

1. PETER GREGG • PORSCHE CARRE
2. MILT MINTER • PORSCHE CARRER
3. MIKE KEYSER • PORSCHE CARRE
4. AL HOLBERT • PORSCHE CARRE
5. STEVE BEHR • PORSCHE CARRE
6. GEORGE DYER • PORSCHE CARR

Leserwahl '83

auto motor sport DIE BESTEN AUTOS DER WELT

Porsche 911 SC Cabriolet: „Bestes Cabriolet der Welt"

S · EV 2660

PORSCHE
FAHREN IN SEINER SCHÖNSTEN FORM

52
Jägermeister

CUP PORSCHE 81

1. Bob Wollek (F) / Jägermeister / Kremer Porsche 935
2. John Fitzpatrick (GB) / Sachs Porsche 935
3. Dieter Schornstein (D) / Vegla Porsche 935
4. Edgar Dören (D) / Weralit Porsche 935
5. Bob Garretson (USA) / Style Auto Porsche 935
6. Bobby Rahal (USA) / Style Auto Porsche 935
7. John Paul jun. (USA) / J.L.P. Porsche 935
8. Harald Grohs (D) / Andial Porsche 935
9. Jochen Mass (D) / Jöst Porsche 935
10. John Cooper (GB) / Porsche 935
11. John Paul sen. (USA) / J.L.P. Porsche 935
12. Dr. Gianpiero Moretti (I) / Momo Porsche 935
13. Volkert Merl (D) / Jöst Porsche 935/908 T
14. Bruce Leven (USA) / Bayside Porsche 935
15. Ted Field (USA) / Interscope Porsche 935
16. Mauricio DeNavarez (Mex) / DeNavarez Porsche 935
17. Roy Woods (GB) / Porsche 935
18. Rolf Stommelen (D) / Andial Porsche 935
19. Jürgen Lässig (D) / Weralit Porsche 935
20. Hurley Haywood (USA) / Bayside Porsche 935

Dr. Ing. h. c. F. Porsche AG Stuttgart-Zuffenhausen · Printed in Germany December 1981 · Entwurf Werbeagentur Stranger · Foto: Reichert

DU CLASSIQUE.

PORSCHE

PORSCHE 911

Performance in itself means little in evaluating the true worth of a car, unless accompanied by reliability and first-class design throughout.

Cross sectional view of the Porsche 911

PORSCHE

FAHREN IN SEINER SCHÖNSTEN FORM

Bring the best
part of your
European
Vacation home

PORSCHE

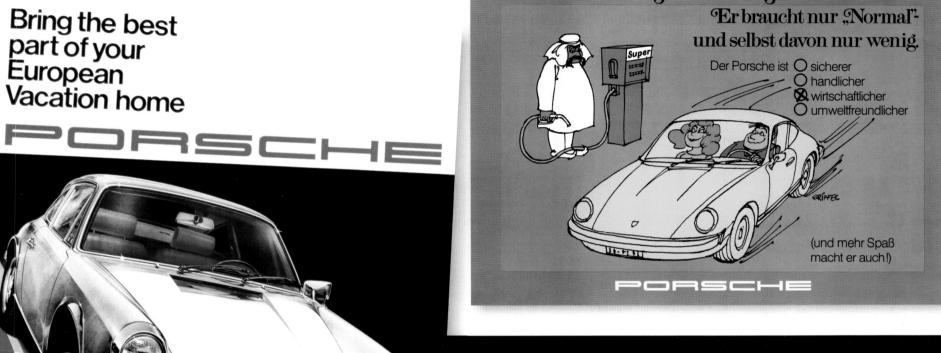

Ein Grund mehr, Porsche zu fahren:
Er braucht nur „Normal"-
und selbst davon nur wenig.

Der Porsche ist ○ sicherer
○ handlicher
⊗ wirtschaftlicher
○ umweltfreundlicher

(und mehr Spaß
macht er auch!)

PORSCHE

MARTINI PORSCHE

There are leaders and there are followers.
Life is really quite simple, isn't it?

This is the latest title in the *Original Scrapbook* series. The other books in the series all have a similar layout and format.

Stirling Moss Scrapbook 1929-1954
by Stirling Moss & Philip Porter

Stirling's formative years from F3 to HWM, and XK120 to 250F. Full of period atmosphere: 160 pages, with over 500 photos. Standard edition £34.95; leather-bound limited edition, signed by Sir Stirling & Philip Porter £75.

Jaguar Scrapbook
by Philip Porter

Something for every Jaguar enthusiast: from the early days of Swallow to the 21st century. Personalities, production classics, company memos, styling exercises and loads of unseen material. 160 pages with over 500 photos. Standard edition £34.95; leather-bound limited edition, signed by Norman Dewis and Philip Porter £75.

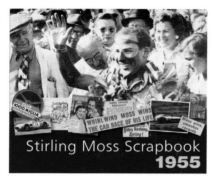

Stirling Moss Scrapbook 1955
by Stirling Moss & Philip Porter

Stirling's 'Mercedes-Benz' year: his first GP victory and his brilliant sports car successes including the amazing Mille Miglia. 160 pages, with over 500 photos. Standard edition £34.95; leather-bound limited edition, signed by Sir Stirling and Philip Porter £75.

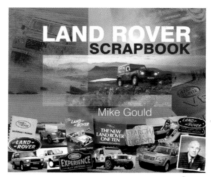

Land Rover Scrapbook
by Mike Gould

Development and production of all the iconic models, plus styling sketches and secret projects; written by an inside man who worked for Land Rover for 30 years. 160 pages with over 500 photos. Standard edition £34.95; leather-bound limited edition, signed by Bob Dover and Mike Gould £75

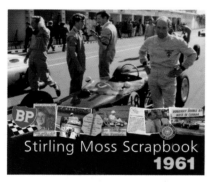

Stirling Moss Scrapbook 1961
by Stirling Moss & Philip Porter

Stirling winning against the odds at the Monaco and German GPs; a 7th victory in the Tourist Trophy, and many other successes. 160 pages, with over 500 photos. Standard edition £34.95; leather-bound limited edition, signed by Sir Stirling and Philip Porter £75.

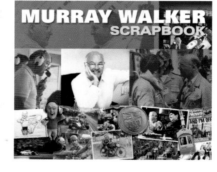

Murray Walker Scrapbook
by Murray Walker & Philip Porter

Everyone has heard his voice; now here is his life story in his words and photos, with fascinating recollections from 80 drivers, friends and colleagues. 192 pages with over 500 photos. Standard edition £34.95; leather-bound limited edition, signed by Murray Walker & Philip Porter £75.

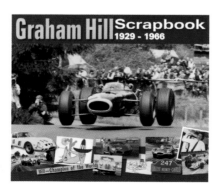

Graham Hill Scrapbook 1929-1966
by Philip Porter

From Graham Hill's beginnings as an unpaid race mechanic to his first world title, plus F2, saloon cars, sports racers, sports cars, GTs and victory at the Indy 500. 176 pages with over 500 photos. Standard edition £34.95; leather-bound limited edition, signed by Damon Hill & Philip Porter £75.

The Automotive Art of Alan Fearnley

Alan Fearnley is one of the world's foremost motoring artists. This book combines over 135 of his superb paintings and drawings, with detailed captions and comments from his subjects including Sir Stirling Moss. Foreword by Murray Walker. 145 pages. Standard edition £45; leather-bound limited edition, signed by Alan Fearnley £95

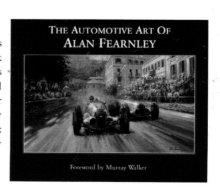

Porter Press International

Each book is published in a standard edition and also a special de Luxe edition: these are limited editions, bound in leather, numbered, hand-signed and supplied with a leather-bound slip case. De Luxe editions are only available direct from the publishers.

Price and availability subject to change without notice